Shaping
School
Culture

Pitfalls, Paradoxes, and Promises

Second Edition

Terrence E. Deal

Kent D. Peterson

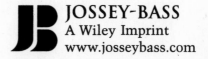

JOSSEY-BASS
A Wiley Imprint
www.josseybass.com

Published by Jossey-Bass
A Wiley Imprint
989 Market Street, San Francisco, CA 94103-1741   www.josseybass.com

Jossey-Bass books and products are available through most bookstores. To contact Jossey-
Bass directly call our Customer Care Department within the U.S. at 800-956-7739, outside
the U.S. at 317-572-3986, or fax 317-572-4002.

Jossey-Bass also publishes its books in a variety of electronic formats. Some content that
appears in print may not be available in electronic books.

Library of Congress Cataloging-in-Publication Data

Deal, Terrence E.
  Shaping school culture : pitfalls, paradoxes, and promises / Terrence E. Deal, Kent D. Peterson. – 2nd ed.
      p. cm.
  Includes bibliographical references and index.
  ISBN 978-0-7879-9679-6 (pbk.)
  1. Educational leadership.   2. School environment.   3. Educational change.   4. Educational leadership–
Case studies. I. Peterson, Kent D. II. Title.
  LB2805.D34 2009
  371.2–dc22

                                                                                              2008053153

Printed in the United States of America
SECOND EDITION
PB Printing   10 9 8 7 6

Contents

The Symbolic Role of School Leaders

Preface

This book represents a second major reworking of an idea that started in 1990 as *The Principal's Role in Shaping School Culture*—a best-seller for the U.S. Department of Education. We revised and published it as *Shaping School Culture: The Heart of Leadership* (1999). We have substantially expanded and developed it into what now appears before you: *Shaping School Culture: Pitfalls, Paradoxes, and Promises*. We have added significant material on paradox, updated and expanded illustrations, and introduced some new ideas. As usual, we received a lot of help from school leaders in rewriting this edition. From across the country and indeed the world, readers of the two previous editions have shared ideas and examples. They once again confirm that stories and examples make a difference to them in how they think about their schools and deal with cultural issues.

It is clearly time to reconsider and rethink the importance of school culture in today's educational environment. Students have the right to the best schools we can provide. There is little doubt that teaching staff and administrators can lead the way to successful cultures in which all students learn. Of late, far too much emphasis has been given to reforming schools from outside through policies and mandates such as No Child Left Behind (NCLB). Too little attention has been paid to how schools can be shaped from within, as our colleague Roland Barth (1991) demonstrates.

Research and examples of excellent practice drawn from both education and business show that top-flight schools are possible in every community. This book pulls together the best that we know about culture to provide insights and examples of ways teachers, administrators, parents, and community can create positive, caring, and intellectually challenging schools.

The importance of school culture and the symbolic roles of leaders in shaping cultural patterns and practices remain at the core of this book. While policymakers and reformers are pressing for new structures and more rational assessments, it is important to remember that these changes cannot succeed without cultural support. The existential tenor of a school is key to achievement and student learning. In this book, we have expanded the research base demonstrating how culture influences school functioning. We also draw on evidence from the world of business, linking culture with financial performance.

In our look at the importance of mission and purpose, we added new material because mission and purpose are central features of culture. We added examples of the types of rituals and traditions found in quality schools. We added new case examples of the ways stories and history are used to build commitment and motivation. We added important new illustrations of symbols in architecture as well as in action. We integrated original case studies of culture building and development into relevant chapters; before, they were separate and seemed to be add-ons. We added considerable case material to the ways leaders shape culture, with new roles and numerous useful examples. We added new ideas about "toxic" cultures—negative places where the rituals, traditions, and values have gone sour and threaten the very soul of a school. We expanded our discussion of the connection between the culture of the school and parents and the local community. We think this topic now receives the attention it deserves.

The book contains new examples and cases collected while we were working with schools and organizations across the globe, including British Columbia, London, Taiwan, Toronto, and Norway. A number of excellent examples from other researchers of schools trying to transform themselves have added rich new illustrations of culture building. We believe that it was important to bring to the fore our previous work on bifocal leadership and paradox. We have drawn from *The Leadership Paradox* in Chapters Thirteen and Fourteen to highlight these ways of shaping culture and leading schools. Even though we added new material, we wanted the book to be readable and concise, with engaging examples from both education and business. We think readers will find the mix of stories interesting.

We focus on the elements of successful cultures and the ways leaders from every level—teachers, principals, parents, and community members—shape a school's identity and image. Successful schools possess leaders who can read, assess, and reinforce core rituals, traditions, and values. Successful schools have leadership emanating from many people—leadership that maintains and supports learning for all students, as well as learning for all staff. Successful cultures have leaders who know deep down in their hearts how important schools are to children and want to make them the best places they can be. Successful cultures have leaders who can cope with the paradoxes of their work and take advantage of the opportunities of the future. In this book, we hope to support, encourage, and nourish these kinds of leaders for schools.

We begin the book by introducing the impact of culture on school reform and student learning. Drawing on both organizational literature and research, we emphasize the importance of culture to achievement and other important educational outcomes.

In Part One: The Elements of Culture, we lay out the elements of culture, the basic building blocks people cobble together in creating a meaningful workplace. In Chapter One, Schools as Tribes, we present a case study of a school that transformed itself by reworking its cultural profile. The school, Ganado Primary, moved from a dismal place to a school with visionary leadership, a deeply held purpose, and rituals and traditions that build commitment and motivation. In Chapter Two we explore the potency of symbols in everything we do day to day. We highlight architecture, mottoes, words, and actions. In Chapter Three we turn back the clock to reaffirm the importance of the past in determining current cultural patterns and ways. Central to any school culture is its history—the past events that have shaped the present. In Chapter Four we turn to the legacy of history: myth, mission, purpose, and values. We underscore the importance of a meaningful purpose and widely shared values in adding spark and vitality to a school. In Chapter Five we show how current stories and tales add to the stream of cultural energy and perpetuate important lessons. We burrow beneath everyday routine to showcase its ritualistic significance in Chapter Six. In Chapter Seven, Ceremonies and Traditions, we ratchet ritual to a more grand and episodic plane. Celebrations put culture on display. We introduce in Chapter Eight the cast of cultural players whose real work outside official duties is keeping cultural patterns and practices intact and on track.

In Part Two: The Symbolic Role of School Leaders, we move from concepts to application. We discuss cultural metamorphosis and transformation in Chapter Nine. Drawing on seven case examples, we demonstrate how leadership can build school culture through consideration to purpose, energy, and all the elements of culture. In Chapter Ten we show what happens when culture turns sour or septic. Drawing on extensive experience in schools, we identify features of the dark side of some schools and provide antidotes for these poisonous situations. In Chapter Eleven we examine the key symbolic relationship among the school, parents, and the community. In Chapter Twelve we describe the multiple roles that leaders take on in the shaping of the culture, including historian, anthropological sleuth, visionary, symbol, potter, poet, actor, and healer. We reconnect the technical aspects of management with the symbolic aspects of leadership in Chapter Thirteen to create the idea of a bifocal principal who thinks both structurally and symbolically. Very few issues in education are either-or, and principals who deal with paradox will find their jobs much less stressful and more rewarding. School leaders who want to build and maintain successful cultures will have to cope with paradox and take advantage of both rational and ethical opportunities they confront. This approach leads to the ideal of a school in Chapter Fourteen, Achieving Balance: Meeting Cultural and Structural Demands, where both metrics and magic apply. These paradoxes and challenges can shape the direction and hope for leaders in this millennium, a topic we explore in the concluding Chapter Fifteen.

Acknowledgments

The Deal-Peterson team has been around for several years. As with any duo, there are others around us who make substantial contributions to what we write. The first to receive our enduring thanks is Lee Bolman. He now teaches at the University of Missouri, Kansas City. His work with Terry Deal seeps into this book in a number of places. Thanks, Lee. You have one of the best conceptual minds in the business.

Thanks also to those whose work made this book possible; our former administrative assistants Homa Aminmadani and Carole Jean Roche both put in hours and hours. We also express gratitude to our many graduate assistants who have moved on to important positions—Valli Warren, Frances Wills, Kubilay Gok, Shelby Cosner, Yi-Hwa Liou, and Nathaniel Bray—who did a wonderful job chasing things down, reviewing drafts, and pushing our ideas.

Over the years our colleagues Allan Kennedy, Sharon Conley, Linton Deck, Bob Slater, Pam Robbins, and Rick Ginsberg have influenced our thinking and clarity. Thanks also to students in our graduate and undergraduate classes and all the school leaders who have shared with us their stories, challenges, and successes. We would like especially to thank Sigmund Boloz and Bob Herring, who shared their stories of school culture building. There is nothing like fresh minds and new blood combined with the wisdom of experience to enrich a book and get your ideas straight.

One colleague, Joan Vydra, deserves special mention. One of the most culturally attuned principals anywhere, she generously shared her experiences and allowed us to adapt a number of contemporary cases she wrote. Thanks also to Gary Crow for helpful feedback and ongoing support.

Our wives, Sandra Newport Deal and Ann Herrold-Peterson, contributed love and support that helped fuel our creativity and energy. Our children—Kent's sons, Erik, Russell, and Scott, and Terry's daughter, Janie—have given us a real boost along the way.

We greatly appreciate the encouragement, support, and patience of Lesley Iura and Christie Hakim at Jossey-Bass.

We dedicate this work to the leaders of America's public schools. They can and do make a real difference in the lives of children. Keep the faith.

Spring 2009   *Terrence E. Deal*
                                                        San Luis Obispo, California
                                                        Kent D. Peterson
                                                        Madison, Wisconsin

The Authors

Terrence E. Deal's career has encompassed several roles, including that of police officer, teacher, principal, district office administrator, and professor. He has taught at the Stanford and Harvard graduate schools of education, Vanderbilt's Peabody College, and the University of Southern California. He lectures and consults internationally with business, health care, educational, religious, and military organizations. He specializes in leadership, organizational theory and behavior, and culture. Deal is the coauthor of over thirty books, including *Corporate Cultures* (with Allan A. Kennedy, 1982)—an international best-seller. His books include *The Leadership Paradox: Balancing Logic and Artistry in Schools* (with Kent D. Peterson, 1994), *Leading with Soul: An Uncommon Journey of Spirit* (with Lee Bolman, 1995), *Reframing Organizations: Artistry, Choice, and Leadership, Fourth Edition* (with Lee Bolman, 2008), and numerous others.

Kent D. Peterson was the first director of the Vanderbilt Principals' Institute and is former head of the National Center for Effective Schools Research and Development. He is currently professor in the Department of Educational Leadership and Policy Analysis at the University of Wisconsin-Madison. He lectures and consults with leadership academies across the United States and internationally. His research has examined the nature of principals' work, school reform, and the ways school leaders develop strong, positive school cultures. Author of numerous studies on principal leadership, he is coauthor of *The Principal's Role in Shaping School Culture* (with Terrence E. Deal, 1990), *The Leadership Paradox: Balancing Logic and Artistry in Schools* (with Terrence E. Deal, 1994), and *The Shaping School Culture Fieldbook* (with Terrence E. Deal, 2002).

Shaping School Culture

Introduction

"If only schools would be run more like businesses." It's a phrase we to hear all too often. It haunts many school principals and teachers, making them feel like they're missing something or following the wrong path. It's difficult to take pride in your work when you are persistently reminded that your efforts don't measure up. But let's take another look at the oft-invoked comparison. What does it really mean? What makes successful businesses tick? Is it structure or strategy? Is it technology or clear goals? Or maybe tighter standards and accountability?

The truth is deeper than these commonplace reasons imply. In business, one thing is crystal clear: *the culture of an enterprise plays a dominant role in exemplary performance*. Highly respected organizations have evolved a shared webbing of informal folkways and traditions that infuse work with meaning, passion, and purpose. The evidence is persuasive; the word *culture* is a staple in business lexicon. Every business leader we've talked to about success mentions it in the first few minutes.

Consider some well-known examples. Howard Schultz, CEO of Starbucks, puts it this way: "A company can grow big without losing the passion and personality that built it, but only if it's driven not by profits but by values and by people.... The key is heart. I pour my heart into every cup of coffee, and so do my partners at Starbucks. When customers sense that, they respond in kind.

If you pour your heart into your work, or into any worthy enterprise, you can achieve dreams others may think impossible" (Schultz & Yang, 1997, p. 8).

Another example. Lou Gerstner's classic turnaround of IBM initially started out as a structural overhaul: "The last thing IBM needs is a vision." But as he burrowed more deeply under the company's public veneer, he realized that striking out in a brand new direction overlooked the real problem. IBM had drifted from the values and ways that had once made it the most successful organization in the world. The strategy then became one of revival rather than reform. Some jettisoned or tarnished traditions needed some attention to restore the sheen of a once renowned history. Gerstner concluded following IBM's newfound success: "I came to see, in my time at IBM, that culture isn't just one aspect of the game—it is the game" (Gerstner, 2002, p. 182).

Or step outside the business world and take a look at the U.S. Marine Corps. In his book *Making the Corps*, Thomas Ricks (1997) points to culture as the symbolic glue that has bonded the Corps together throughout its heralded military campaigns. He says, "Culture—that is, the values and assumptions that shape its members—is all the Marines have. It is what holds them together. They are the smallest of the U.S. military services, and in some ways the most interesting. Theirs is the richest culture: formalistic, insular, elitist, with a deep anchor in their own history and mythology" (p. 19).

There are countless other examples in a variety of enterprises. The point is that education seems to be learning the wrong lessons from mediocre businesses that focus on only making a profit and measurable short-term financial goals. Educators are being pressured to adopt practices that the best organizations shy away from. If schools want to emulate other successful organizations, then parents, teachers, and administrators need to take a look at their local traditions, folkways, and dreams. And this look has to be a sustained, fine-grained scrutiny, not a brief superficial glance.

Another valuable lesson to draw from businesses such as IBM is how quickly cultural traditions can weaken or stray. Starbucks confronted this predicament in 2007. Schultz's book, *Pour Your Heart into It*, was published in 1997 when the company was envied by other businesses and its product dominated the consumer's coffee palette. Starbucks growth was phenomenal (100 to 123,000 stores in ten years), as were its profits. But a memorandum from Schultz to senior executives in 2007 highlighted a sinister side of success:

> Some people even call our stores sterile, cookie cutter, no longer reflecting the passion our partners feel about our coffee . . . stores no longer have the soul of the past and reflect a chain of stores vs. the warm feeling of a neighborhood store . . . . It's time to get back to the core and make the changes that are necessary to evoke the heritage, the tradition, and passion we all have for the Starbucks experience." ("Big Quiz," 2007)

Many of Starbucks growth-induced changes seemed innocuous since rationally they seemed superior to old ways. Automating espresso machines assured a more consistent cup of coffee brew but undercut the artistry and image of the local barista. Sealing coffee beans in airtight pouches maintained freshness at the expense of a store's signature aroma of fresh coffee. In sum, Starbucks growth and automation merged to "[sacrifice] the 'romance and theater' of the coffee shop experience for efficiency and profit" ("Show Tracker," 2007). The company closed all of its stores one afternoon in 2008 to reculture and retune Starbucks baristas. Time will tell whether or not the coffee purveyor can restore the heart of the enterprise. But it is clear that the renewed focus was on the core values of the organization, reconnecting to its history and lore.

If people are looking for a parallel between business and schools, the experiences of IBM and Starbucks suggest a promising place to start. Like Starbucks and IBM, schools have drifted from traditional cultural roots. But in schools this shift had been caused by legislative mandate as much as by local neglect.

For decades, educational organizations have been pummeled by external reform initiatives. Most of these well-intended efforts have striven to make schools more rational and technically advanced, emulating what people assume to be more like successful businesses. Standardization, test scores, and research-based methods have replaced local discretion, faith, creativity, and teacher ingenuity. The unintended result is the unraveling of symbolic fibers that once gave a hallowed enterprise passion, purpose, and meaning. What were once joyful places of promise and hope have too often become mechanized factories bent on producing only a small fraction of what a well-educated person needs and what the community wants. As a U.S. Department of Education spokesperson remarked in 2007, "If it can't be measured, we're not interested in it."

This book seeks to staunch the symbolic wandering and unraveling in schools by reemphasizing the importance of culture and how its tending and nourishment can lead to better performance—not just on test scores but in the full array of social, emotional, and communal outcomes we expect schools to attain. Many of these are not easily quantifiable or measurable, but they are important. Their attainment must be accepted, in large part, on faith and trust in those who teach.

Consider a situation in Ethiopia. Ethiopians believe that the Ark of the Covenant was brought to their country for safe-keeping. It resides in a small chapel, attended by a monk whose only name is "keeper of the ark." How he assumed the role or how he will be replaced when he dies is a mystery.

He is the only one who has seen the Covenant. Even the country's top religious leaders have never laid eyes on the holy treasure. They don't need to. His Holiness of the Ethiopian Orthodox Church (a Princeton Ph.D.) says: "It's no claim, it's the truth.... I'm still forbidden from seeing it. The guardian of the ark is the only person on earth who has that peerless honor"

(Raffaele, 2007, pp. 40–41). Others concur. A monk: "We don't need proof because it's a fact. The monks here have passed this down for centuries.... It's the tabots (replicas of the ark's tablets) that consecrate a church, and without them it's as holy as a donkey stable" (p. 42). An Archbishop of the Orthodox Church notes: "These stories were handed down through the generations by our church leaders and we believe them to be historical facts.... That's why we keep *tabots* in every church in Ethiopia" (p. 42).

In contemporary America, such unwavering faith seems almost inconceivable. We want tangible proof even when the subject of interest is unquantifiable. Yet many of the country's top businesses operate on faith: "We have faith that our intangible beliefs and values will ultimately yield financial success." Culture in successful organizations arises in the yeasty crucible of meaning somewhere between mystery and metrics. It is the glue, the hope, and the faith that holds people together: "Nothing that is worth doing can be achieved in our lifetime; therefore we must be saved by hope. Nothing which is true or beautiful or good makes complete sense in any immediate context of history; therefore we must be saved by faith. Nothing we do, however virtuous, can be accomplished alone" (McCain & Salter, 2008, p. 338). This heartening way of thinking should chart our future course to better schools: reviving the soul and spirit of a noble and vital enterprise.

School Culture and Its Heritage

The concept of schools having distinctive cultures is not new. Willard Waller wrote in 1932: "Schools have a culture that is definitely their own. There are, in the school, complex rituals of personal relationships, a set of folkways, mores, and irrational sanctions, a moral code based upon them. There are games, which are sublimated wars, teams, and an elaborate set of ceremonies concerning them. There are traditions, and traditionalists waging their world-old battle against innovators" (p. 96). His observations are still relevant today.

Parents, teachers, principals, and students have always sensed something special, yet undefined, about their schools—something extremely powerful but difficult to describe. This ephemeral, taken-for-granted aspect of schools is often overlooked and consequently is usually absent from discussions about school improvement. For decades terms such as *climate* and *ethos* have been used to try to capture this powerful, pervasive, and notoriously elusive force. We believe the term *culture* provides a more accurate and intuitively appealing way to help school leaders better understand their school's unwritten rules and traditions, norms, and expectations. The unofficial pattern seems to permeate everything: the way people act, how they dress, what they talk about or consider taboo, whether they seek out colleagues or isolate themselves, and how teachers feel about their work and their students.

Beneath the conscious awareness of everyday life in schools, there is a burbling of thought and activity. The underground flow of feelings and folkways wends its way, beckoning people, programs, and ideas toward often-unstated purposes: "This invisible, taken-for-granted flow of beliefs and assumptions gives meaning to what people say and do. It shapes how they interpret hundreds of daily transactions. The deeper structure of life in organizations is reflected and transmitted through symbolic language and expressive action. Culture consists of the stable, underlying social meanings that shape beliefs and behavior over time" (Deal & Peterson, 1990, p. 7).

The concept of culture has a long history in the exploration of behavior across human groups. Anthropologists first developed the concept to explain differences among the unique, all-encompassing ways of tribes, societies, and national or ethnic groups. Later, other social scientists applied the concept to patterns of behavior and thought at work. Formal organizations have clearly distinguishable identities manifested in organizational members' views, deeds, and customs. The concept of culture helps us understand these patterns—how they came to be and how they affect performance.

Of the many different conceptions of culture, none is universally accepted as the one best definition. One scholar defines culture as the web of significance in which we are all suspended (Geertz, 1973). Others define it as the shared beliefs and values that closely knit a community together (Deal & Kennedy, 1982). Another suggests simply that culture is "the way we do things around here" (Bower, 1966).

Schein (1985) provides a comprehensive definition, calling it "a pattern of basic assumptions—invented, discovered, or developed by a given group as it learns to cope with problems...that has worked well enough to be considered valid and, therefore, to be taught to new members as the correct way to perceive, think, and feel in relation to those problems" (p. 9). He views shaping the culture as one of the most important things that any leader must attend to.

Complex symbolic entities do not develop overnight. School cultures are complex webs of traditions and rituals built up over time as teachers, students, parents, and administrators work together and deal with crises and accomplishments (Schein, 1985; Deal & Peterson, 1990). Cultural patterns are highly enduring, have a powerful impact on performance, and shape the ways people think, act, and feel. Everything, and we do mean everything, in the organization is affected by the culture and its particular form and features.

Culture and Productivity: The Research Base and Impact

In the business world, evidence across multiple studies documents the significant role culture plays in financial performance. Kotter and Heskett (1992) compared top-performing firms with less successful ones in the same business environment. They found that those with strong cultures attuned to prevailing business conditions outperformed their counterparts in several ways: revenue increased by an average of 682 percent compared to 166 percent; the workforce grew by 282 percent versus 36 percent; stock gained value by 901 percent contrasted with 74 percent; and income rose by 756 percent, eclipsing that of 1 percent in less cohesive firms.

In a major study, Collins and Porras (1997) found similar results in their study of visionary companies—places where cultural values infused all aspects of everyday practice. They compared these visionary companies with other top-rated firms ("comparison companies" they called them) and with average performers. A look at the long-term financial performance of these three groups tells a dramatic story:

- Shareholders who, in 1926, invested $1 in the general stock market (average companies) would have accumulated $415 in growth and dividends by now.

- Shareholders who invested the same dollar in a more select portfolio (above-average companies) would have earned more than twice that amount—$955.

- Investors whose 1926 dollar was placed in visionary companies would today see a portfolio worth $6,356.

In business, culture stands out as a strong predictor of financial results. But does this same culture-performance link apply in education? Again, let's look at evidence.

In the late 1970s and early 1980s, studies of effective schools consistently acknowledged a climate and ethos that was purposeful and conducive to learning (Levine & Lezotte, 1990). A clear mission focused on student learning fostered high expectations for all students, focused the work of staff, and generated motivation to learn.

In a landmark British study, Rutter and his colleagues (1979) established school "ethos" as a prime contributor to academic achievement. As in other studies of successful schools, they discovered that the underlying norms, values, and traditions were factors in achievement gains. The ethos, or culture, was a crucial factor in success.

Later studies of school change have identified culture as critical to the successful improvement of teaching and learning (Rossman, Corbett, & Firestone, 1988; Fullan, 1998; Leithwood & Louis, 1998). In study after study, where cultural patterns did not support and encourage reform, changes did not take place. In contrast, things improved in schools where norms, values, and beliefs reinforced a strong educational mission, a sense of community, social trust among staff, and a shared commitment to school improvement.

Over time teachers in such schools developed a group sense of efficacy (a belief that they could become better) that generated energy to improve (Goddard, Hoy, & Hoy, 2004). This culturally supported empowerment encouraged the use of data, and engagement in planning, problem solving, and professional development. Culture was a key factor in the enhancement of more effective practices.

In a study comparing public and private schools, Bryk, Lee, and Holland (1993) found that a sense of community (similar to our concept of culture) was a key factor in cultivating a sense of excellence in private schools. Teachers in these communal schools were, compared to those in public schools, more satisfied with their work, seen by students as enjoying teaching, and less likely to be absent. Students were less likely to misbehave (for example, by cutting class, being absent, or disrupting class), were less likely to drop out, and showed higher gains in mathematic achievement.

The researchers' conclusion is echoed in the work of Johnson (1990), who demonstrated the superior strength and cohesion of culture in private schools relative to their public counterparts.

In a longitudinal study, McLaughlin (1995) discovered tremendous variation in schools, even departments, serving similar populations but with a different cultural sense of community. For example, a school with 80 percent Latino students (School A) and a school with 80 percent African American students (School B) demonstrated strikingly different levels of performance, even though they served students from comparable socioeconomic backgrounds. School A had a drop-out rate of 60 percent between the ninth and twelfth grades. Most grades fell in the D or F range, with very few As. Only 20 percent of the students went on to higher education. Teachers lamented their fate in having to work in the school.

In contrast, students in School B scored in the top quartile in mathematics, were first in the district in language arts, and showed well in music and the performing arts. By all measures it was a top-performing school. The difference, according to McLaughlin, was that School B had developed a learning community—a culture focused on learning that motivated staff and students. It was a place of cohesion, passion, commitment, and extensive interactions among teachers.

An extensive study of school restructuring showed conclusively that changing the structure of schools (transforming governance, time use, and grouping) is not enough (Newmann & Associates, 1996). To succeed, both new structures and a professional culture are needed. In a five-year study, the researchers documented that success flourished in schools with a primary focus on student learning, a commitment to high expectations, and social support for innovation, dialogue, and the search for new ideas. Also present was an "ethos of caring, sharing, and mutual help among staff, and between staff and students, based on respect, trust, and shared power relations among staff" (p. 289). The culture enhanced and bolstered structural changes, thus leading to success in instructional practice and student learning.

Contemporary research continues to point to the impact of school culture on a variety of important outcomes. In a major meta-analysis of research on leadership and student achievement, Waters and associates (2004) discovered a strong correlation between aspects of school culture and how well students performed. Student achievement was related to a shared set of core beliefs, a focused and clear sense of purpose, recognition of staff and student accomplishments, intellectual engagement, and celebrations of success. Although structures fostered connection, discussion of purpose, and school improvement, it was clear that these were deeply embedded in the culture of values, stories, ceremonies, and celebrations (Waters, Marzano, & McNulty, 2004).

Research on distributed leadership suggests that effective leadership is "stretched" over the staff—not just formally delegated to a few. To work, distributed leadership must be deeply embedded culturally, not just sketched in a structural blueprint (Spillane, Halverson, & Diamond, 2003).

Research on school improvement and change points to the central importance of the culture in enhancing curriculum, instruction, professional development, and learning—for both students and staff (Louis, 1994, 2006; Fullan, 1998; Abplanalp, 2008). Core norms and values are also central to initiating improvement, planning, and implementation. There are several reasons. First, a school with a strong, shared sense of mission is more likely to initiate improvement efforts. Second, norms of collegiality are related to collaborative planning and effective decision making. Third, cultures with a strong dedication to improvement are more likely to implement complex new instructional strategies. Finally, schools improve best when small successes are recognized and celebrated through shared ceremonies commemorating both individual and group contributions (Louis, 1994; Fullan, 1998; Abplanalp, 2008).

Research (Kruse, 1996; Newmann & Associates, 1996; Lambert, 2002; DuFour, 2007) on professional learning communities reinforces the centrality of cultural elements in school success, including the following:

- A shared sense of purpose

- Teacher involvement in decision making

- Collaborative work around instruction

- Norms of improvement

- Professional learning by staff

- A sense of joint responsibility for student learning

This research strongly buttresses the central role of culture to school success. All of these studies and others we have not cited point to the multiple ways school culture fosters improvement, collaborative decision making, professional development, and staff and student learning.

Functions and Impact of Culture

Culture affects all aspects of a school. It influences informal conversations in the faculty lunch room, the type of instruction valued, how professional development is viewed, and the shared commitment to assuring all students learn. Several examples illustrate its pervasiveness.

Culture fosters school effectiveness and productivity (Purkey & Smith, 1983; Levine & Lezotte, 1990; Newmann & Associates, 1996; Leithwood & Louis, 1998). Teachers succeed in a culture focused on productivity (rather than on maintenance or ease of work), performance (hard work, dedication, and perseverance), and improvement (continuous fine-tuning and refinement of teaching). Such a culture helps teachers overcome the uncertainty of their work (Lortie, 1975) by providing focus and collegiality. It provides motivation to persevere in the demanding work of teaching thirty students in a small, usually isolated, space. It encourages, sanctions, and rewards professionals in the constant task of improving their craft.

Culture improves collegiality, collaboration, communication, and problem-solving practices (Little, 1982; Peterson & Brietzke, 1994; Kruse & Louis, 1997; DuFour, 2007). Schools that value collegiality and collaboration offer a better opportunity for the social and professional exchange of ideas, the enhancement and spread of effective practices, and widespread professional problem solving.

Culture promotes innovation and school improvement (Little, 1982; Louis & Miles, 1990; Deal & Peterson, 1990; Kruse & Louis, 1997; Waters, Marzano, & McNulty, 2004). Toxic cultures that harbor mediocrity, inertia, and apathy are unlikely to be innovative. In contrast, schools that encourage change and risk taking foster people who seek innovative practices and experiment with new approaches. In positive cultures, staff plan and implement new practices.

Culture builds commitment and kindles motivation (Schein, 1985, 2004). People are motivated and feel committed to an enterprise that has meaning, values, and an ennobling purpose. Motivation is strengthened through rituals that nurture identification, traditions that intensify connection to the school, ceremonies that build community, and stories that convey the heart and soul of the enterprise.

Culture amplifies the energy and vitality of school staff, students, and community. It has long been known that social climate and culture influence the emotional and psychological orientation of a school. Many say that the context is infectious. This is especially the case in schools that are optimistic, caring, supportive, and energetic. Staff, students, and community are likely to take on those same characteristics. But the opposite is also true. Some school cultures are toxic. The social milieu is so negative that even the positive individual can become discouraged or disheartened.

Culture focuses attention on what is important and valued (Deal & Kennedy, 1982; Schein, 1985, 2004). Rules, job descriptions, and policies can influence what a person does. Yet unwritten rules, informal expectations, and rites and rituals may be even more meaningful precursors of positive action and sustained progress. Unstated, often hidden, assumptions and expectations are embedded in cultural patterns and become more intensified over time. With meaningful values, daily work is centered on important issues of quality instruction, continuous refinement of teaching, and accelerated learning.

Symbolic Leadership

With evidence from both business and education highlighting culture as a critical aspect of cohesion and performance, what's holding us back from strengthening school cultures? Why do standards, testing, and accountability continue to play such a dominant role in educational improvement and reform? Part of the explanation lies in the prism through which we view schools.

Bolman and Deal (2003) have identified four lenses, or "frames," people rely on to size up and act in response to situations. A *human resource* frame emphasizes people's needs, skills, and the importance of a caring, trusting climate. A *structural* mindset emphasizes goals, efficiency, policies, a clear chain of command, and results. A *political* take highlights a world of scarce resources, power, conflict, negotiations, and compromise. Finally, a *symbolic* disposition spotlights meaning and the symbols, rituals, ceremonies, stories, and other emblematic forms on which faith and hope are anchored and communicated.

In education, some viewpoints are more prominent than others. For example, policymakers rely heavily on structural suppositions in developing mandates for school reform. Nearly all reform initiatives of the past three decades have emphasized goals, restructuring, uniform standards, or standardized tests. Conversely, school leaders—teachers and principals—tend to read and respond to day-to-day challenges from a human resource posture. Although some principals (especially in high schools) and superintendents may be more structurally oriented, the human resource way of viewing situations is more familiar. Although political views are renounced publicly as distasteful or pathological, people incessantly rely on power and influence, pressure, and coalitions behind the scenes to get what they want. Finally, the symbolic and cultural side of schools is too often viewed as "soft," mystical, or as a superficial postscript.

The neglect of the symbolic aspect of schools does not square with ideas of what successful leadership is all about. One of the most significant roles of leaders (and of leadership) is the creation, encouragement, and refinement of the symbols and symbolic activity that confer meaning. The late Lou Pondy (1976), who studied business organizations, pointed out that the effectiveness of a leader is in the ability to make actions meaningful to others.

Edgar Schein (1985), an organizational psychologist, states the case for cultural leadership even more forcefully: "There is a possibility underemphasized in leadership research, that the only thing of real importance that leaders do is to create and manage culture and that the unique talent of leaders is their ability to work with culture" (p. 2).

In this book we examine the ways leaders shape culture to create a cohesive, meaningful, nurturing, social milieu for teachers to teach and students to learn. Leadership in robust cultures is dispersed among teachers, administrators, parents, and students. Together they read, shape, and continuously renovate the culture of their school.

Schools' Need for Improvement

There is widespread consensus that America's schools need significant refurbishing. The proposal that schools should be revamped to more closely resemble businesses is also frequently invoked. But when discussion veers to what the make-over should look like and how the renovation should proceed, the shared consensus twists to sharp disagreement. We think that schools should, in fact, resemble businesses. But popular reasoning is often flawed. We see it differently.

Our reason: *top businesses have developed a shared culture with a deep set of values*. A successful company's culture pumps meaning, passion, and purpose into the enterprise. Company leaders know that success flourishes only when people are committed, believe in the organization, and take pride in their work. Such organizations become beloved institutions where people pour their heart and soul into everyday ritual and routine.

The same passion and purpose must become true of our nation's schools. Although values, folkways, and traditions will take form to reflect the unique character of educational institutions, the human side of good organizations may be worth emulating. In education, the risk of not doing things right is even higher. A poor-quality product or service can be recycled, but a young person who does not learn or who drops out is hard to salvage—a lost treasure. Top-drawer teaching and learning can never flourish in a sterile or toxic environment.

The evidence is persuasive. The challenge is real. The need for some leaders to step forward and take the necessary risks to build positive school cultures has never been greater. If Starbucks' CEO can pour his heart into a cup of coffee or IBM's Gerstner fall in love with a company, so too can school leaders pour their hearts into or fall in love with their schools and student learning. If Starbucks and IBM can polish tarnished and neglected cultural ways into a gleaming promise of new meaning and opportunity, there is no reason schools cannot take a analogous tack, a step into building deep, positive cultures.

Part I

The Elements of Culture

1

Schools as Tribes
The Power to Transform

The tiny community of Ganado is in northeast Arizona's high desert. It is nestled in the midst of an expansive reservation twenty-seven miles from Window Rock—the largest town in Navajo lands. This is picturesque country, dry and beautiful, dotted with traditional hogans and small homes. To outsiders, the town of Ganado would be one of the last places expected to house an award-winning elementary school. The town has one of the highest unemployment rates in the country. Forty-six percent of the families do not have running water, and 35 percent across the district's one thousand square miles have no access to electricity. Despite the odds, Ganado Primary School is the town's pride and joy and has been continually recognized for its excellence.

Our first edition featured the special ethos of Ganado Primary based on our visits, examination of documents, and interviews with students, parents, faculty, and Sigmund Boloz, the school's principal for almost twenty years. We have chosen to update the case and add new themes because the school continues to thrive. Ganado Primary was identified as a School of Excellence in 1997, received the Arizona A+ award three times, and persists in serving its students and community with a dedicated professional community and unique culture. The school continues Boloz's tradition of success secured by a strong positive culture.

Ganado Primary School: A Desert Jewel

The school's large, modern building is centrally located, visible both from the main road and the small town. Its color blends with the high desert and fits well with the history and spirit of the community. The school's entry courtyard features a small-scale sculptural likeness of Spider Rock—a spiritually significant, 800-foot vertical sandstone pinnacle rising from Canyon de Chelly. The sculpture beckons students to enter a way of life that involves a deep sense of community history and traditions, an unwavering present-day focus on learning and literacy, and a lucid image of the future.

The school was not always a source of community pride. Over twenty-five years ago, Ganado Primary had one of the worst school buildings in Arizona. Designing and constructing the new school was the beginning of a new identity: a distinctive set of cultural ways and practices that are anchored in tradition but still embrace modern standards. The school's culture engages teachers in ongoing learning about their craft, communicates high expectations for students through lively programs and celebrations, and involves parents as equal partners in the learning experience. It also envelops students with symbols, support, and significant others as they go about their business of growing and learning. The combined symbols of student achievement and Navajo traditions make the environment caring and meaningful. The fusion of modern practices and ancient tribal ways connects the school historically and organically with the local community.

A walk through Ganado reveals a visual portrayal of the school's cultural values and assumptions. A visitor entering the school experiences an inviting, open area dominated by the depiction of Spider Rock. More than mere adornment, the replica represents a sacred place and time in Navajo history. According to tradition, the actual column of sandstone in Canyon de Chelly is where

Spider Woman gave the Navajo the knowledge of weaving. Today, this symbolic spire signifies that Ganado Primary is a historically anchored, sacred place that conveys knowledge and skills that are part and parcel of being a Navajo. It signals to the community that the school is part of its heritage, traditions, and future, a symbol of respect and appreciation for Navajo ways.

Inside the building, one immediately is struck by a massive red Ganado Navajo rug hanging in the front hallway. The rug—woven in the distinctive Ganado style—pulls one into the unique Navajo way of life. It is beautiful, complex, and emotionally warming. It draws you into an image of community and school working together in harmony. Nearby walls are adorned with awards for educational excellence won by staff and students, as well as academic work demonstrating a wide array of student accomplishments. But, fitting local values, displays are a symbol of community pride—neither boastful nor excessive.

The school's architecture and design blend symbol and purpose. The school was designed collaboratively with architects to serve educational needs and to send an emblematic message. It is a fusion of modern educational equipment and methods with symbols of the traditional ways of the Navajo people. The school is configured in four units or quadrants. Each quadrant houses a team of teachers and a cohort of students—a design that reinforces the closeness of staff and makes students feel part of a cohesive group.

Each quadrant denotes one of the tribe's four sacred directions and represents a core value. The east is associated with white, dawn, spring, critical thinking, and a clear mind. The south is associated with blue, daylight, summer, one's purpose in life, the roles of staff, and the importance of keeping oneself nourished. The west is identified with yellow, twilight, fall, the waning of light, suppertime, and interpersonal relationships and connections. The north is associated with black, night, winter, the importance of respect and reverence, personal values, and how life fits together in harmony (Witherspoon, 1995, p. 13; personal conversation with Sigmund Boloz, 2008). The deeper meanings of these four cardinal directions play out in the school and reinforce the learning and social mission of the school

At Ganado, dawn is celebrated through the start of the day and the opening of school. Daylight and summer represent growth and sunlight, one's learning roles during the day. Twilight reminds one of relationships in the school and within family. Night reinforces the importance of reflection and contemplation, an important element to planning and thoughtfulness. The four quadrants are represented throughout the school in the colors of the blinds in each classroom and in stories told and retold in group settings. All these elements—architecture, mission, colors, stories, and relationships—combine to form the Ganado culture.

Other unique architectural features also reinforce cultural and instructional values of Ganado. For example, the library is located in the center of the building, a point signaling the centrality of literacy. It displays thousands of books in open view as students travel from one part of the school to another. Writing displays reinforce literacy. Small reading corners invite students to curl up with a book. Hallways are airy and light. A room used for meetings, reflection, and community gatherings is shaped in the form of a hogan—an ancient Navajo home design with deep symbolic significance, still common in rural areas.

In the meeting room, traditional wooden posts holding up the ceiling seem perfectly in harmony with modern paraphernalia: books, scanners, camcorders, and computers. Hallways are adorned with numerous expertly hung Navajo rugs woven in the red geometric design favored by local weavers. The rug represents "quality, attention to detail, care, skills, learning, creativity and tradition" (personal conversation, S. Boloz, 2008), all values of the school. The floor in the lunchroom mirrors the patterns in the Ganado rug on display in the foyer—again reinforcing cultural traditions and tying the school together with common themes.

Architecture and artifacts vividly represent the school's core values and basic beliefs as embodied in the school's mission statement during Boloz's years:

> The Ganado Primary School's mission is to provide opportunities for children to make sense of their world, to respect themselves and others, to respect their environment, and to appreciate and understand their cultural and linguistic heritage. Children, teachers, and administrators all bring varying points of view, resources, expectations of and assumptions about the world, and ways of dealing with their daily circumstances. Our mission is to help everyone negotiate their experiences with the content of the classroom, instructional style, and the social, emotional, physical, and professional interactions of school life. We believe that a relaxed atmosphere where surprise, challenge, hard work, celebration, humor, satisfaction, and collegiality is the natural order of the day for all.
>
> Care must be taken to insure that sound philosophical, developmental, and cultural understandings of children are at the heart of decision making in the classroom and the school. The question, "What is it like to be a child?" underlies staff development, matters of curriculum, parent involvement, and instructional approaches. "What is it like to be a teacher?" is an equally valid question. What is true about our mission to children is true for teachers and staff as well.

The school's mission is reflected in a reflective piece written in 1997 by then principal Sigmund Boloz. It sketches a portrait of his core obligations:

The C Diet

My job is

to keep the compass

to massage change

to build credibility: *a positive image for the school in the eyes of the* community

to cultivate *my staff*

to ask the compelling *questions*

to be an advocate for children

I build the culture *of the school*

curriculum consensus constituents community

I see my job as building my staff. I strive to build:

confidence *in themselves, in their decisions and in their teaching*

courage *to take risks and to break new ground*

compassion *for children and others*

character *to always do their personal best*

competence *that they know the current trends*

capacity *to learn new things*

commitment *to our mission*

clarity *a good focus on the whats and the hows*

consciousness *to bring thinking to a higher level*

communication *open lines of dialog*

collaboration *share expertise*

connectedness *bonding to each other and our mission*

collegiality *professional interactions*

challenge *to keep staff on their cutting edge*

critical thinking *thoughtfulness*

creativity *to implement innovations*

curiosity *actively seek better ways*

contentment *feel accepted*

Other key values are played out in the culture of Ganado. Central among Navajo educators is the importance of honoring relationships and harboring a deep feeling of moral responsibility to oneself and to others. In addition, in Navajo culture all tribal members are to work toward "living well" in harmony and balance. As Eder (2007) notes, living well means " . . . wholeness; continuity of generations; one's relationship to the beginning, to the past and to the universe; responsibility to future generations; life force; and completeness" (p. 279). As we have seen, these are core values of Ganado educators and are reinforced in efforts and actions to jointly ensure that all children learn.

Ganado's Mission and Rituals

The school's mission and purpose cast a shadow far beyond architectural form, artifacts, and the written word. The school year is packed with rituals and ceremonies for everyone—students, staff, parents, and elders. These engaging rites reinforce core values and beliefs.

Four times a year, Boloz held a "Once Upon a Time Breakfast" meeting. He invited students, teachers, and parents to bring their favorite books and celebrate literacy while they enjoyed food, drink, and read together. This activity bolstered the professional community and emphasized literacy as a vital part of life.

Students were acknowledged on a regular basis for their growth and learning. During the "Celebrating Quality Learning Award Ceremony," a significant number of students received awards for writing, quality work, citizenship, dance, drama, or for progress in mastering the Navajo language. Each student was recognized and parents or caregivers joined them at the front for applause, the award, and a photograph. Parents and teachers joined with children and celebrated together what they had collectively accomplished to make the school special. After the awards, reporters from the school newspaper conducted interviews and took additional photos for the articles that appeared in the coming issue. Frequently the award that students received was a Ganado T-shirt proudly worn at school. These celebrations reinforced cultural values by anointing champions who exemplified the purpose and successes of the school.

Learning to read earned major celebration throughout the school year, thus signifying its centrality in the school's mission. A T-shirt was designed that said, "I can read guaranteed," reinforcing widespread attention on the recognition and deciphering of written words. Reaching 3.0 on Accelerated Reader was the measure of success celebrated with the ringing of a bell and the presentation of the T-shirt in the lunchroom, where the whole school would applaud the accomplishment. A photograph of the student and teacher memorialized the event and was placed on the wall for public attention.

Parents also learned at Ganado—through workshops on important topics and a series of year-long classes leading to a general education degree (GED)—and were feted in frequent events as their learning progressed. Parents are snugly woven into the texture of Ganado. They are respected, supported, and made to feel welcome at any time.

A Culture of Learning

At Ganado everyone is a learner: students, teachers, parents, and administrators. The value of learning and improving is part of what keeps the school moving forward. Boloz met often with teachers from one of the four units for a "curriculum conversation." Together, they explored new ideas by discussing articles or books, viewing DVDs of new approaches, or observing individual teaching episodes. The dialogue offered fresh perspectives on curriculum, instruction, and learning. Teachers were esteemed as professionals, always seeking innovative ways to serve their students. As Boloz noted, "You need to be thinking, learning, be a model in your class." Staff deepened this commitment to self-improvement by reading, attending workshops, and staying abreast of new developments in their fields.

Over time routine meetings have become ritual gatherings to share ideas on literacy ("Reading Achievement Meetings") or examine progress on the school improvement plan ("The Instructional Improvement Committee"). Small meetings are held to discuss an individual student who is struggling.

These ritualistic occasions are focused on improving instruction and serving children, but they also reinforce trust, collaborative decision making, and a shared sense of purpose. Staff have become more of a team, more skilled at diagnosing and solving learning problems, and more committed to the school and its community. There is a sense that if any children fail, the school and staff have botched the job.

Child-focused curriculum and instruction are prized and reinforced through voluntary focus groups that pursue relevant topics in depth. Sometimes topics originate from teachers' direct observations of classroom needs, but they are also prompted from close examination of performance data. For example, ten teachers might examine new techniques for teaching poetry; another group might discuss alternative ways of teaching writing to first-graders. The meetings are lively, focused, and collegial. They simultaneously build skills and a sense of community—all core values and expectations of the culture.

Everyone at Ganado is dedicated to learning. An "Early Childhood Academy" for classroom aides provides new ideas and conveys a sense of importance among the school's paraprofessionals. Classroom aides are immersed for a full week in early childhood concepts and classroom techniques. All who participate receive book bags with the academy name and year prominently displayed, symbolizing their responsibility to carry newfound knowledge back to the school.

As former principal Sig Boloz noted: "We marinate students in literacy and activities in the classroom. And we marinate our staff in new ideas, new dialogues, and new approaches." His successor continues the legacy of finding ways to reinforce learning and nurture a sense of professional community.

Another staff ritual is "Teachers as Readers." The school provides time for teachers to eat together and talk about what they are reading. Individuals bring a new book or article that they want to share and discuss with colleagues. Leadership for the sessions is distributed, thereby reinforcing the sense of professional responsibility.

Students as Leaders

Students are also active shapers of cultural ways. The "Tour-guide Program," for example, is an ongoing tradition. First- and second-grade students guide visitors around the school, highlighting student work, explaining the presence of community weavers, and showcasing school awards. The petite guides are articulate and well prepared to enlighten visitors about the special features of the school and the unique values they share. Youthful guides become both purveyors and consumers of their own culture and history.

Students help others become more proficient readers and are the editors, photographers, and writers for the school newspaper. They are engaged and energized by the school.

Although learning is important, it is also important that students have fun. Activities that promote learning must also be engaging and fun, making the classroom culture a joyous one.

Another important tradition that supported kids and built ties with the community was the "Caring Adults" program. Everyone was encouraged to volunteer who was willing to identify a student who seemed lost or in need of some attention. The adult took the time to talk with the student, ask about his or her interests and work, listen to the student read, or just check in. Almost everyone had someone; the principal had several, the head custodian had five on his list, and the secretary, clerks, and food service workers all pitched in. Students with emotional needs or who were going through tough times had access to an adult who acknowledged that they existed, took an interest in them, and made sure they connected daily. This invisible platoon of adults was there to help kids. The program not only helped the individual student but it also built a deep sense of purpose and commitment to children as a whole.

Ganado Lore

History and stories are significant cornerstones of the school culture, just as stories are a key part of Navajo culture. Almost everyone in the Ganado community is a storyteller. They tell stories of change and renewal, celebrating the transformation of the school from one of the worst to one of the best in Arizona. They share tales of the conferences and training programs that have kept their school fueled with new ideas and innovative instructional approaches. They spin yarns of parents once excluded who now work in the school, get their GEDs, and come to early-childhood conferences. The narratives tell of reaching goals, overcoming obstacles, and working together as a community. The school's treasure trove of stories becomes glue for the staff, sets expectations for new hires, and provides the stuff of celebrations for parents and community.

Ganado's Cultural Network

There is a strong informal network at Ganado Primary. The social system is filled with role models and individuals who keep stories and information flowing. One of the first school superintendents was appreciated as a special person at Ganado. A Navajo, he had been there for thirty years and was credited with a good heart; some say perhaps he cared too much. When he visited the school, children flocked to see him and wrote to him through the school post office—and he responded. In the early years, Grandma Taliman was another character in the cultural network, and she was a foster grandparent for many children. She visited with staff and children and brought the attention, caring, and sense of legend that only the elderly can offer. She made people feel good just by being a quiet, understanding anchor to the past and a reminder of how community values came to be.

Ganado is full of heroes and heroines. Some are parents who learned to read themselves and then helped their children. Some are staff members dedicated to becoming great teachers. Many others are students whose deeds exemplify the school's values and purpose. As Boloz remarked, "A good administrator has to have heroes—people who embody important values" (S. Boloz, personal conversation). Many people have been heroes and heroines in Ganado; they have "carried the flag" in various areas, with different groups, at different times. Sometimes they have been teachers, sometimes parents or community members. Principal Boloz is now retired from the school but remains an icon and is fondly remembered. His words, deeds, and commitment are constant reminders of the school as a beloved institution.

Ganado also has its subcultures. The four units are tight-knit family subcultures and miniprofessional communities. Staff often have breakfast and lunch together and talk about curriculum and other educational matters. Teachers in the units take special pride in "their kids." Each cluster is its own small neighborhood. Students feel connected, cared for, and part of the school as a whole. School is another family for many.

Other core norms are deeply embedded in the culture. Staff are always asking, "What does the child need?" They assume that everyone is working together; clearly problem solving is a joint venture at Ganado. Kids are always at the center of decisions in the school. Knowledge is valued and the expertise and intelligence of teachers is respected and upheld. Learning by everyone is a virtue, not a requirement. Creativity and new ideas are revered resources to be nurtured. Finally, the school is considered another family for children, not as a replacement for the core family but as a place to provide continuity to caring relationships in the community.

Ganado did not instantaneously change from worst to first. It took twenty years of hard work, leadership, and a communal desire for something better. The school's successes continue based on the same commitment. Staff and students continue to be zealous learners, active problem solvers, and creative architects of a culture in which history is a foundation for the future, current accomplishments are recognized, and children are the center of the universe and tomorrow's promise.

Ganado Primary is an example of a school possessing the necessary elements—the blueprint and building blocks—every school assembles to build a cohesive culture that gives purpose, vitality, and direction to an educational enterprise. School cultures—no matter whom they serve—offer, like tribes and clans, deep ties among people, and the values and traditions that give meaning to everyday life. In the next chapters, we explore the elements of culture in more detail and see how culture shapes behavior, focus, and success. It makes no difference whether the school is large and urban, well funded and suburban, or poor and rural, the challenges are very similar. Unless America changes its course and focuses on meaning more than metrics, our schools will never realize their full potential.

2

Artifacts, Architecture, and Routines

Symbols of Culture

As the principal assumed her new post, she remembered the promise she had made to herself during the interview to get rid of Mr. Meany. Mr. Meany, the middle school mascot, resembled a cross between a warlike gremlin and a grumbling troll—a rather terrifying creature. To her and others on staff, the mascot represented precisely the opposite of what she wanted the school to be—a warm, nurturing, and peaceful place. She bided her time until the Thanksgiving break. On Friday, with the help of other allies on the staff, she removed the large figure from the school's foyer and took Mr. Meany to the basement. Once school resumed, she felt quite pleased with herself. No one mentioned Mr. Meany's absence. She assumed he wasn't missed and started to think about how the school would come up with a new mascot—one that was more in tune with the cultural values she had in mind.

Between Thanksgiving and Christmas, however, there was an unusual amount of buzzing and whispering in hallways and in the teachers' lounge. Whenever she approached such gatherings, the conversations abruptly ended. Something was wrong, but she couldn't put her finger on what it was. Over Christmas she asked the custodian to come to her office. She asked him if he had any idea what was amiss. He came right to the point: "You kidnapped Mr. Meany and buried him in the basement. Mrs. Smith rescued him and now has him hanging on the wall of her classroom." The new principal and her supporters received their first lesson in the role symbols play in school culture. Meaning is in the heart of the beholder.

What Are Symbols?

Symbols represent intangible cultural values and beliefs. They are the outward manifestation of those things we cannot comprehend on a rational level. They are expressions of shared sentiments and sacred commitments. Symbols infuse an organization, a nation, a tribe, or a family with meaning, and they influence our thoughts, motivation, and behavior. Anyone who doubts the power of symbols in our modern world should review the controversy around "Joe Camel," the animal caricature that the R. J. Reynolds tobacco company used in their advertisements for Camel cigarettes. Joe Camel was viewed by parents and the public as a prime factor in encouraging teenage smoking. One of the stipulations included in a proposed settlement with U.S. tobacco companies was that the use of Joe Camel, or any other animal likeness, in advertising be prohibited.

But one also remembers the power of symbols to inspire feelings: the AT&T networked world, the American flag, one's local sports teams, religious iconography, and the Red Cross. These symbols immediately call up images and feeling, memories and significance. Symbols in schools also are powerful elements of culture.

Symbols are cultural rallying points. They represent those intangible values and beliefs that are difficult to express. Architectural forms convey values, as do the symbols and signs that adorn walls. And leaders are living logos; through their words and deeds they signal what's really important.

The Power of Symbols

Symbols, as representatives of what we stand for and wish for, play a powerful role in cultural cohesion and pride. Attachment to shared symbols unifies a group and gives it direction and purpose.

As our new principal quickly discovered, removing cherished symbols, irrespective of their potential negativity, carries great risk. Tampering with important signals and signs is like playing with fire. In designing buildings, creating displays, naming schools, or choosing logos, we must be mindful of the signals being sent. Symbols play a more prominent role in schools than many initially suspect. What is often labeled as fluff is more often the stuff of leadership and culture.

Symbols and Signs—Messages and Meaning

Schools have a panoply of symbols and signs scattered throughout classrooms, hallways, and gathering places. This rich mix of symbolic artifacts makes schools either meaningful sanctuaries for students and celebrations of accomplishment, or dead and empty vessels of bureaucratic control. Some of the more obvious symbolic artifacts include the following:

> *Mission statements.* In Joyce Elementary School, messages and symbols of purpose and mission are displayed everywhere. Enlarged for easy visibility, the mission statement hangs in the main hallway. Posters exhorting students to greater achievement adorn classrooms and gymnasiums. Teachers wear school pins to communicate their belief in students. In another elementary school, the school pin worn by teachers is in the form of a frog. It represents the transformation of frogs to princesses and princes; the school embraces transformation as its core purpose. The school's Web site is an important place to display and discuss the mission statement and perhaps to translate it into a motto that is easier to remember.

> *Displays of student work.* Good schools usually festoon the halls with displays of the hard work of students. Examples of student work are ubiquitous in good schools. Hallways become galleries celebrating student creativity and accomplishment.

Banners. Banners exhorting students to work hard, do well, let their intelligence shine through, and excel also adorn halls of many schools. At Nativity School, they also are displayed proudly during the opening and closing ceremonies. Bright, colorful symbols help remind people of the deeper purposes of diligent effort in the service of learning.

Displays of past achievements. In Ganado Primary, student work is put on show universally. In addition, awards that the school has received (of which there are many) are prominently exhibited. T-shirts and book bags from various early childhood conferences are arrayed chronologically along with the awards. Superbly crafted rugs donated by local weavers decorate the walls. Sports achievements are also prominent.

Symbols of diversity. In a Wisconsin elementary school, the creativity of new immigrants is merged with the values of their new home. The walls are adorned with intricate and beautiful Hmong stitchery, some featuring images of an American eagle. In another school, the flags of every nation represented in the community are raised each morning in front of the school. The cultural diversity of the Madison Memorial High School in Madison, Wisconsin, is represented prominently in life-sized plaster sculptures of teenagers from many ethnic and racial backgrounds. The display stands prominently and proudly as a symbol of shared community.

Awards, trophies, and plaques. Athletic awards, trophies, and records of the season's scores in various sports are traditional representations of the value of athletic competition. But more and more schools are recognizing, with equal relish, the academic and artistic successes of students and staff. In many schools now, beautiful display cases accommodate trophies, plaques, and academic honors of the school, and these are larger and more prominent than the sports trophy case.

Halls of honor. Audubon Elementary School is known for its "Hall of Honor," where every award received by a student or teacher is matted and framed. Newspaper articles featuring the school or a staff member are added to the mix when they appear. Copies of published articles, interviews, or poetry written or published by staff or students are also on display. The hallway is a powerful and visible testimony to the hard work and accomplishment of individuals and teams within the school.

Mascots. We opened the chapter with an example that shows how deeply mascots fit into people's emotions and their ideas about what things mean. School mascots are tangible symbols that represent intangible values; they are the spirit that welds a school into an organic whole. What is the message behind the mascot? What values, skills, traits, and attitudes are found in the mascot? Is it a fighting Badger, a strong Mustang, an energized bear Cub, or a skilled Red Hawk? It is the meaning behind the mascot that is most important.

Historical artifacts and collections. The history and traditions of a school are important symbols of longevity and sustained purpose. Schools with no clear sense of history are disconnected from the past; they are rootless and lack meaning. As a counterexample, one school displays textbooks of bygone eras (from McGuffey readers to current trade books), the tools of writing from the past (from Esterbrook fountain pens to BIC ballpoint pens to retired computer screens), and the photos of groups of children from years past. The display reinforces a shared embrace of roots and historical progress by tying past and present together in a shared culture.

Symbolism of the Physical Plant and Architecture

The physical environment and architecture of schools speak volumes about cultural values and beliefs. Students and staff spend much of their time encased in a physical environment of walls, halls, and spaces. Children, in fact, spend more than fourteen thousand hours inside a school building over twelve years of schooling. The physical setting and the school's symbolic appearance have a lot of time to exert an influence. As Cutler (1989) points out, the architecture of schools reflects important beliefs as to what schools are about and the meaning they hold for students and for the community. In the late nineteenth century, schools were often fashioned after factories, communicating a working atmosphere of efficiency and production. Later, many schools were designed to look like castles. They had towers, limestone decorations, dark oak stairways, and monumental paintings in the halls. Evanston Township High School in Illinois is a classic example of a castle for learning with towers, limestone, and brick.

More recently, architects have worked closely with educators and have constructed schools that communicate a more personal, intimate learning environment with strong ties to the community. The Ganado Primary School, as we have learned, was designed to be quite functional, but with symbolic ties to Navajo values and traditions through the blueprint based on the Four Directions, symbolic colors, and tribal patterns. These trends in architectural design reflect an evolution in the way we think about education.

The symbolism of architecture reinforces culture in four major ways:

>*Architecture signals what is important.* A school that has a small library or gigantic gymnasium sends a clear message of priorities. In some schools the largest and most luxurious sections are the athletic facilities. At Ganado Primary, visited in Chapter One, the library is large, airy, and in the middle of the school. It conveys the central importance of reading and learning to the school's success.

>*Architectural elements of schools can tie a community together.* Where the design, colors, and other elements used in the

building connect to a community's ethnic or cultural heritage, it tightens the bonds between the school and its community. In a New Mexico Pueblo, for example, a school principal fought a successful battle with a superior over whether the school's perimeter would be enclosed by a metal chain-link fence or encircled by an adobe wall in the architectural tradition of the Pueblo. Her stance was dictated by her strong belief that the school should reflect community values (Martinez, 1989). At Ganado the four sections of the school mirror the four quadrants of Navajo values and spirituality.

Architecture provides a message of deeper purposes and values. The size, grandeur, complexity, and spatial arrangements of a building communicate significant messages about what's important and what really matters. The Oneida Nation Elementary School near Green Bay, Wisconsin is shaped like a giant turtle. The turtle remains central to the nation's creation story in which the people were carried on its back to Mother Earth. The hopes and dreams of the community and children are now symbolically carried on the turtle's back in the form of the school. The turtle and teaching are now inextricably linked.

Architecture motivates staff, students, and community by forging pride in their school. If it is dilapidated, dirty, or poorly landscaped, a school becomes an eyesore rather than a symbol of pride. The tall sculpture of Spider Rock outside in the front of Ganado Primary School represents a holy place to the Navajo people. It also symbolizes the knowledge students receive and is a key source of school pride.

Even the physical appearance of the school grounds can send a message. At Joyce Elementary School in Detroit, the small yard in front is carefully manicured by the joint efforts of staff, students, and community. The small patch of grass and flowers represents the care and attention given to students and is a pleasant oasis in a neighborhood that is otherwise dotted with boarded-up homes. Memorial High School in Madison hosts a modern public sculpture that allows the diverse student body to sit together in peace and celebration of variety.

Schools built by the Cuningham Group in Minneapolis and other architectural firms reflect the architects' understanding of the power of symbols; these firms have focused on making architecture a visible symbol of a school's underlying values and purposes while providing spaces that are beautiful and functional.

School Names as Signals and Signs

Even though not all schools are named for an actual person or place (large urban areas often provide only numbers; for example, PS 142), many names offer clues to both students and community about the school's meaning and cultural values. The significance of some names has been lost to historical neglect, thus losing a prime opportunity to build a sense of rootedness, cohesion, and identity. In contrast, the John Muir School in Madison, Wisconsin, bestows symbolic power with its name. Each year features a John Muir week, when the values of the famous environmentalist are highlighted and recognized. These commemorations tie students and teachers to values the school holds most dear. Names can have national or international meaning—Malcolm X, Cesar Chavez, John F. Kennedy—or they can have local significance, that of a dedicated educator who guided the district through difficult times or a principal who passed on too early after a life of dedication to students. Finding the significance behind a school name can enhance awareness of the source of values and beliefs.

Living Logos—Symbolism in Daily Routines

What is a living logo? Principals and other leaders broadcast powerful symbolic messages as they go about their daily routines. They transmit meaning and ideals in all the seemingly mundane things they do. Leaders, both formal and informal, convey important messages and meanings in their words, actions, and nonverbal announcements. Their work lives are placards, posters, and banners of symbolic meaning.

This symbolic signaling occurs through the things they read, words they use, issues they raise, ideas they float, and the things they get upset, exuberant, or frustrated about. Other indicators are the educational books they buy, read, and talk about, the workshops and conferences they attend, the things they notice and discuss when visiting a classroom, and the things they write about. Types of symbolism conveyed by the actions of leaders include the following:

> *The symbolism of action*. How principals spend their time sends a powerful symbolic message. John Flores, a strong instructional leader at Visitacion Valley Middle School in San Francisco, talks to dozens of students while taking a visitor on a tour of classrooms. Barbara Karvelis spends time on the playground at Edison Elementary School in San Francisco connecting with students, talking with parents, and leading the Pledge of Allegiance, even though she has administrative reports to finish. Interested attendance at cocurricular activities sends a message of inclusiveness. Participation in professional development workshops shouts the importance of life-long learning. What leaders pay attention to in their actions sends a strong message of core ideals.

> *The symbolism of the school tour*. School leaders are onstage as they tour the school, talk to students, share ideas with teachers, and visit classrooms. Meandering makes time for brief exchanges "on the fly." What leaders do or say as they step into a classroom signals what they care about.

> *The symbolism of intellectual engagement*. Charles Baker reads history and philosophy, as well as the most current educational books. He constantly talks about the ideas he finds. Having

a bookshelf filled with important educational books sends a message very different from that of a bookshelf of policy manuals from the central office.

The symbolism of writing. Sigmund Boloz, former principal of Ganado, wrote poetry about teaching, learning, and schools. He wrote letters to students who have written him to encourage correspondence via the school post office. Some principals put pen to paper in a column in the school newsletter to acknowledge accomplishment and appreciation, as well as telling stories of achievement. Some principals rely on blogs and podcasts to get their messages out.

The symbolism of communicating ideas. Debbie Meier (1995) speaks eloquently about new ideas in secondary education and keeps a journal of issues and dilemmas. Her memos to staff, students, and parents are profound discussions of issues in the school, from school violence to trust and from instruction to assessment. Using local radio shows to answer questions and regular podcasts to talk about educational ideas and new programs are also useful modes of communication.

The symbolism of advocacy. As a principal Phyllis Crawford was an articulate and continuous advocate for her school, pressing the central office and the local community to support innovative staffing and approaches that serve students. She could describe the core values of the school to any age group and did so at every possible opportunity. Often school leaders press for resources, support, and flexibility for their programs, all of which signal their commitment to the school's mission.

The symbolism of collegial sharing. Teacher-leaders in Audubon Elementary discuss content from innovative workshops while preparing their daily materials for class. In other schools, staff meet in the morning over coffee to share instructional ideas or seek help on problems. At Stevenson High School, sharing and collaboration symbolize and reinforce their professional learning community. Expectations for this level of collegiality are part of the hiring process and early socialization into the school culture.

The symbolism of greetings. A staff member is a living logo at an elementary school in San Francisco as she greets non-English-speaking parents with a big smile, words of greeting in their own language, and a cup of coffee. The quick "hello," the pat on the back, a question about how a project is going, or other greeting can jumpstart the morning for a student or staff member. Without warm greetings a culture can wither; and teaching can become a job rather than a calling.

The symbolism of song. At Nativity School, an original song written in the 1930s by a student still inspires and motivates. In another urban school, staff and students each month select a popular song that communicates hope and self-respect and evokes the potential in everyone. The lyrics are reprinted and used as part of a reading program; the message is discussed to build self-esteem and motivation.

The symbolism of joy, laughter, and fun. At Visitacion Valley Middle School in San Francisco, administrators, teachers, and aides are often smiling, laughing at student jokes, and approaching situations with humor. They send messages of joy rather than epistles of incarceration. In other schools, administrators and staff share funny stories to get through hard times and to remember the humanity of teaching. Even routine morning announcements can be fun if presented as a poem, rap, or song.

The symbolism of storytelling. In one school the teacher-storyteller recounts the history and events of the school to all visitors to the building. Similarly, at Ganado Primary, student tour guides in vests escort guests around their school while proudly recounting the school's history and successes. Stories are a deep symbol of history and longevity. Retelling positive or funny ones seldom gets tiresome, and each retelling is often enriched with embellishments.

The symbolism of professional learning. Staff who talk about educational reform, new curriculum possibilities, and innovative instructional techniques send a message and model the value of learning new ideas, growing professionally, and seeking new ways to serve students. In some schools it is a badge of honor to be the teacher chosen to share a new technique.

The symbolism of recognition. Administrators and staff leaders wear the school colors, fasten badges proclaiming the chess club regional winners, or talk about the successes of the school to communicate pride in achievement and effort. Recognition that is honest, authentic, and from the heart is always appreciated. Quick e-mails or handwritten notes of appreciation reinforce values and show gratitude for doing a good job.

Educators, students, and community connect in powerful ways to the symbols, artifacts, and logos of a school. They identify with these seemingly mundane but, on a deeper plane, invaluable signs of their institution with emotions and sentiments that last a lifetime. School leaders need to think twice about their school's artifacts, architecture, symbols, messages, and signs. In their daily contacts and communications, they also need to be aware of what their deeds and actions say to others. Symbols, signs, and signals link everyone to the deeper purposes and meaning of the school. In Chapter Three, we see how school leaders pull these elements together to build different but powerful cultures.

3

History

The Value of Lore and Tradition

Objects in the mirror are closer than they appear.

In 1991, the West Palm Beach School District launched the new school year with a nostalgic trip down memory lane. Rather then being regaled with reports of new policies and plans for the coming year, several hundred administrators revisited their past and were reminded of how present cultural mores and ways came to be. Following introductory remarks by the superintendent, school board president, and an external consultant, they were assigned to groups based on the decade they joined the district: 1960s, 1970s, 1980s, or 1990s. They were given an hour and a half to sort through the events of their decade to pinpoint that generation's legacy to the district's traditions. As the groups started to work, the entire 1960s contingent walked out. The reason: during that turbulent decade, the district experienced a teacher walk-out; a few scars remained. Other groups laughed at old practices they remembered, cried at the loss of a colleague or program, smiled at remembered successes with challenging students, and reconnected on an emotional level to their early careers in the district and their schools.

After lunch, each group presented the essence of their decade—their contribution to the district's culture. For an hour and a half, the district's heritage was recounted through raps, skits, songs, and poems. Old-timers reconnected with old memories; newcomers learned for the first time how things came to be. Everyone experienced a common bond in the pageant of history—the district's cultural roots and the deeper accomplishments and values that had pulled them through tough times. As the event ended, Joan Kowal, the superintendent, laid out her hopes for the approaching year—a new beginning grafted onto the solid stock, commitment, and sense of community fabricated over the decades.

The past is closer to us than it often seems to be. It affects us more than we think. Because Americans value newness, we often neglect our roots, creating, as some historians see it, the United States of Amnesia. What went before not only shapes the present, it also outlines the future. As we look back to the past, we see roots embedded in the mythic bedrock shoring up existing cultural patterns and practices:

> All people and institutions are the product of history (defined as past events). And whether they are aware of it or not, all people use history (defined as an interpretation of past events) when they make choices about the present and future. The issue is not whether people use a sense of the past in shaping their lives but how accurate and appropriate are their historical maps.... (Tyack & Cuban, 1995, p. 6)

All schools have histories. They begin even before the site is selected and doors of the new building are opened. To the extent that memories are revisited from time to time, the founding nucleus of beliefs and values remains stable and the accumulation of key experiences around the core story is communal. Otherwise, the ethos of the school becomes splintered into subgroups and the school is vulnerable to the educational fads of the moment. Without a well-known historical map the school loses its way.

Several years ago in Beaverton, Oregon, a scenario similar to West Palm's played out. The district was growing at a rapid pace, adding new staff, and experiencing the uncertainty of new leadership. Cultural divisions between seasoned veterans and newcomers were obvious, and the place needed some glue to bind people together. The chance came at the district's kick-off event. Administrators assembled, assuming that it would unfold as usual: an outside speaker, a few team-building exercises, and a speech by the superintendent. Instead, they were loaded onto yellow school buses and transported to a local winery. As they walked off the bus, they saw tables labeled by decades. People assembled around the table that represented the year they joined the district. The district's rapid growth was evident in the large size of the group relatively new to the school system. Scribes, preassigned to tables, passed out relevant artifacts—pictures, newspaper articles, school annuals. Each group prepared a presentation for the larger gathering. From early beginnings to current realities, the history was recounted through drawings, poems, songs, and dramatizations. The decade-by-decade accumulation of traditions and ways was now shared by everyone. As the sun set behind the historic building, administrators reboarded the buses and returned home. The next day, the superintendent laid out his hopes and dreams for the coming year, connecting his vision to events and lessons from the past.

Comparable cultural histories have played out in numerous places. All are not a grand event such as West Palm's or Beaverton's. The Fairfax School District, for example, created a video of its history from early beginnings through the decades. The video is a portable archive that can be used to orient new staff or acquaint parents with the district. Whatever form they take, such reminiscences often reinforce the dedication and commitment to the deep spiritual purpose of education, but also revisit difficult and challenging times. Cultural histories serve a deep symbolic and social purpose so the future can be based on core values and filled with hope.

Fortifying Cultural Roots

Past events may influence present cultural practices in dramatic fashion. Learning the history is critical to acquiring a robust understanding of the culture of a school—it is not simply an occasional social gathering of old storytellers. Knowing one's history replaces amnesia with mindfulness; rootlessness with purpose and direction.

One of the first things a physician or psychotherapist does prior to an appointment is to review a patient's history. It is an important step in making an accurate diagnosis of a current condition by understanding the physical and psychological grounding of the present situation. Likewise, before tinkering with a culture leaders need to initiate, one way or another, an in-depth and comprehensive history of their school.

Most often, it is wise to make this a public event rather than a private undertaking with inclusion of all adults, or students, who work in the building. There are many approaches. A school principal in New York State, for example, turned over half a day of the opening day staff-development event to veteran teachers. Their job: recount the school's fifteen-year heritage. The staff had prepared extensively with old photos, videos, and artifacts from prior curricula. After the successful event, the principal observed: "It had a profound influence on newcomers, but an even stronger impact on the old-timers. I guess the only thing worse than not hearing about the past is knowing the history without anyone to tell it to."

Monona Grove High School used passage into the new millennium and the completion of the new high school as an opportunity to do an archeological excavation into layers of the past four decades. The effort was dramatized with songs from the various eras and humorous stories of the now-defunct technology that once captured the school's attention. Although remembering the songs of the 1970s brought warmth to the group, it was often the memories of dedicated and caring staff that moved the group more profoundly. The history "lessons" connected the staff to echoes of the foundation on which the school was built and provided a bridge to cherished possibilities and dreams that would now seep into new hallways and classrooms. Without history the building was simply a new structure. With a historical map, it charted a meaningful innovative course that was rooted in what came before. Revisiting old roots pulls some things forward, revitalizes traditions that unknowingly have been allowed to wither, and helps people let go of outdated or unpleasant memories best left behind.

Histories can be part of transitional ceremonies, marking significant temporal passages. At the Nativity School the seventy-fifth anniversary of the founding provided not only an opportunity to recognize changes and accomplishments of the past years but also to reconnect to the values built up over time. Staff and administrators from prior eras were invited, artifacts of the four decades were assembled, and a monograph of the school's history prepared. The cover of the written history was graced with a collection of old photos, report cards, and memorabilia. The event brought together grandparents and children, retired staff and greenhorns, and continues to serve as a history of the first seventy-five years.

Nurturing the Future

Cultural patterns and traditions evolve over time. They are initiated as the school is founded and thereafter shaped by critical incidents, forged through controversy and conflict, and crystallized through triumph and tragedy. Culture takes form over the years as people cope with problems, stumble onto routines and rituals, and create traditions and ceremonies to reinforce underlying values and beliefs.

What are the forces that nudge a culture in one bearing or another? Formal and informal leaders articulate path and purpose through their words and deeds; crises and controversies forge new values and norms in the crucible of tension and strife. People, through their everyday activities, spin out unstated rules governing relationships and conflict. Planned change, although often of mixed success, leaves its traces and mementoes, agendas and materials. Cycles of birth, death, and renewal bequeath a rich deposit of secrets and sentiments.

Dealing with History

Like those facing grave illness (Kübler-Ross, 1970), organizations have varied responses to the past. Some negative cultures perpetuate anger about unsettled slights, missteps, fads, and bad leadership. Other organizations are in denial, suffering from historical amnesia about what happened in the past. Wounds are left to fester, infecting the present with a pessimistic, negative tone. Still others use the past as a springboard to the future, embracing events that formed their unique circumstances and learning from experience. A positive understanding and acceptance of what came before can be an important grounding for future decisions. An example from business illustrates the potential of fusing the past with current realities and future possibilities.

Delta Corporation was a culture "going downhill": sales were down, costs were soaring, and stockholders were grumbling; no new products loomed on the near horizon. Internally, things were a mess. The company's 3,500 employees and managers were clustered into distinct subcultures and silos, each with its own version of negativity. In the middle management group, a "Golden Fleece" award was given to the researcher who developed the idea with the least bottom line potential. Early followers of Harry, the creative founder, were partitioned into the Leper Colony. Their hero was Serendipity Sam, the engineer who had amassed more than his share of Golden Fleece awards. Harry's replacement was hired to staunch the downward spiral. She envisioned blending old and new in a culture where "engineers could fly" as a way to revive the once creative and productive enterprise (Owen, 1987).

Her first move convened thirty-five representatives from across the company in a management retreat. She opened the meeting with stories of Harry and the Garage Gang (now the Leper Colony). She called attention to one of Harry's first successful inventions, displayed prominently in the middle of the room. Most of the participants had never seen the primitive machine. During the break, Harry's first effort became a magnet:

> Young shop floor folks went up and touched it, sort of snickering as they compared it with the sleek creations they were manufacturing now. But even as they snickered, they stopped to listen as the Leper Colony recounted tales of accomplishment. It may have been just a "prototype," but that's where it all began. (Owen, 1987, p. 172)

After the break, subgroups shared their hopes for the company, then reconvened as a whole group arranged in a circle around Harry's machine. As they compared notes from the small group discussions, Serendipity Sam suddenly erupted with an idea for a new product:

> The noise level was fierce, but the rest of the group was being left out. Taking Sam by the hand, the CEO led him to the center of the circle right next to the old prototype. There it was, the old and the new—the past, present and potential. (Owen, 1987, p. 173)

The CEO asked Sam to slow down and put his ideas into words the whole group could understand. Calmly and clearly, he spelled out what he was thinking. Everyone begin to pitch in, elaborating the concept:

> The group from the shop floor . . . began to spin a likely tale as to how they might transform the assembly lines

in order to make Sam's new machine. Even the Golden
Fleece crowd became excited.... (Owen, 1987, p. 174)

In one intense moment, the old spirit was brought forward and
grafted onto a new initiative fusing the once disparate subgroups
together in a common quest.

Back to the Future

Our view is that, in large measure, past is prologue. A learning
organization is one that mines past and present experiences for
important lessons and principles, for stories and legends that can
energize current labors. Through trial and error people learn what
works and what doesn't. Across time, triumphs and tragedy accrue
in cultural codes—a legacy of shared wisdom that lets people know
what is the best or right thing to do. Recounting history through
stories and events transmits these important precepts, giving meaning to cultural practices and ways and laying a foundation for the
future.

Without roots, an organization drifts from one fixation to
another, often repeating past mistakes and failing to learn from
either victory or defeat. Fashion and fascination replace purpose
and planning. As an example, a Broward County, Florida, principal
was describing a past year's disaster. She was trying to instill in
teachers a sense of empowerment so they could take charge and
make decisions on their own. She arranged for a consultant from
a local bank to offer a day-long session on empowerment. In the
midst of the session, teachers revolted and asked the consultant to
leave. His message wasn't seen as relevant or of much help. The
principal was devastated and vowed never again to try to empower
the school's teachers. As her story ended, an observer said, "Wait
a minute. Didn't that event demonstrate that teachers could take
charge? In trashing the empowerment session, teachers empowered
themselves. What a great lesson—as long as it is made explicit.

You thought you failed. In fact, you were a resounding success. Why not write the history that way?"

Exhuming the Past

How does history affect the culture of schools today? As we noted in the definition, the elements and character of culture are initiated in response to circumstances, forged and shaped over time, and crystallized by repetition and reinforcement (Deal & Kennedy, 1982; Schein, 1985, 2004; Collins, 2001). Culture develops as people cope with problems, establish routines and rituals, and develop traditions and ceremonies that strengthen and sustain values and beliefs. Eventually core assumptions become mores—informal rules of behavior—that are strictly enforced through social sanction.

History is reconstituted in a variety of ways. Existing documents—old annuals, official papers, or minutes of meetings—are a rich source. So are artifacts: trophy cases, pictures on walls, statues, or architecture. Spending time with informal priests, historians, or storytellers yields a treasure trove of times past.

In addition to poking around, listening, and keeping an open mind, a school leader can get an initial reading of a school's history by observing and asking a few key questions:

How long has the school existed?

Why was it built?

Who were the first staff and administrators?

Who has had a major influence on the school's direction initially and over time?

What were core values on which the school was founded?

How have the mission and values changed over time?

What critical incidents occurred in the past, and how were they resolved, if at all?

What were the characteristics of past principals, teachers, and students? How have they changed? Have community demographics shifted?

What symbolic messages was the school's architecture supposed to convey?

How many generations of staff and students have moved through the school?

How were curriculum, instructional practice, and technology initially viewed by staff? How have instructional approaches been reinforced or transformed?

How has the school responded to past decades' various reform efforts?

Questions on special topics offer further guides to the examination of a school's history:

Leadership. Formal and informal leaders help provide bearing—a sense of purpose and mission. Who were the formal and informal leaders of the school? What did they stand for? What new approaches, structures, or ideas did they bring? If the school is relatively new, who were the founding principal and teacher-leaders? Was leadership shared with staff, distributed over various roles? Did formal leaders built credibility or trust with staff, students, and community?

Crises, conflicts, and controversies. Crises, conflicts, and controversies forge cultural patterns and practices by hardening beliefs and assumptions in the crucible of strife. What were the major crises, controversies, or conflicts that staff faced over time? What was the source of the difficulty? How did staff resolve the conflicts? Did frustrations and hostility go underground, fomenting lingering anger and scars? Did staff and administrators address differences directly and honestly, developing conflict resolution skills? Did part of the staff leave on account of the disagreements or simply become toxic saboteurs? When differences cropped up, was some accommodation or compromise reached to heal wounds and rebuild a sense of community? Are the issues still a persisting source of negative memories, toxic stories, and painful reminders?

People, personalities, and relationships. The individuals and personalities of people who inhabited an epoch in the school's history establish customary ways of interacting with others. These norms promulgate unstated rules for relationships and communication. How did people treat others—with respect, disdain, or distance? What kinds of relationships developed over time, and were they exclusive or inclusive? Did staff establish trust and caring as ways of being or did they deem distrust and avoidance as the preferred approach? Is there a sense of shared mission or is the school divided into silos and warring factions?

Birth, fading, death, and renewal. All schools have ongoing cycles of birth, failing, death, and renewal among people, values, policies, and programs. How these critical transitions are navigated affect future states of affairs. How were new programs, approaches, or instructional philosophies initiated, implemented, supported, and, at times, ended? How was the sadness of losing a popular staff member (through firing, death, or retirement) dealt with? How was the loss of a student to accident or illness addressed? What happened to favored programs or methods as the school took on new programs, instructional techniques, or governance plans? How were the past crises or changes in the community (loss of employer, change in composition, decline in population, a wave of foreclosures) handled? What are the residual feelings associated with all these major crises?

Changes, modifications, and adjustments. Change is never easy. The aftermath of positive and negative changes lingers in memories, sometimes for decades. Modifications of goals or educational philosophies, instructional practices, schedules, and methodologies are often mishandled. They can surface as barriers whenever new changes are suggested or begin.

School restructuring, improvement, reform. One of the most prevalent historical artifacts of education has been a string of "scientifically based" or simply fashionable reforms (the acronyms provide a smattering of these initiatives—ESR, OBE, MBO, SBM, CSLR, SFA, SLC, NCLB, PLC—as do names: open classrooms, restructuring, standards-based reform, accountability). The history of these programs form the soil in which new reforms sprout or die. Many of the well-intended improvement efforts employed similar features and elements (though often with different nomenclature). And as each reform wave crashed onto school culture, prior efforts were often ignored, denied, or buried. New names were put on school reform files or appended to old plans.

One should ask many questions about reform. How was the reform initiated and by whom? How was core staff involved in the identification and decision about the new program? What supports for implementation and evaluation were in place—if any at all? How did the staff deal with the natural implementation dip and frustrations of new practices? Did trust or mistrust of the change process ensue? How did the reform end—was it an amicable divorce or a nasty demise? Are the reforms of the past viewed as sick attempts to be fashionable or noble attempts to improve?

Prior reforms are in the rear view mirror of every school. Knowing the past's legacy is central to moving forward. Teachers carry the emotional and intellectual scars and social history of improvement efforts in their heads and hearts. Whether conscious or not, these early memories of programs and events are part of the cultural heritage, the foundations on which new programs are built.

Sometimes prior foundations are strong, clear, and positive, as in a Southern elementary school where collegial planning was a revered part of their remembered past. Planning was seen as enjoyable, social, and fun so when central office mandated a structured data-driven decision-making program it was tailored into the school's ongoing practice. The school thrived on the new software because as modified it fit what they were doing already. But more often historical reform foundations are made of quicksand or resemble toxic dumpsites.

Negative experiences with reform over the years, if not addressed, will consume or sabotage new efforts. For example, in one district OBE (outcomes-based education) had been forced on schools with no explanation or connection to existing core values and customary practices. Needless to say, later state standards-based reform efforts met with bitter, hostile, passive aggressive sabotage. Schools are still fighting the new reform initiatives, even though in many respects the curriculum is reasonable and compatible with the shared mission of the school. Unpacking, understanding, appreciating, and dealing with the history of change is crucial to future success. Ignoring past experiences is fraught with danger and predictive of calamity.

In almost all previous labors to improve schools, we have emphasized rectifying or reforming existing deficiencies. We concentrate on replacing traditional ways with more modern, up-to-date practices. That was the mindset of business leader Lou Gerstner as he assumed the responsibility for setting IBM on a new course (described in the Introduction). But the deeper he dug into IBM's history the more he realized he was on the wrong track. The problem wasn't that IBM needed to adopt new ways. It had drifted from original cultural values, traditions and spirit that had once made it one of the world's most admired and profitable businesses. His prime challenge was to reach back and pull forward discarded or forgotten patterns and practices, buff them up, and move ahead with refurbished old rootstock.

A comparable revitalization is long overdue in our nation's schools. Under the banner of school reform, we have for so long sought to make schools more rational and rigorous that we have muted their spirit and vigor. Like IBM, schools have drifted from the cultural values that once made education a proud profession and gave parents and the public confidence and faith that schooling prepared young people for a successful career and a productive life. Reconnecting with historical roots is a fundamental step in shaping school culture. Successful schools nourish and adjust the heritage that brought them to the present. In doing so they reconfirm Burton Clark's (1972) observations of the reason unique colleges succeed. They relied on a saga or historical narrative to unite faculty, students, administrators, staff, and alumni into a "beloved institution." That is also possible in schools, but only if we savor the heritage that the times of yore offer to the present and future. At the turn of the century, a British educator said of the American school system: "The American school is radiant with a belief in its mission, and it works among people who believe in the reality of its influence, in the necessity of its labors, and the grandeur of its task" (Tyack & Hansot, 1982, p. 3). Now may be the time to consider a move back to the future.

4

Myth, Vision, and Values

Discovering a School's Highest Calling

A school's purpose and mission serve as bedrock of its culture. The embedded values are often embodied in a unique founding story or myth. Nike provides a memorable example:

Bill Bowerman was a track coach who wanted his athletes to have everything conceivable to make them winners. A large part of this was making sure that they were mentally and physically prepared to compete. But he also wanted them to have the best equipment available. Adequate running shoes were one of his concerns, but there was nothing in the existing marketplace to fit his high standards. His epiphany came one morning as he watched his wife prepare breakfast. As the waffles came off the iron, he saw the basis for a new design for running shoe soles.

He experimented with a waffle iron and liquid rubber until his vision found form in a prototype. That became the basis for Nike's waffle sole, which is still found on many of the company's running shoes. This became the corporation's founding myth and core story (Fog, Butz, & Yakaboylu, 2005, pp. 53–54).

Comparable founding narratives survive in Southwest Airline's original concept sketched on a cocktail napkin, Proctor and Gamble's mistaken batch of soap that floated, and 3M's determined employee who invented Post-it® Notes. Tales of origin also exist in education; for example, Teach for America and the search for a way to serve disengaged youth through Middle College High Schools in Guilford County, North Carolina (personal conversation, Terry Grier, 2007).

But not all myths or core stories arise around an organization's early beginnings. Predicaments also breed guiding legends. A local Domino's Pizza outlet hit a retailer's nightmare—a hungry crowd of customers and a shortage of pizza dough. The local franchisee called headquarters and a private jet was dispatched laden with the scarce commodity. Employees locally did everything possible to stretch the inventory, but to no avail. The dough ran out before customer orders could be filled. "For an entire month afterwards, employees went to work wearing black mourning bands" (Fog et al., 2005, p. 14). The outlet had failed to deliver but the company and local workers gave it their best shot. The core story of dedication to service was reinforced—"the best pizza delivery company in the world"—and the incident became a part of legend.

Core stories pass on a vision or visual image of what the company stands for and show what people can do to realize a vivid picture of the present and future. Martin Luther King Jr.'s vision was expressed as a dream. It pictured how racial relations might be if the country were to live up to its venerable creed. His vision, as he stated, was "deeply rooted in the American dream." Sigmund Boloz, principal of Ganado Primary School, and Bob Herring, principal of Nativity School, had visions for schools that would transform their communities, achieve the seeming unattainable, and foster both achievement and social justice.

Too often we think of visions as grasped from thin air by an individual who can foresee a bountiful future. In reality visions emerge serendipitously from experience. People know the history of the Kelloggs, who, in searching for a healthy food for patients, were interrupted during one of their experiments, and as a result their boiled wheat turned cold. When they rolled and baked it, it flaked, thus laying the foundation for Kellogg's breakfast cereals. Visions are reinforced in the same way: 3M's Scotchgard™ process was discovered and developed by an employee as the result of a chemical that was accidentally spilled on a material that proved impervious to soap and other solvents. Post-it® Notes were created with an experimental glue that failed its intended purpose because it didn't stick very well. Such stories buttress the company's dedication to "innovation at all costs."

Similar accounts abound in other notable businesses: the Nordstrom manager who gave a customer a refund on tires the company didn't sell; the Ritz-Carlton doorman who hired a cab to catch a guest at the airport who had forgotten his suitcase; Johnson and Johnson's decision to pull Tylenol from the market when only a few bottles had been poisoned; BMW's rise from the financial depths of 1959 when a series of poor decisions brought the company close to financial ruin.

Every tightly knit human group anchors its existence in a unifying myth or a core story that orients the group's worldview and channels behavior. Without such an existential anchor or compass, the enterprise wanders aimlessly, like a rootless tumbleweed changing course with each shift in wind direction, fashion, or bandwagon. Schools are no different. Without a core story the efforts of people become fragmented and find refuge in subgroups, bureaucratic routine and minutiae, or toxicity (unified by "devils" and negative images).

A unifying myth or core story spells out how the group came to be, why it exists, the beliefs and values it holds most dear, and what would be lost if it ceased to be. The long history of a school and its deeper sense of purpose and direction are incorporated in its core story. Burton Clark (1972) referred to this root narrative as an organization's saga, a story "between the coolness of rational purpose and the warmth of sentiment found in religion or magic . . . [it] includes affect that turns a formal place into a beloved institution" (Baldridge & Deal, 1975, p. 98).

As in businesses, these unifying narratives arise in new beginnings or crises. Ganado's core story centers on the needs of students, the belief that linking school and community tightly will enhance learning, and the staff's deep sense of responsibility for developing literacy. This narrative was reinforced by the story of Spider

Woman and how she came to the spire in Canyon de Chelly that later became known as Spider Rock. She brought to the Navajo people the art of weaving and knowledge. Today the myth is perpetuated by the replica of the spire in the school's entry. The school's basic purpose is to pass on knowledge to the new generation in a kind and caring atmosphere.

As a counterexample, the school district in Edina, Minnesota came to its core story in a difficult circumstance. Their new superintendent, who had replaced a legend, committed suicide. Her death prompted a deep inner search for the glue that held the district together. A committee produced a set of values that were winnowed down in interviews with teachers, parents, students, and members of the community. The final credo: "Edina. We care. We share. We dare."

The mythic side of a school is the story behind the story. The core story sits at the center of what life in the school is all about. It looms as a school's existential anchor—its spiritual source, the wellspring of cultural traditions and ways. In this chapter we use such concepts as mission, purpose, values, and beliefs to approximate the meaning behind the myth or core story to get to the deeper calling, higher worth, or greater cause of an educational enterprise.

Mission and Purpose in Schools

At the hub of a school's culture are its mission and purpose—the revered focus of what people do. Although not easy to define, mission and purpose trigger intangible forces that inspire teachers to teach, school leaders to lead, children to learn, and parents and the community to have confidence and faith in their school. Mission and purpose shape and reflect what the school hopes to accomplish, desires that vary from place to place. Most important is that people share beliefs of what the school wishes to realize. Study after study has reinforced the power of a shared sense of mission to guide decisions, motivate innovation, strengthen commitment to the calling of education, and energize collaboration. Charter schools, for example, "reflect the profound impact of [the founders'] personal beliefs and life history on the school's mission, passion and instructional practices" (Deal & Hentschke, 2004, p. xi). Public schools with a strong sense of shared purpose are equally affected.

The struggle to come to terms with mission and purpose is often manifested in mission or vision statements. These are noble attempts to get to the core of what a school seeks to bring about—its sacred mission or ennobling purpose. But in efforts to reach for this deeper mythical level, too often schools produce abstract documents that have little to do with what really matters or what people do on a day-to-day basis. In many cases they are vague statements written in haste and rarely remembered or lived. In a large urban high school, for example, the assembled staff was asked to describe the school mission. After a long silence, the principal replied, "It's written on the wall outside the auditorium—our school philosophy." A request for someone to tell what was on the wall resulted in silence.

Mission and purpose run deep. People need a medium that will help people connect viscerally and emotionally with the school's reason for existence, its higher calling. Mission declarations are often merely words without any real meaning and are frequently stored in some distant computer file rather than held deeply in one's heart. Authentic purposes speak to hearts as well as heads. Achievement scores, for instance, are poor substitutes for what schools can contribute to young lives and a vibrant, democratic society. To paraphrase a quote from Fog and associates (2005): if a school does not stand for something more profound than raising achievement levels, then it probably does not make a memorable difference to teachers, students, or parents. Put on a spiritual plane, a school needs a deeper soul. Without soul, flesh and bones have no purpose, but without flesh and bones, soul has no substance or way to enact purpose.

Purpose and the Meaning of Success

Definitions of success, as Schein (1985, 2004) notes, reflect the purposes of organizations, such as schools, and vary from place to place. These missions can run from the mundane to the deeply purposeful. Sometimes schools emphasize purposes that ignore or avoid the centrality of learning for all students. These less than positive missions include the following:

> *Achieving extracurricular success.* In some schools, how well the football team does is a fundamental measure of what makes a successful year. As is so vividly detailed in the now-classic *Friday Night Lights* (Bissinger, 1991), a school and its community can be obsessed with winning in athletic contests. The mission and point of the school reside in the Friday night football games. This same emphasis can also carry over to the performance of the school band ("Our band has been in the Macy's Thanksgiving Day Parade three times") or other extracurricular activities ("The school yearbook has won highest honors five years running"). In some schools, emphasis on athletics or other activities outshines academic success or character development.

> *Performing well.* Some schools value the teaching process. Success is achieved when teachers and others believe they have done a good job. Too often judgments are formed on lessons well presented or classrooms well organized and under control. Sometimes successful teachers are engaging presenters—sages on stage—or skillful managers. But great performances can fall flat in the larger scheme of things. Teaching is successful only when students learn what they need to know to thrive. Ultimate success can only be determined long after the classroom performance has ended. That is why judging teachers on classroom evaluations made once a year falls short of

measuring the significant difference teachers can make. Kidder (1989) captures a shortfall too often true: "Teachers usually have no way of knowing they have made a difference in a child's life, even when they have made a dramatic one" (p. 313).

Learning for the elite. Some schools measure success by the number of students accepted at Ivy League colleges or designated as National Merit Scholars. Cultural values put emphasis on the success of top students. One school felt a sense of accomplishment when teachers produced double-digit numbers of National Merit Scholars in one year. In reaching this pinnacle of success, however, the needs of many other students were ignored. Students who are not part of the elite lose motivation, as staff spend most of their time and energy serving the needs of the highest-performing students. The rest eke by or drop out.

Surviving, or not making waves. Some schools define triumph as just getting by, surviving another day, week, or year. The accent is on keeping the pond placid without visible problems or undercurrents. Teachers are happiest when left alone. The focus is on just making do. Students know that if they don't make demands or rock the boat, they'll probably be promoted and receive their diplomas at graduation time. That's what many parents really care most about.

Embracing the new flavor of the month. For some schools, accomplishment is defined as being first with the latest. Instituting a new instructional approach, using new technology, or trying whatever currently is in vogue is what counts. It doesn't really matter what or whether students learn. More important is that something innovative is in the works. Change itself becomes the shared mission. Being up to date and in the vanguard is regarded as the emblem of excellence.

On the more positive side, the mission of the school can embrace a broader sense of purpose, such as the following:

Building a professional learning community. Some schools have worked to establish a professional learning community with a profound commitment to learning for all, both students and teachers; establishing programs to serve the social development of students; fostering a deep sense of responsibility for student learning; and forming strong collaborative and collegial interchanges that strengthen the profession and hasten innovation.

Significant learning for students in toto. Some schools pour heart and soul into seeking and attaining high standards of universal learning. In these cultures teachers focus on diverse learning needs, from the most highly successful college bound to those who will find meaningful jobs in the trades, service sector, or other places of work following graduation. Time and attention are spent working on learning across the board. Celebrations are convened when students succeed at whatever route they have chosen to follow. Success is defined by how many students reach their learning potential.

Purpose and mission do many things for schools. For example, they define what actions ought to occur; they motivate staff and students by signaling what is important and what will be rewarded; and they steer the allocation and distribution of resources according to what is considered important or valuable.

Values, Beliefs, Assumptions, and Norms

Myth, mission, and purpose give generalized guidance to what people work toward on a daily and weekly basis. Other concepts used to capture the deep mythical underpinning of school culture include values, beliefs, assumptions, and norms. Each is a related, often overlapping, way to get at the sacred calling of an educational enterprise. Sometimes used interchangeably with mission and purpose, values, beliefs, assumptions, and norms all have a special contribution to make in capturing the symbolic glue that holds a school together.

Values are the conscious expressions of what an organization stands for. Values define a standard of goodness, quality, or excellence that undergirds behavior and decision making and influences what people care about (Ott, 1989). Values are not simply goals or outcomes; values capture a deeper sense of a school's priorities. Without an existential commitment, everything is relative; values focus attention and define success.

Beliefs are how we comprehend and deal with the world around us. They are "consciously held, cognitive views about truth and reality" (Ott, 1989, p. 39). Beliefs rest on faith rather than evidence. They mediate the connection between cause and effect. Beliefs originate in group and personal experiences and are established through history and its interpretation. Beliefs are powerful in schools because they represent core understandings about student capacity (immutable or alterable), teacher responsibility for learning (little or a lot), expert sources of teacher knowledge (experience, research, or intuition), collaboration (useless idea or core principle), and the link between teaching and learning (direct or incidental).

Assumptions are sometimes viewed as the preconscious "system of beliefs, perceptions, and values" that guide behavior (Ott, 1989). They are deeply embedded in a cultural tapestry, and they shape thoughts and actions in powerful ways. A school may have underlying assumptions about certain types of children (either that they can't learn or that they always do), about the nature of teaching (it's an art or a craft), about change and improvement (why change or we are always finding new approaches), or about the nature of curriculum (it's a sequential body of knowledge or a set of central issues). Cultural assumptions are hard to assess because they are so closely aligned with myths and at times even harder to change.

Norms consolidate assumptions, values, and beliefs. They are unstated tokens and taboos governing behavior, dress, and language. These mores or informal rules become "behavioral blueprints" that people are obliged to follow; they are "organizational sea anchors providing predictability and stability" (Ott, 1989, p. 37). Normative conventions develop as the staff in a school discover and reinforce particular ways of acting and interacting. They are bolstered by signals and sanctions when individuals overstep normative bounds.

In some schools, for example, norms govern what teachers are expected to wear (jeans versus dresses for women and trousers for men), how one treats parents (as pawns, enemies, or partners), what one should talk about during prep periods (new cars or instruction), whether one should share a new successful practice with colleagues (or keep it to yourself), and how often a teacher should attend workshops on instruction (seldom or often).

Positive norms vary from school to school. Kilmann (1985), Saphier and King (1985), Deal and Peterson (1994), and others have identified the following *positive norms* that are found in schools:

Treat people with respect.

Be willing to take on responsibilities.

Try to initiate changes to improve performance.

Encourage those who suggest new ideas.

Be conscious of costs and the use of resources.

Speak with pride about the school and your unit.

Enjoy and be enthusiastic in your work.

Be helpful and supportive of others.

Share useful information and new ideas.

Solve problems together when they occur.

Place the needs of students above personal agenda.

Find ways to expand one's own learning.

Be trustful, authentic, and honest.

Feel a sense of responsibility for student learning.

But negative, dysfunctional norms also exist. These same researchers have identified the following *dysfunctional norms*:

Don't disagree with the principal.

Don't make waves and remain in your silo.

Treat women and minorities as inferior.

Put your school down.

Hide new ideas and information from others.

Treat colleagues poorly.

Look busy and innovative when you're not.

Reward or recognize others on the basis of politics.

Laugh at and criticize those who are innovative.

Grouse constantly about everything.

Distrust colleagues.

Do what will serve personal needs. Worry about students later.

Identifying the positive and negative norms or mores is a key task of principals and teacher-leaders. It is key to address these honestly, reinforcing the positive and working to transform the negative, a task that we turn to in a later chapter.

The Remystification of Schools

Each school chooses its own language to capture deep-seated cultural commitments. Some focus on ennobling purpose and sacred mission. Some review and reinforce important assumptions.

Others try to consolidate and communicate core values and beliefs. Still others stand back and take a look at unstated norms that may help or hinder the educational process.

The problem is that today's internal and external pressures nudge schools away from time-honored cultural values or ways. The trend is toward standards and measurement as the only way of assessing the impact of teaching and the effectiveness of schools. Policymakers, parents, and the public want tangible proof that schools are getting the job done. Scores on standardized tests are becoming the only acceptable evidence that students are learning what they need to know. The narrow gauge of achievement tests captures only a small slice of what students take away from their time at school. As a result evidence of success is spotty, tied at times to ethnicity or socioeconomic standing that students bring with them rather than important learning that may be taking place. The cry for tangible evidence and the relative lack thereof undercuts confidence or faith in schools. Over time it erodes teachers' belief in their ability to make a difference. What they once hoped for in a career falls victim to a constricted version of what education means.

They key challenge is this: How do we recapture the magic and myth of education? How do we restore a core story that enables teachers to believe in their importance and convinces the public that schools are worthy of their confidence and support? Some believe the path to these ends is rational, in other words that seeing is believing. Show people results on achievement tests and they will once again have faith in schools. We advocate another direction—that believing is seeing. How do we reinvigorate the tradition of schools as shaping the next generation so that teachers believe in themselves and the public rediscovers the hope it once had?

The key here lies in the culture of schools—the shared meaning these essential institutions create. The bedrock of cultural vitality and stability lies in the optimistic myths, missions, purposes, values, beliefs, assumptions, and norms that, deep down, people cherish. Some reformers in recent memory have concentrated on the demystification of schools: to get better, make them more rational and narrow. We and other writers see another possibility, that is, to reembrace the mythology that launched the public school system in this country: school should be a place to create a sense of community; each student should be able to realize his or her potential; each teacher should feel fulfilled; each parent should experience joy in watching their child learn and grow. Restructuring or setting new standards will not achieve the level of success that reformers hope for without remystifying and reviving the cultural worth of schools and classrooms.

5

Stories and Tales

Passing Along the Vision

Stories are for eternity, when memory is erased,
when there is nothing to remember except the story.
T. O'Brien (1998)

History is an aggregate of stories about people and events sorted in terms of their epic character and enduring influence. Everyday stories cluster into and merge with an organization's core story. These larger-than-life myths or historical narratives that stand the test of time become a profound part of the culture and social capital of an organization. One also finds vivid experiences each day that become parables or stories.

Through telling and retelling, these "little stories" carry values, convey morals, describe solutions to dilemmas, and shape the patchwork of culture. Sometimes they provide comic relief; other times they offer poignant testimony to core values and treasured beliefs. They can portray the process of daily work and the dreams for the future. These small stories fill the hallways, teachers' lounges, and conversations with the latest about what's going on.

Too often, these compelling tales have a short lifespan and dwindle away shortly after the event occurs because no one spots their cultural significance and keeps them alive through retelling. It is everyone's business to tell stories; it is the role of leaders to keep the stories positive and long-lasting.

Every organization spawns stories that tickle the fancy, warm the heart, and say a lot about what the enterprise really means. Here is an example from business:

> An American businessman left his hotel in Stockholm to catch a plane for a trip to Copenhagen. Upon arriving at the boarding gate he discovered that he had left his ticket in his hotel room. He explained his bind to the SAS representative at the counter. She smiled and handed him a boarding card, "Don't worry Mr. Petersen, here is a temporary ticket, and you're set to board. Just tell me the room you were in and where you'll be staying in Copenhagen. I will take care of everything." She contacted the hotel and a porter retrieved the forgotten ticket. The gate agent sent a SAS car to pick it up. She sent it ahead and upon arrival at his destination a SAS employee greeted him: Mr. Petersen. I have your ticket. Here you go. (Fog et al., 2005, pp. 132–133)

This episode is not unusual at SAS, with its reputation service as a businessperson's airline. Former CEO Jan Carlzon called such encounters with customers "moments of truth" in which the company demonstrates its commitment to getting people to their destinations on time.

Another example of such a story is this one from education:

> Samuel was a challenge. Only seven years old, he was chronically truant. When he did come to school he obviously hadn't bathed for days and his clothes were ragged and torn. We got him some new clothes and did our best to make him feel safe and loved while he was at school. Those needs met, it was time for him to learn to read. I worked with him for several weeks and then it happened. He volunteered to read in a group. After

Samuel struggled through the first sentence, he raised
his eyes from the page to look at me. Unable to contain
the joy I felt, my tears flowed freely as he beamed at
me with the first smile I'd ever seen on his face. The
breakthrough had occurred. (Wright, 1999, pp. 178–79)

For this teacher, the "moment of truth" came with the first
sign that a student previously written off was on his way. But
in education, the magic of times when a teacher reaches out
and touches a student isn't always obvious at the moment. It
may take years to realize his or her long-term impact, but every
educator knows when an important breakthrough has occurred.
These special moments, these simple truths, occur regularly in
schools and deserve to be highlighted, told, and retold to reinforce
and focus the culture on its special mission.

Another situation comes to mind. It had been a particularly
tough day for a retired high school teacher. His wife was unhappy
because they could not afford to take a European cruise with their
friends. For this and other reasons, he was beginning to question
whether he had picked the wrong profession. And then, as if by
magic, there it was: an e-mail from a student he'd had in class thirty
years ago. It read:

I hope you are the Mr. Jones who taught me at Sunset
High years ago. I have been trying to chase you down
for a long time. Your name came up when a bunch of
us were sitting around at a dinner party talking about
people who permanently affected our lives. I told them
about the controversial sex education course you and
another male teacher taught. I was raped at age 12
and for three years until your class I did not know if I
was pregnant (ignorance of the times), had syphilis and
might die, or if all sex was violent and angry. You brought
me into reality without even knowing it and allowed

me to develop a healthy attitude toward "normal" sex
and to avoid lifelong psychological problems as a result
of the rape. Many times teachers are not even aware of
the impact they have on their students. I wanted you to
know. Thanks.

Such stories reveal the soul of teaching. There are thousands of
these life-shaping incidents happening in schools each day. Sewn
together they form a core story: making a profound difference in
young lives. Tracy Kidder put it succinctly: "Many people find
it easy to imagine unseen webs or malevolent conspiracy in the
world, and they are not always wrong. But there is an innocence
that conspires to hold humanity together and it is made up of people
who can never fully know the good they have done" (Kidder, 1989,
p. 313). Just as SAS exists to make travel pleasurable and reliable
for those in business, schools are established for the primary purpose
of making growing up a happy, engaging, fun learning experience.
It is through stories that the culture of a school is conveyed to
students, teachers, parents, and the community.

Resurgence of Stories

For some time, the role of stories in organizations has been marginal-
ized by a pervasive fascination with logic and numbers. People
outside school are often repeating: Just give me the facts; we don't
have time to tell tales. Only recently, momentum has shifted.
Probably linked to the well-documented connection between culture and productivity, businesses are taking stories seriously. Told
inside, stories reinforce a unique identity among managers and
employees: that of "who we are and what we stand for." Broadcast
outside, stories communicate special brands or images to customers
and the general public.

In *Made to Stick*, Heath and Heath (2007) examine what makes
ideas understandable, memorable, and influential. Not surprising,
concreteness, simplicity, emotional appeal, and inciting action

made their short list. In a nutshell, what makes ideas stick is stories. Their book is full of examples that illustrate their point. One of the most poignant comes from the Subway sandwich company:

> Subway stakes its identity on healthful food. To empha-size this avowed pledge, the chain launched an adver-tising campaign, "7 Under 6"—seven of its subs with less than six grams of fat. The campaign was relatively successful but paled in comparison to its next effort, the story of Jared. Jared Fogler weighed 425 pounds. His health had deteriorated to a point where dieting became mandatory. Intrigued by Subway's ad, he tried a turkey sub and liked it. Subway's sandwiches thereafter became the anchor of his self-conceived diet plan: a foot-long veggie sub for lunch, a six inch turkey for dinner. He lost one hundred pounds in three months. His unique approach to weight loss attracted media attention and, at 180 pounds, he became Subway's foremost spokesman.
>
> Consumer response to Jared's story was immediate. Sales jumped 18 percent in 2000, another 16 percent in 2001. The slogan "7 under 6" was catchy but couldn't compete with a good story about a real person: "Numbers aren't concrete . . . not many of us will be floored to hear that a sandwich has less than 6 grams of fat, so we don't need much convincing. It's not emotional and it's not a story." (Heath & Heath, 2007, p. 223)

This is not an isolated example of the superiority of narrative: when people hear a speech, only 5 percent remember the facts; 63 percent remember the stories. Humans are hardwired to remember and act on the basis of a story. That's just the way it is and always has been whether in early tribal cultures, in locker rooms, in organizational boardrooms, or teachers' lounges.

In recent years, the number of business books on the subject of storytelling has mushroomed. Consider some of the titles: *Managing by Storying Around*, *Around the Corporate Campfire*, *The Story Factor*, *Storytelling in Organizations*, *The Leaders' Guide to Storytelling*, *Story Telling: Branding in Practice*, *The Power of Storytelling*, *Squirrel Inc*. One of the best-selling business books of the new millennium, *Who Moved My Cheese*, is a story about mice; another book on change tells a tale of penguins. One of the widest-selling books on leadership, *Leading with Soul* (Bolman & Deal, 2001), by one of the authors, is conceived of as a story. As a discursive essay it would not have captured the heart of readers in the same way. Stories engage us in visceral ways.

Businesses are moving in this expressive direction for pragmatic motives. If you want to communicate, motivate people, lead effectively and thrive economically it's hard to beat a good story. Costco's CEO, Jim Senegal, makes no bones about the role of stories in his wholesale business:

> What else have we *got* besides stories? That's really what hits home with people; it's what brings meaning to the work we do. And when you have real examples like our success in selling Calvin Klein jeans, that's what really resonates. A picture is worth a thousand words and a story told appropriately is priceless. Telling one of our stories speaks volumes about our philosophy and our values. (Clark, 2004, p. ix)

Schools have always been fertile ground for stories. And many leaders use stories to send their message inside and outside the walls of the school. But for some reason (perhaps the new federal and state laws focusing on test scores) education seems to be moving away from this powerful part of the culture. We live in a world of standards and metrics. The education literature is filled with numbers, techniques, and formulas. Professors shy away from telling "war stories." We seem hell-bent on emulating what many modern businesses, particularly those most productive, are moving away from. This seems particularly ironic for schools that abound in good stories. We need data and analysis and metrics, but we may have to relearn the need for storytelling as well.

Stories as Solutions

When you talk to administrators, teachers, and other people in leadership positions, the same complaints crop up again and again: How do I get people to listen? How can I encourage people to remember? How do I persuade people to believe what I say? How do I convince people to care? What can I do to motivate people to act? (Heath & Heath, 2007, p. 246). These problems bedevil teachers in classrooms as well as CEOs in large companies. Storytelling offers some commonsense solutions.

Take the problem of getting people to listen. In a world awash with information, trying to grab people's attention is never easy. Stories, myths, or legends can help. Joe Wyatt, former chancellor of Vanderbilt University, faced this daunting challenge each June at the university's graduation exercises. At Vanderbilt it is customary for the chancellor to give the main commencement address. With thousands of people sitting outside on a sultry Nashville summer midmorning, there are more distractions than anyone can fathom. During one of his commencement speeches, most people were engaged in their own private diversions. Then he segued into a story about one of the graduating seniors. Papers came down, people stopped talking, and all eyes and ears were focused on Wyatt's words. It seemed that this young woman wanted to do something special for the graduates of the School of Education. She went to some wealthy alumni and got enough money to buy each graduating senior a beautiful, long-stem iris, the school's symbol. Prior to the event the faculty committee in charge read about her plans in the campus newspaper. This violated the university's "no adornment" policy.

She persisted in the face of intense opposition, and the procession of seniors into the ceremony, each carrying a blue iris, confirmed her inspired strategy.

The chancellor applauded the act and then read a letter from an alumnus who had also read about the controversy in the university's newspaper. It described how the event had touched the previous graduate's heart and renewed ties to his beloved alma mater. As the chancellor read the letter, all seniors in the graduating class raised their irises on high. The crowd's appreciative and emotional reaction was obvious.

But Wyatt's story did more than get people to listen; it almost guaranteed that they would remember. Because the story was about someone who deliberately violated university policy, the irony of the chancellor's authoritative blessing made the incident believable. Moreover, it emphasized how much he, the young lady, and the alumnus cared for the institution—certainly a sentiment contagious to the crowd. And finally, the story undeniably encouraged at least two groups to act: students to do the right thing and then "take the heat" and alumni to give generously to such a wonderful cause. One vivid story solved several persistent problems and helped reinforce a sense of community.

Who Stories Are About

Stories in schools single out exploits of teachers, students, staff, administrators, and parents for special attention. This broad-based inclusion stitches all constituencies into a shared cultural quest.

Students are natural progenitors of wonderful stories. They have not yet learned to clamp their behavior or thoughts. Some of their escapades are hilarious, as we hear in these stories from practice:

> For several weeks, the first grade teacher had been working with students on the alphabet. So far, she was pleased with her progress. Until one of her students ran up to

her during recess. "Miss Martinez, Johnny just called me a bad word." "What word?," the teacher inquired. "You know, the A-word." "What's the A-word?" "You know the A-word; it's so bad I can't say it." "Just tell me; it will be all right." "But Miss Martinez, it's the A-word, I can't say it." "Why don't you just whisper it to me?" The little girl put her mouth close to the teacher's ear and said quietly, "He called me a bitch."

Many times, stories about students are poignant:

In a Texas school, a student had never won an award before. But he qualified for a faithful-attendance award. His attendance was not perfect but still exemplary. Just before the award ceremony, the student was diagnosed with cancer. All he could talk about was how much he wanted to receive his "prize." Tragically, two days before the event he passed away. The school invited the parents to receive the award posthumously on behalf of their son.

Schools are overflowing with stories of teachers who made a difference:

Penny was an eleventh-grade transfer student. She moved to the new school because her mother had died. She had few friends and was an unhappy loner, still affected by her mother's death. Miss Clemens, her English teacher, took a special interest in Penny and stimulated her interest in literature and poetry. Ten years later Penny, now in graduate school, wrote Miss Clemens a letter reflecting on her earlier experiences:

Those years were some of the very darkest of my life, and I didn't like myself or believe I would make it most days. I struggled to fit in and find an identity and meaning for myself and my life . . . You spoke a language of intellect and beauty about literature, and thus about life, that reawakened a love of learning and sustained me through the worst of times. The transforming impact your class had on me planted an internal reason to endure and strive that I am still building on today. Your interest in me as a person and student demonstrated hope and compassion, which I had little of at the time. You could not fathom how much that meant to me. (Wright, 1999, p. 165)

But school support staffs also have an impact on young people. Their influence often goes well beyond their official responsibilities. A bus driver recently commented on the full scope of his work:

My assigned responsibility is to get kids to and from school safely and on time. But my real job is to get them to school and then back home with a good attitude. I'm the first person to see them in the morning and the last to see them in the afternoon. (personal communication)

A principal tells a story about a special custodian:

Custodians at my school are truly respected and held in high regard. Johnny, one of the custodians, was working alone on a Saturday night after an event. He was pushing the risers together in order to clean thoroughly underneath them. In so doing his arm got locked between the risers and Johnny was stuck overnight. The next morning, when a dedicated teacher came in to complete some weekend work, he found Johnny, counting the ceiling tiles to keep him awake. The teacher called 9–1–1, but Johnny's arm could not be saved. Years later, the students would see Johnny working diligently each and every day to keep their school clean, even though he had "special needs" (along with his physical disability). He would scrub with one arm and use his prosthetic arm to hold the rag between it and his shirt. Still, Johnny would learn the names of students, and try to learn about their interests, too. That school was spotless, not only because the custodial staff was excellent, but also because students often followed Johnny's lead by taking pride in a clean school. Oftentimes, Johnny would be honored at school gatherings for his dedication to the organization and its individuals. The students and the staff throughout the school community love and respect Johnny. (Love, 2008)

School principals are squeezed by federal and state requirements, the needs of teachers, and district rules and regulations. Since they are responsible for most paperwork, they have less contact with students, who are one of the main sources of their own satisfaction. They also seldom talk with their compatriots—other principals. One of the situations principals find draining is dealing with irate parents. Tension around such thorny encounters is best relieved by telling and listening to stories. At an administrators' meeting, an elementary principal broke up the crowd with this story:

She was having a particularly rough day. She was a new principal in a tough situation—a rural school with a history of problems. At day's end, she discovered that two female students, kept after school by their teachers, had missed the bus. In a rural setting this poses a problem because the only alternative transportation is provided by parents, who were informed of the situation. The irate father arrived in his truck. He was a little man with a big temper. The principal first saw this as a real opportunity to establish her authority and do some

> P.R. but changed her mind as the father screamed in
> her face. "Where's the principal, I want to give her a
> piece of my mind." The principal smiled and replied
> calmly, "I'm sorry, she's not here right now." (personal
> communication)

This story is funny, but it also reinforces the values of creativity
and humor. All administrators have been in similar situations.
Stories allow them to appreciate the common predicaments that
everyone shares and to chuckle about what they convey about life
as a school leader.

Parents are often the subject of stories. But they also can
generate some good ones:

> A group of leaders from schools in North Dakota were
> invited to share stories about their work. After a lengthy
> silence, an older woman stood up and said: "I'm not a
> school leader, I'm a parent. But I want to tell you about
> my son. He was a very poor student, not very motivated,
> periodically in trouble. He turned in an assignment to
> one of his middle school teachers. She turned it back,
> telling him he could do better. It made a difference. The
> next year, Mr. Ames, a biology teacher, did the same
> thing but also invited my son to take a biology field trip.
> Later my son graduated from college and is now a high
> school biology teacher. I thank all of you. You really can
> make a difference." (personal communication)

When given an opportunity, the public can also contribute
tales. Most often these concern a favorite teacher from their time
as students. The executive director of a biomedical corporation
told this one:

> For the first three years of elementary school, I had to
> be pried, crying, from a viselike grip on my mother's
> legs. I didn't want to leave my mother and I certainly

didn't want to go to school. Then in third grade it all changed. Mrs. Grosenbeck was my teacher. There was something about her that made me feel safe. One day she complimented me on something I said. For some reason it changed my life. I actually began to feel smart. I'll never forget her. I tried to Google her a couple of weeks ago, but couldn't locate her. Maybe she passed away. I just wanted to tell her what she did for me.

Sally Dutra, a well-known thespian and author, writes about her most memorable teacher:

He was short and pudgy (like the Pillsbury Doughboy with a goatee) and he was fond of sitting on a chair backward while he directed a show. He had a nervous "snort-sneeze" that would quietly slip out of his nose without warning, but instead of making us laugh somehow we all understood it had more to do with nerves than a medical condition. ... With great compassion, brilliant insight, and a genuine kindness, Mr. Martello helped unlock a part of my soul and direct me in a lifelong pursuit. He built up my self-esteem by encouraging me to believe in myself and step forward in life to pursue my dreams. (Goldberg and Feldman, 2003, pp. 23–24)

This smattering of stories is just the tip of a large collection about schools. Together they convey a very different image of education than what currently dominates people's thinking. Standards and metrics have eclipsed the magic of stories, thereby eroding a crucial pillar of culture. With this erosion many people have lost faith in schools, educators struggle with believing in themselves, and students close down in a sterile, irrelevant environment. One remedy is telling more stories and convening more occasions where tales can be spun and memories regenerated.

Gathering People Around the Educational Campfire

America's best companies—3M, Southwest Airlines, Mary Kay Cosmetics, Nike, FedEx, Costco, Armstrong International, to name a few—regularly gather their employees to tell and hear stories:

> Great leaders know that workers need more than lofty mission statements and industry buzzwords. To understand and appreciate what their organization stands for, workers need to hear about its people, its values, and its history. And they periodically gather the "tribe" around the corporate campfire (the boardroom, annual meeting, holiday events, etc.) to recall the legends and share new tales. By touching the hearts as well as the minds of their employees, customers, and stakeholders, they leave a legacy of experiences that inspire generations. (Clark, 2004)

Some schools and districts have taken the same route. Beaverton Public Schools, for example, convened an annual "Pits and Berries" storytelling time at its administrative retreats. For two hours, over two hundred principals, supervisors, and district office personnel would swap tales of the best (Berries) and worst (Pits) moments of the preceding year. Stories were first told at tables, and then tables joined other tables, working up to the final judging when an applause meter decided the winner in each category. Two examples from prior sessions capture the content of the narratives.

A winner from the "Berries" category:

> A third-grade boy was sent to the principal's office because he refused to do his work in class. He said he would rather suck snot from a dog than do his assignment. The principal told him to wait while she had an opportunity to ponder the situation. She strolled

to the cafeteria to talk to the boy's grandmother, the school's cook. She asked her for suggestions of what to do. The custodian was there eating his lunch. Hearing the situation, he chuckled and said, "My dog's in the boiler room." The principal retrieved the little Lhasa apso, with a runny nose, and returned to her office. The boy was still there, attended by a learning specialist. She put the dog in front of the startled boy and said, "Go ahead." He said "What?" She said, "Go ahead, you can either return to class and do your work, or suck the snot out of this dog." The boy sat for awhile looking at the dog and then said, "I think I'll go back to class." That evening, his mother asked him how his day at school had gone. He replied, "I found out today that my principal has a sense of humor."

A "Pits" champion:

A new principal had arranged to take a group of his teachers to lunch. He wanted to make a good impression, so had purchased a new sport coat and slacks and borrowed his father-in-law's late model car. On the way to pick up the teachers, he stopped at a drive-through car wash just to make sure everything was perfect. As the car started through the wash sequence, he realized that the windows were still down. In an unfamiliar electronically sophisticated car he had no idea what to do to roll them up. His bumbling attempts were to no avail. The principal and the car went through the entire cycle; both soaked through and through. He did his best to clean the car but realized he would have to go home to change clothes. Now late, he changed clothes and sped to the lunch date. On the way, he realized that in all the excitement he forgotten to relieve himself. He pulled into a gas station, ran to the restroom. As he flushed, the "rogue urinal" back-splashed, dousing him with water. He then realized that his plan to get things off to a great start would rank among the worst days of his life.

Over the years, stories accumulate and the triumphs and tragedies become part of the school lore. The beauty of stories is that they are ripe for multiple interpretations to convey all the important lessons that can be taken away—lessons that will stick because they come from stories.

Convening the educational campfire is not hard. Just putting people in a circle and inviting them to tell stories is all it takes. At first, people are reluctant, but then the magic transpires. People lean into the group and the energy level escalates as people discover that storytelling is an innate human quality. Each "little" story becomes part of the cultural fabric drawing people together under a shared canopy of meaning and spirit.

The Positive Role of Stories

Stephen Denning is one of the prime movers in reviving the art of storytelling in organizations. In *Leaders' Guide to Storytelling*, he presents a "storytelling catalogue" that outlines the different roles stories can play (Denning, 2005):

Sparking Action

Communicating who you are

Communicating who the company is—branding

Transmitting values

Fostering collaboration

Taming the grapevine

Sharing knowledge

Leading people into the future

Barry Lopez sums it up poetically in *Crow and Weasel* (1990):

> Remember only this one thing
> The stories people tell themselves have a way of taking
>   care of them
> If stories come to you, care for them
> And learn to give them away when they are needed
> Sometimes a person needs a story more than food to stay
>   alive
> This why we put stories into each other's memories
> This is how people care for themselves (p. 13)

Stories are the language of leadership. In spotting and telling tales, principals actively shape the culture of their schools. People in education are experiencing a crisis of meaning in part because they are starving for stories. Teachers hunger for belief that they make a difference, a craving that bigger salaries will never fully satisfy. The public longs for faith that schools are preparing young people for tomorrow's challenges. Stories rather than standards and stanines offer the more promising hope that the confidence of parents and the public can be restored. The enactment of rituals adds another important dimension.

In summary, the ways leaders engage the culture through history and stories is the key to success or the basis of failure. Whether one leads a church, a corporation, or a school, understanding and using history and stories is foundational to shaping strong cultures. Ritual, as the next chapter elaborates, provides a behavioral accent to meaningful prose.

6

Rituals

Embedding Purpose and Meaning

Her name was Mrs. Krantz. She taught fifth grade. Every day, after lunch, she would read to us for half an hour. We were often tired, sweaty and still bubbling with energy. But as we sat at our desks with heads down, we were spellbound by the adventures of Nancy Drew and the Hardy Boys. We calmed down as we were transported to other worlds, each a unique construction of someone's imagination. We never wanted her to stop, especially in the midst of a riveting situation. But reluctantly, with renewed energy and focus, we would plunge into the afternoon's lessons. She never missed a beat the entire year. We loved the freedom of the noon recess, but were also eager for it to end—with another episode from the adventures of people we longed to be. Looking back on it, the afternoon story time gave us something in common and unique from other fifth grade classes. Every day after lunch, Mrs. Krantz reading a story. You could count on it.

Imagine our lives without ritual. Do away with morning coffee, the noon lunch break, the evening social hour, the late-night walking of the dog, or whatever special parentheses you look forward to daily and life isn't the same. It's a chilling thought; our daily or weekly rituals provide a welcome chance to reflect and connect, gain perspective and engage in comforting and meaningful routine. We renew ourselves, bond with others, and experience life's fundamental significance in our everyday liturgy. Rituals are central to our existence.

Think of the hollowness we would create if we were to cancel traditions such as Halloween, Thanksgiving, Christmas, Cinco de Mayo, Hanukkah, Kwanzaa, Easter, Passover, summer picnics, county fairs, or New Year's Eve. Without ritual to honor traditions, mark the passage of time, graft reality and dreams onto old roots, heal our losses, and reinforce our cherished values and beliefs, our very being could become empty, sterile, and devoid of meaning.

Without rites to note accomplishments or offer symbolic recognition of small wins and incremental improvements, the chance to renew hopes and spirit would decline. Without ritual, any culture will wither and die. Without periodic expressive events, nothing makes much sense and we lose our way. Joseph Campbell identifies the risk: "When you lose ritual, you lose a sense of civilization; that's why our society is so out of kilter" (Campbell, 1991).

Think about the impact on Catholics when Latin was abolished from the traditional liturgy. Most parishioners did not understand the unfamiliar words, but they found meaning in the protocol and repetition. The change interrupted their spiritual communion. In *Hunger of Memory*, Rodriguez (1982) writes:

> I cannot expect the liturgy—which reflects and culti-
> vates my faith—to remain what it was. I will continue
> to go to the English Mass. I will go because it is my
> liturgy. I will, however, recall with nostalgia the faith
> I have lost...I go to mass every Sunday. Old habits
> persist. But it is an English Mass I attend, a ritual of
> words. A ritual that seeks to feed my mind and would
> starve my somewhat metaphorical soul....I cling to the
> new Catholic Church. Though it leaves me unsatisfied,
> I fear giving it up, falling through space. (pp. 107–109)

Ritual allows us to act out in a collective setting what otherwise is unseen and hard to touch or comprehend. In doing so, we touch base with our core values and bond with each other. "Rituals reveal values at their deepest level . . . [People] express in ritual what moves them most, and since the form of expression is conventionalized and obligatory, it is the values of the group that are revealed" (Moore & Meyerhoff, 1977, p. 32). Rituals are the key to understanding the essence of culture.

Ritual is to culture what a movie is to the script, a concert is to the score, or a dance is to values difficult to express in any other way (Deal & Kennedy, 1982). The repetition underscores, renews, and rekindles our sense of purpose and direction. When we lose connection with ritual, we lose our way.

Everyone has their personal rituals. And we understand ritual as a sacred component of our religious liturgy. Now, let's shift from our personal or religious lives to life where we work. The U.S. military, for instance, is packed with rituals. This is especially true for fighter pilots, who risk injury and death encased in a winged steel weapons platform. One of these important rituals is enacted as an aircraft is passed from a crew chief who readies the plane for a pilot who flies it:

The ground ceremony is a ritual we have formalized to signify the handing off of the aircraft to the pilot where the pilot is assured his aircraft is ready and safe for flight . . .

1. The first salute is a courtesy greeting that signifies respect between the aircraft mechanic and his pilot.
2. The handshake takes the greeting to a new level and is the personal bond between the mechanic and his pilot.

3. The second salute after the pilot has operationally checked the aircraft signifies the aircraft's airworthiness and that the aircraft is now in the hands of the pilot.

4. The thumbs-up is the personal gesture wishing a good flight to the pilot.

(R. Mola cited in Reed, 2001, p. 5)

These actions and gestures bond mechanic and pilot, building trust and respect through a ritual that occurs over and over again.

Without such rituals governing important interactions among people, any organization would become a confusing cacophony of actions that make little sense or simply a set of bureaucratic procedures. A ritual is "a complex type of symbolic behavior that usually has a stateable purpose, but one that invariably alludes to more than it says, and has many meanings at once" (Moore & Meyerhoff, 1977, p. 5). The shared enactment of a ritual bonds people to one another and signifies and solidifies their membership in a special group.

Rituals in Schools

Imagine schools without such symbolic interludes. In the world of education, with its multiple challenges, complex goals, and significance to communities, ritual is probably more important than in a business with a tangible product or service that is easily measurable. Schools run largely on faith and hope—those aspects of organizations that are hard to touch but central to internalized meaning and motivation. Students and teachers don't leave their humanity behind when they come to school—they bring their personal problems, conflicts, hopes, and dreams to the classroom. They need special moments in the daily tasks of teaching and learning (themselves rituals) to reflect on what's really important, connect with one another, and feel the common spirit that makes seeming routines less like assembly line work and more like spiritual communion.

In the past few decades, in the name of educational reform, we have managed to sterilize schools of the symbolic forms and acts that help culture survive and thrive. We have transformed many schools into factories for learning facts and academic skills. Some ritual and ceremony has fallen victim to pressures for time to drill and practice. Some has been dismissed as fluff or frills in favor of structure and rationality. A lot has just been overlooked and ignored, allowed to wither away because of the fear of accountability or the narrowing of the social curriculum.

More than ever, we need to revive ritual as the spiritual fuel required to energize and breathe life and a deeper sense of purpose back into our schools. Learning is fostered in large part by strong traditions, frequent ritual, authentic celebrations, and poignant ceremonies to reinvigorate cultural cohesion, connect to a higher purpose, and focus on broader educational ends.

As we have seen, rituals are procedures or routines that are infused with deeper significance. They help make common experiences uncommon events; they serve to elevate the daily learning to a higher level. Every school has hundreds of routines, from the taking of attendance in the morning to the afternoon's egress procedures; from inviting a student to answer a question on the board to teachers sharing instructional wisdom after school. But when these routine events are intimately connected to a school's mission and values, and linked to the calling of teaching rather than the obligations of content coverage, they summon spirit, energize one's professional soul, and reinforce cultural ties.

Let's look at a couple of examples. In a rural midwestern school, food service workers make toast for staff and students every Thursday morning—even though it's not in their official job description. As a routine it feeds people and provides carbohydrates and calories, but as a ritual of "breaking bread" together, it energizes the communal spirit for the coming day. It provides time to share how the week is going, get support or advice, or laugh at a funny incident. A recent attempt to eliminate the morning ritual failed, because hundreds of former staff recalled the fond memories and wanted the tradition to continue. It did.

A large urban high school staff meets for coffee, bagels, and doughnuts once a week to share stories about their experiences with new curriculum ideas and to renew relationships and recharge batteries with colleagues they see only occasionally. These are more than informal times for chit-chat. They are social rituals that bond the group together and spotlight the purposes of their work and the needs of their students.

Rituals become significant traditional events with special history and meaning. The traditional encounter unfolds year in and year out. Traditions provide a vital tie to the past, reinvigorate the present, and offer a welcome promissory note for a robust future. Special events touch the hearts of parents and others in the community who can recall with feeling their own experiences in school. When people honor traditional rituals, it gives them a cultural foundation to weather challenges, difficulties, and change. Rituals are the daily comings and goings that create the mortar that binds people and activities; rituals provide behavioral glue that holds a school together.

Some events take time to progress from routine to ritual. In a Pennsylvania school district, the new superintendent convened staff for the opening of school. Prior to launching into his remarks, he placed a brass oil lamp on the lectern and said, "Before beginning, I'd like to light the lamp of learning." He lit the lamp and then gave his address on the importance of teaching and learning, the district's primary mission. No one commented on his symbolic act the first year or when he repeated it a second time. Before schools' opening the third year, he received a flood of requests: "You are going to light the lamp of learning, aren't you?" It is now a tradition involving teachers, students, and staff in the annual lighting of the lamp.

Types of Rituals

Schools have a variety of rituals that do culture's symbolic work. Here are some examples.

Greeting rituals are value-embedded ways of connecting people. At Audubon Elementary School the workroom is filled with teachers each morning, and greetings are boisterous, usually taking place over homemade treats. At Ganado Primary, visitors to the school are taken around by energetic Navajo tour guides who show them student work, rugs from local weavers, and awards the school has received. These petite guides wearing special vests tell the stories of the school and its purpose. In a Beaverton, Oregon, elementary school the official greeting of teachers and students is an animated "high five"—a behavioral testimony to the school's commitment to "Reach for Excellence." Bob Herring, the principal of Nativity School, uses unique rites to greet students and staff in the morning and to bid them goodbye in the afternoon.

Transition rituals shore up symbolic ties to bridge changes in people, practices, or procedures. Transitions are as hard for organizations as they are for individuals. Letting go of old ways and embracing the new is made easier through value-laden rituals. In one school, traditional textbooks had given way to trade books in language arts. The staff gathered to remember the best and the ridiculous of the old texts. They were then boxed up and sent to a needy traditional school in another state, symbolically paving the way for introduction of the new materials. A set of the old books was kept in the school museum.

In another school, older technologies—from fountain pens to iMacs—are placed in a special cabinet to show the chronological progression of writing technology used in the school. The display shows the continuity of different instruments all aimed at the same objective—literacy.

Battle preparation rituals gird people with the armor and pluck needed to face threatening challenges. Prior to going on patrol, police officers participate in "roll call." Besides bringing them up to speed on the latest developments, or hot spots, this ritual prepares them to face tough situations on the street, many involving life or death. Pep talks in locker rooms prior to athletic contests prepare teams for competition. The late Vince Lombardi of the Green Bay Packers was renowned for his pregame speeches. When he first became the Packer's head coach, players anxiously awaited his locker room appearance. He didn't show up until three minutes before game time, and then burst through the double doors. His penetrating eyes went from player to player. He began: "Gentlemen, all eyes on me. This season you have three things to think about and three things only: Your family, your religion, and the Green Bay Packers." The players almost tore the walls down to enter the stadium. The Packers rolled over the opponent and Lombardi was on his way to become a legend.

Similar rituals can motivate students to give their all. Before state-mandated tests, a school's staff and students gather around an enormous cake with "We Will Succeed" written in huge letters across the top. The rite prepares staff and students to do their best in the face of a challenging, high-stakes examination. In another school, teachers and administrators fill care baskets with cards, notes, stuffed animals, and other small items of comfort when students are facing graduate exams or other stress-filled challenges.

Initiation rituals connect newcomers to a school's community. Rites of initiation can be as simple as a significant introduction of a staff member's past successes and special attributes at the first faculty meeting. Or they can be more complex: meaningful indoctrination events that involve reflection on professional values and philosophy, shared group participation at commonly attended conferences, or extensive discussions of the history and core values of the school. In a New York elementary school, old-timers—veteran teachers who have been at the school for an extended period—take over the newcomers' entry into the culture. They share the school's history and traditions. As the principal observed of the rite's impact: "It's worked both for the newcomers and old-timers. The only thing worse than not learning the ropes is having great traditions to share but no audience of initiates." Introduction rituals in a midwestern middle school reinforced the "differentiated instruction" philosophy of the school. All the new staff were introduced with multimedia presentations involving unusual graphics, creative diagrams, and a variety of music—making the newcomers feel welcome and appreciated. Staff look forward each year to the introduction rituals.

School improvement rituals signal the importance of collegiality and change. With the renewed interest in systematic school improvement, more and more administrators and faculty are regularly meeting together to plan needed changes. Some schools emphasize data-driven decision making and methodical planning because they are required. But resolute cultures see these activities as opportunities to build bridges to a deeper sense of shared purpose. All meetings in one school start by reviewing the mission, discussing the needs of students, and reflecting on the primary purposes of education. The focus is on the school's concept of teaching and learning rather than simply satisfying federal, state, or district mandates. Use of evidence is a ritual related to the core values of the school, not simply a requirement. Empirical data on student achievement is only one aspect of continuous self-reflection. The sentiments and judgments of teachers and parents matter more.

Rites of passage rituals furnish needed support and compassion when things end. In a Florida elementary school, teachers and students create "Big Books" featuring the year's special events, surprises, and accomplishments. Poems, pictures, and stories fill the commemorative document that is ceremonially placed in the library. Student teachers are ritually anointed by similar goodbye tomes. Similarly, Nativity School cements ties and copes with endings by recognizing contributions people have made to the school and releasing balloons symbolizing memories and hope into the spring sky.

In a Chicago elementary school, teachers became concerned that the school year ended without some sort of recognition of the sadness that teachers and students felt acutely if not consciously. They put together an ending ritual. With all students assembled in the multipurpose room, teachers entered one by one singing a familiar farewell song from *The Sound of Music*. The students squealed and clapped as each teacher sauntered across the stage waving goodbye. But another layer of the event was bittersweet, students losing their teachers and teachers their students at the end of a meaningful school year. The ritual provided a way to recognize the sadness while smoothing the way to the joys and liberty of summer vacation.

Playful rituals provide opportunities for people to let their hair down and laugh. Ruth Elder, an elementary teacher and a graduate student at Vanderbilt University, focused her doctoral work on humor (R. Elder, personal communication). Her documentation of the benefits of laughter was impressive. Positive attributes included reducing stress, improving communication, aiding bonding, softening we–they boundaries, and sparking creativity. In the world of business, Southwest Airlines has consistently confirmed the value of having fun at work. In schools, accountability and high-stakes testing have taken their toll on playful rituals. A principal recently remarked, "I'm devoting several days this year as times that children in my school can be children." Sig Boloz brought fun and playfulness to Ganado Elementary even as he focused on literacy.

Classroom Rituals

Mrs. Krantz, profiled in the chapter's opening, seemed to intuitively grasp the importance of classroom rituals. The classroom, as the school, needs ritual to accomplish its contributions to a place full of meaning and passion. As an example, Mrs. Elizabeth Harris begins and ends each day with a ritual:

> Harris starts her second-grade class each morning with a song. One of her children's favorites is "Peace Is Flowing Like a River." She begins instruction by asking, "What are we going to be our best at today?" Students start volunteering things, both instructional and noninstructional, at which they intend to excel. "I'm gonna be good at lining up for recess," shouts another. "I'm gonna be good at doin' my own work and minding my own business," says a little girl. As the students recite their goals and expectations for the day, Mrs. Harris encourages them with a smile or a comment, "Oh, you are? Well, that's very good!" or "I just know you can do that."
>
> At the end of the day, Harris reconvenes her students to have them assess how well they met their goals. Each student is given an opportunity to describe what she or he did to be successful during the day. Students report on successes and reflect on ways they could have been even better at some things. Harris constantly tells them how good they are. (Ladson-Billings, 1994, p. 48)

The rituals in Mrs. Harris's class illustrate the multiple roles rituals play in human groups: building enthusiasm, reinforcing values, bonding people together, recognizing accomplishments, and conveying an organization's worth to interested constituencies. The morning ritual in Mrs. Harris's class creates an all-day learning culture. The day's ending ritual sends students home primed to tell parents what they have learned, thereby shoring up the community's confidence and faith in the school.

Rituals are periodic meaning-filled interactions that are key to reinforcing, renewing, and reenergizing cultures. Ceremonies, the subject of the next chapter, are larger, more complex social gatherings that build meaning and purpose in a more elaborate way.

7

Ceremonies and Traditions
Culture in Action

Five thousand women leaned forward in their seats, hanging on every word of Reva's speech accepting Mary Kay's Sales Person of the Year Award. She was suffering from breast cancer and removed her wig covering her bald head as she spoke. She concluded with: "Ladies, if I can do it so can you." With that the crowd came to its feet with thunderous applause, not a dry eye in evidence. The large pipe organ in the cavernous auditorium began playing "The Impossible Dream." Another dramatic moment in a lavish Mary Kay ceremony celebrating the company's "You Can Do It" spirit. But more was to come. The next morning featured a speech from an evangelist, reinforcing the company's commitment to "God first, family second, career third." Mary Kay Ash had requested that the evangelist's wife accompany him on stage. She was obviously not used to being in front of large crowd. He gave his speech and received sustained applause. Then Mary Kay handed the microphone to the wife. She looked shocked and started to tremble. Then, as if by magic, she launched into an inspired extemporaneous speech, "I set my goal last night after hearing what Reva said. If she can do it I can too." The crowd went wild. In less than twelve hours, two dramatic enactments of the "can do" spirit of Mary Kay Cosmetics had been displayed—and one of the reasons for the company's accomplishment in transforming housewives into businesspeople succeeding for themselves and contributing to the company's economic productivity.

Ceremonies are complex, culturally sanctioned events in which organizations celebrate successes, communicate values, and rec-ognize the special contributions of employees. Even without the lavishness of a Mary Kay seminar, schools can strengthen cultural bonds through ceremonial occasions of their own design.

Each season of the year provides an occasion to communicate ceremonially the full of meaning glue that binds an educational enterprise together. Before classes begin in the fall, the staff of a large urban high school gather to pool hopes, ideas, and dreams for the coming year. This shared experience creates connections that last throughout the year, despite the serendipitous ups and downs of the academic calendar.

In another school the staff host a unique evening, featuring student artwork matted and displayed. Parents and community members are invited to appreciate and celebrate students' creativity. Special awards are given to parents and others in recognition of their cooperation and help. The contribution of teachers is singled out for special attention in a carefully and artistically designed brochure that outlines the evening's festivities. The ceremony knits a diverse community together in celebration of the collective successes of children. It builds, bonds, and cements the school's sense of pride and esteem.

Types of Ceremonies

Schools with upbeat cultures convene ceremonies to bring people together, connecting them to treasured values and reinforcing core purposes. These grand events happen periodically or in response to notable triumphs or tragedies.

Opening-day ceremonies rebind staff to the school and its mission. Beginning a new school year always conjures up both anticipation and dread. Kick-off events reinforce core values, remind people of the hard yet rewarding year ahead, and renew their commitment to the growth of young people. Staff and parents represented on a school's council come together for a beginning-of-school potluck. Each person brings a dish that represents something they did over the summer—Texas chili from a parent who attended a summer conference in Houston or an Irish stew from a teacher whose summer was devoted to developing a new teaching module on immigration. Eating good food and trying to "read" the food's deeper meaning creates fun times and renews ties for the coming year.

At Brown University each academic year is begun with a ceremonial opening of the gates to welcome entering freshmen. At graduation, four years later, the gates will swing open again to send seniors on their way to new adventures and careers. The gates are opened only twice a year, thus making entering for the first time or leaving at graduation special occasions.

At an elementary school the mission statement is reviewed each fall. It is refined or reworded to match current challenges. As needed the statement is redone in calligraphy by a local artist and signed by teachers, students, and administrators. This makes the mission statement a living covenant, vital, connected to everyday experience, and evolving. It is tattooed on people's hearts and minds and reflected in their behavior rather than gathering dust as it hangs on a wall.

Seasonal ceremonies take advantage of cyclical merriment outside the school. Reitzug and Reeves (1992) found in one school that the principal, Mr. Sage, has a Thanksgiving assembly in which he cooks and serves a large turkey, using the activity to teach about weights and measures but also to renew teachers at a ceremonial time in the middle of the first semester.

Management ceremonies ease the hard work of formulating plans and developing new programs. Professionals often gather and make improvement plans through brute force of rationality. But infusing these times with a collaborative spirit and shared collegiality fosters even greater accomplishment. A Kentucky high school working to restructure its educational programs held its planning retreats at the principal's rustic cabin. The principal, a strong and insightful leader, knew the importance of shared thinking and planning. But she also recognized the other side of the equation. She cooked incredible food and encouraged play as the core planning council hammered out new directions. They often referred to their gatherings as "an advance" rather than a "retreat." In a Connecticut school, it was not a rustic cabin but a hotel with a reputation for lavish buffets that made the planning retreat a meaningful group tradition. There was hard work to do, but it was a collegial effort, sharing leadership and fun.

Integrative ceremonies provide ways to meld the various social, ethnic, and religious groups in a school. As schools become more and more diverse ethnically, socially, and economically, they need to rediscover or invent familiar traditions that knit people together—integrative customs that help everyone develop understanding and appreciation for others. At Piccolo Elementary School in Chicago, African American students learn Spanish songs to sing during Cinco de Mayo; Hispanic students learn rap to participate during African American week festivities. These are more than music lessons, as students develop friendships and learn about different values and ways. In the Tucson, Arizona, school district, opening day brings all its employees together to kick off the new school year. At various places in the large arena, student groups are featured in traditional cultural dress, playing ethnic music. The music and costumes create an expansive, expressive milieu that helps unite diverse subgroups in a shared commitment to building a cohesive learning community.

Recognition ceremonies pay tribute to the special accomplishments of individuals and groups, thereby forging pride and respect. Schools, like other organizations, too often avoid recognizing and celebrating important accomplishments. Sometimes it is not part of tradition; quite often, negative members of the culture want to diminish praise to hide their own mediocrity. But successful cultures find ways—both small and elaborate—to celebrate, commemorate, and salute the accomplishments of others. For the school, this heightens the feeling of being on a winning team, of being part of something greater than themselves. In one middle school, each month the "Super Stupendous Award" (an actual trophy found at a garage sale but with a new plaque) is presented to a staff member who has lived the values of the school and helped someone to better themselves.

In the Beaverton Elementary School mentioned previously, the daily "high-five" rites are supplemented from time to time by a special recognition event. Teachers, students, and parents gather in the school's "hall of fame" to recognize those who have shown notable merit in "reaching for excellence." The principal calls a student forward, reads the accomplishment, and paints the student's hand. The student slaps the wall with a high-five, leaving an imprint. The principal then writes the student's name and his or her accomplishment on the wall. The hallway is a graphic depiction of where the school is heading.

There are many other examples of acknowledgment events: student awards ceremonies, volunteer lunches, graduation ceremonies, and honor roll dinners. At Joyce Elementary in Detroit, students who make the honor roll attend a formal ceremony with their parents. This ceremony has been held yearly for over a decade. Students, caregivers, parents, and staff come dressed in their finest clothes, share an elaborate meal, and hear the prideful, complimentary words of their principal and community leaders. Students receive a medallion of achievement and a T-shirt with every honor student's name emblazoned on it. Teachers write a personal comment about every child for the banquet book, which is ceremonially presented to each student. Photographs capture the event, thus creating a memory trace of the accomplishments that graces many refrigerators in local homes. In a community facing great challenges, the honor roll dinner is a powerful message of hope, accomplishment, and pride.

In Guilford County, North Carolina, superintendent Dr. Terry Grier implemented an Advanced Placement Diploma program to encourage students to take more rigorous classes. Students who took five AP classes and scored 3 or higher on each were invited to a year-end "Cool to Be Smart" celebration. After speeches and cheers, recognition of hard work and future success, each student is given a car key—one of which actually opened a brand new car donated by a local car dealer. Academics and hard work are clearly valued by the district in this event.

Like many schools, Audubon Elementary has a yearly art auction, but theirs is also a time to recognize achievements of other sorts. A printed brochure describes the auction but also lists the accomplishments, awards, and grants received by staff and students for the past year. This brochure is an artifact and symbol of the triumphs and hard work of school members.

Homecomings are for alumni, who gather to tell stories of hard work and success. Returning graduates show a connection to past lessons and verify that their hard work has paid off. In a high school located in a low-income area, adults who have regular jobs return to remind students of the possibility of economic success. In another school, returning graduates offer to mentor struggling students as a way of giving back some of what the school gave them. As an interesting twist on the homecoming theme, an elementary school invited graduates from previous years to attend opening day festivities. Teachers were shocked and pleased at the achievements of some of their more "troublesome" students. Public tributes from students thanking teachers for contributions to their lives generated renewed commitment to making the new school year another challenging opportunity to shape young lives.

Special ceremonies mark the beginning or end of unique events. Transitions are important times in the lives of people and of schools. They mark the beginnings and endings of unique temporal and social events. Transitions need to be acknowledged ceremonially. Otherwise they go unnoticed and their importance and meaning are lost.

Successful cultures find ways to highlight transitions to reinforce and build cultural values. One school celebrates the end of a planning year with a brief talk about accomplishments and challenges, followed by the awarding of pens and coffee cups to the members of the planning committee. More and more schools are holding reading "challenges" to encourage summer reading. Principals mark reaching the goals in many bizarre but symbolic ways. Some have been known to eat fried worms, kiss hairy pigs, or spend the day on the roof to celebrate the school's reaching its reading goals. Adding an exclamation mark to the end of special events or activities can buoy spirits and bolster values.

Memorial ceremonies are times to remember the contributions and trials of others. Most strong cultures remember those who went before. It is a way to recognize the contributions of others and connect to the history of one's school.

Some schools bring back retired teachers who developed core curricular approaches or implemented special literacy programs. Other schools remember those who faced tragedy. At East High School in Madison, Wisconsin, students and staff place flowers on a fence where several students were killed by a reckless driver. Other schools have named scholarships or awards for student leaders who died tragically in war or in the line of duty in their professions. In a Wisconsin school, a scholarship is given each year in honor of an Irish teacher who died of cancer at a young age. The award certificate is wrapped in green and khaki—just like the green and khaki that appeared in some item of clothing the teacher wore almost every day of his career.

Elements of Successful Ceremonies

Each ceremony works effectively if it communicates deeper values and purposes, is well organized and well run, and has a touch of grandeur and specialness. Successful ceremonies often combine a meaningful set of elements (Trice & Beyer, 1985; Deal & Peterson, 1994; Deal & Key, 1998):

A special and value-linked purpose

Symbolic clothing and adornments

Symbols, signs, banners, or flags

Stories of history, accomplishment, or unusual effort

A distinctive manner of speaking or presentation

An invocation of deeper purpose and values

Attention to who is invited and where they sit

Recognition of those who have shown exemplary commitment

Appropriately chosen and varied music

The effective use of media, film, or visual displays

A carefully selected, attractive setting

Special food or drink that represents quality

Value-filled language and commentary

Meaningful symbols and artifacts of past and present

Ritual acts and ongoing traditions carefully enacted

The recounting of the core legends or stories about the school

Successful ceremonies are carefully designed and arranged to communicate values, celebrate core accomplishments, and build a tight sense of community.

Traditions

Traditions are significant events that have a special history and meaning and that occur year in and year out. Traditions are like bookmarks in the passage of time; they reinvigorate the culture and symbolize it to insiders and outsiders alike. They take on the mantle of history, anchored in an ancient past. When people have traditions that they value and appreciate, it gives them a foundation to pause, remember, connect, and weather challenges, difficulties, or change.

There are numerous types of traditions in schools, including

Traditions that build professionalism. It is important to nourish professionalism and effort for one's students. This can happen in many ways, for example by holding retreats where energetic, collaborative planning occurs, by holding professional conferences at the school that spotlight innovative teaching by existing staff, or by acknowledging professional accomplishments in words or displays.

Gatherings where the community recognizes in story, songs, or awards the special and significant contributions of others. At one school, staff hold a storytelling contest in which they recount stories of success or humor that occurred either that year or long ago. Awards for the best story are highly sought after. When Fran Vandiver was principal of Coral Springs Middle School in Florida, many faculty meetings began with the presentation of coffee mugs to staff who had made some special attempt to serve students. Strong cultures are filled with traditions to mark special occasions, reinforce values, and perpetuate rituals that provide connection.

Traditions and Ceremonies: Two Cases

School leaders develop rituals, traditions, and ceremonies that fit their staff and communities.

A Unique Launching of a School Year

Steve Ladd, new superintendent of the Elk Grove School District, had an idea for a different kick-off of the 2007–08 school year. First he outlined it to some of his administrators, who thought he was crazy. But then the idea began to catch on and take shape. A small representative group of administrators fleshed out the particulars of the event.

The Elk Grove School District is located in one of the fastest growing communities of suburban Sacramento. The current population is 150,000 and growing rapidly. It is situated so close to Sacramento, California's capitol that it feels like part of the city. The district itself comprises sixty-two schools, enrolling 61,728 students, who are taught by 3,541 certificated teachers, with a classified staff of 2,370. Student demographics: 28% white, 22% Latino, 20% African American, 20% Asian, 10% other.

The original idea was eventually crystallized into an Administrative Leadership Day to kick off the new school year. The day's theme was "The Courage to Lead in Times of Change." Over two hundred of the district's leadership team, including school board members, attended, all voluntarily giving up a Saturday.

At eight o'clock in the morning, the group assembled for tai chi exercises and a burrito breakfast in Old Town Sacramento. Following breakfast the superintendent introduced the day's event: "Today we are taking a walking journey from our past, through our present, and on to our future. You have been assigned randomly to a group of ten of your colleagues. Our beginning point is our past, which is why we are in Old Town. From here, we will walk to the state capitol building to capture the essence of present time challenges. From there we will stroll to Crocker Park for a barbeque lunch and a visit to the Crocker Art Museum. The theme there is cultural competence, a look through the lens of the interpretive world from which we envision our future. Leadership is a mixture of courage and art. But it also takes teamwork to realize our potential, and our last stop will be Raley Field for a presentation from Tony Asaro to tell us how the River Cats baseball team won the championship this year. Now, on to our journey. Find your group and move ahead to the capitol."

Watching the large procession of school leaders snake through the streets of Sacramento toward the capitol was like observing a lively pageant in action. People were swapping stories, grumbling about legislative interference, and getting to know people with whom they had never spent much time.

At the capitol, the groups reassembled in a legislative hearing room, the source of many of their current challenges. A retired administrator, the district's informal historian, Elizabeth Pinkerton, presented a colorful account of the community's history beginning with the Miwok Indian tribe and ending in 2000 when the city of Elk Grove was incorporated. For each period, she indicated the values *(in bold italics)* that were passed on:

> In the beginning, Miwok Indians set the stage for Elk Grove Unified School District. They showed great ***Respect and Caring*** for their families, the environment and their future. In 1807 Spanish explorers came to visit. They decided the area was too wet and marshy.... The Spanish showed **Common Sense** in abandoning what did not work. In 1846, an important event took place in the corral of Martin Murphy, just south of Elk Grove. Mexican soldiers boarded a large number of horses for the night in the corral. The horses were part of reinforcements for an uprising of American settlers the Mexicans were trying to contain. A group of settlers released the horses during the night, marking one of the events that led to California's independence and eventual statehood. The settlers took the **Initiative** and did what they believed they had to do. In 1850, California was awash in gold and swamped by people consumed by instant treasures. Others were attracted by business opportunities to fulfill the needs of miners. James Hall opened a hotel/stage stop, naming it Elk Grove. His **Motivation** in creating the stage stop birthed a later

city. In 1853, the San Joaquin School was established, the first public school in Sacramento County. The farmers of Elk Grove took on the **Responsibility** of assuring a quality education for their children. In 1868 The Central Pacific finished its Sacramento-Stockton-San Francisco line. Initially the tracks missed Elk Grove by a mile. An enterprising merchant used his **Problem Solving** skills to get the tracks moved—today's Main Street and Old Town. In 1893, the residents of Elk Grove voted to form the Elk Grove Union High School District. This led to the building of the First Free Union High School in California. This took great **Effort** on the part of residents but they were planning for the future of their children. 1906 saw the establishment of California's first rural library in Elk Grove. The effort was spearheaded by Harriet Eddy, principal of the high school at the time. She showed great **Confidence** in moving forward to do what needed to be done. In 1959 the Elk Grove elementary schools were unified with the high school in the Elk Grove Unified School District. This effort took great **Teamwork**. Elk Grove became a city in 2000, an initiative that required **Perseverance and Hard Work**. This is our legacy to bring forward and carry on. (Elizabeth Pinkerton, handout to administrative group, September 2007)

Following the presentation of the district's history, an outside consultant highlighted the school district's history and the realities that schools currently face and presented a variety of ways to frame the challenges. The emphasis on culture and its elements gave people a new lens for connecting roots with existing cultural ways and using the past and present as a springboard to the future. With a reminder of the purpose of the day's journey, the groups wended their way to Crocker Park for a barbeque lunch. During lunch, groups rotated through the Crocker Art Museum, where docents used art pieces to illustrate how artists communicate through symbols. This linked to the challenge of imaging a future for the district and reinforced the artistry of leadership. The primary purpose of the museum experience was to expand the administrators' pallets of options in leading schools in changing times.

Raley Field, home of the Sacramento River Cats, was the final destination. As during their previous jaunts, the groups bantered back and forth, picking up on various themes so far. The purpose of this last stop was very clear: realizing that the district's potential was going to require teamwork, everyone pulling together in a common quest. A better example was almost impossible to stumble on: the River Cats had just won their division championship. And as a feeder team for the Dodgers, they had won their final games without some of their major stars, who had been called up to fill holes in the Dodger's major league roster.

The groups sat in a section of the large stadium, with Tony Asaro speaking from the field of play. Asaro, the ball club's spokesperson, eloquently and enthusiastically conjoined the efforts of the River Cats franchise and the school district. To him, success in either endeavor demands that everyone works together toward the same end. Stars don't make a team; a team makes stars. For the River Cats, success is obvious by looking at the scoreboard in centerfield. For the school district, accomplishment is distributed across the growth and development of thousands of students the district serves. The district's impact is harder to summarize in a single score but is more essential to the Elk Grove community than the win-loss record of its baseball team.

Following Asaro's presentation, Superintendent Ladd pulled together the day's highlights in a stirring challenge for the coming school year: "Building on our past, courageously dealing with current demands, and working as artistically inclined leaders on a culturally united team toward a promising future." The group then met in functional teams to discuss "what next?"

From all quarters the day was a smashing success. Several outcomes were highlighted: the fact that everyone had sacrificed a Saturday gave people a renewed sense of "we" as a district; walking with a group of people randomly assigned provided a chance to develop new relationships across previously closely drawn boundaries; at the day's end, the chance to meet in teams helped focus on the coming year; everyone had fun. To Superintendent Ladd, the day "helped anchor us to the core of what we are doing."

Integrated, Yearlong Traditions

Bob Herring is principal of the Nativity School in Cincinnati, Ohio. The school is urban and serves a diverse clientele from kindergarten through eighth grade. The principal, along with his staff and the community, keep the school's over seventy-five-year history alive and well by filling the school year with ritual and tradition. The year's beginning and end have significant, linked ceremonies filled with history and meaning. Interspersed throughout the year, the school connects through smaller, focused traditions.

These religiously based symbolic events start before the first day of school. Herring gathers new eighth graders ahead of time to plan the opening ceremony—one deeply connected to the school's mission. A procession with banners heralding the values of the school kicks things off. Students deliver readings and reflections on the coming year. All new staff are introduced, from administrators through custodians; they are given a bouquet of flowers and introduced to the community. A band made up of students, alumni, and friends of the school plays music and provides background to the festivities. All new students are asked to come forward—from thirty-five-inch-tall kindergartners to upper-level students—to receive a ceremonial carnation and school button from one of the eighth graders that recognize their membership in the school. The principal recounts some of the school's over seventy-five-year history, tells about leaders and graduates who have been exemplars, and invites everyone present to partner with the school in its quest for learning and the "right" life. The ceremony ends with an environmentally safe balloon launch representing, as the principal says, "We're here, we're open, and we're ready to go!"

The school year ends with equally elaborate ceremony. Again, the band of students, alumni, and friends plays for the assembled standing-room-only crowd. Tall, colorful, festive banners symbolize the core purpose and values of the school. Staff who are leaving are called forward individually to receive flowers, thanks, and applause. Their contributions are noted and cheered. Prayers of thanks are given to all those who have touched the lives of the students. Staff and parents are thanked for their support and love. The principal and staff look back on the year, recounting stories of caring, of challenges overcome, and of accomplishments achieved. A gospel story is read that reminds students not to hide their talents under a bushel basket. Graduates then talk of what it means to them and how they will use their talents for good and let their light shine in the world. A call to the new eighth graders charges them to be leaders and to keep the values alive. A procession outside takes participants to a final balloon launch—a symbolic freeing of the hopes, possibilities, and spirit of the new graduates.

Throughout the year rituals and traditions fortify the school's core values. On Founders' Day the contributions of early principals and teachers are recounted in stories and song. Alumni return to narrate their own memories of Nativity. The school song, written in the 1930s by a student, is sung and cherished. Each monthly faculty meeting ends with a "Good News Report"—a ritual sharing of positive accomplishments. School assemblies are times for fun and contemplation of service to each other and fidelity to communal values. The final faculty meeting is filled with awards for staff: awards for perseverance through difficult times, for implementing new traditions, for serving especially needy students. Each staff member tells a story of his or her contributions. These events throughout the year are concluded by a major ceremony in the spring.

The Nativity School leaders make rituals and traditions an important feature of their community. They build commitment and reinforce core values throughout the year while buttressing the culture by powerful ceremonies at the beginning and end of the school term.

Rituals, traditions, and ceremonies imbue routines with zest and vigor, symbolizing what is important, valued, and significant. They provide everyone a chance to reflect on what is important and to connect as a community. These are renewing and enriching parts of a school's life. They are typically planned and pulled off by an informally sanctioned network of cultural players.

8

Conveyors of Culture
Positive and Negative Transmitters

Keeping the culture intact and on track is a primary duty of those in official positions. But they get a lot of help from a cast of informal helpers. Every school has its network of unofficially sanctioned players whose important responsibilities never appear in an organizational chart or in authorized job descriptions (Deal & Kennedy, 1982; Deal & Peterson, 1990). The scope of their work unfolds behind the scenes, often underground. This off-the-record but widely acknowledged network is most often positive, supportive, and important to success. But in some schools the unendorsed set of connections can be negative, turning the atmosphere toxic. The mix of these roles varies from school to school but most often includes a wide array of people who keep the culture humming and heading in the right direction.

The Supportive Cultural Network

Priests and priestesses are the guardians of cultural values and beliefs, letting neophytes and veterans know cultural ways and sharing the history and traditions at special occasions. One school's priestess made sure that new hires were up to speed about how things had come to be but also knew intimately the current core values. Priests and priestesses are also the keepers of confidences and hold regular "confessionals." They create a safe haven for staff and students but also make sure that significant "secrets" find the ears of those in charge—always without attribution. Priests or priestesses sanction stories that crystallize and convey intangible values and beliefs. One local school priest was also the storyteller, given the podium at the yearly art show to recount the parables and accomplishments of the past year and to remind the school of how far they had come. His narrative-studded "homilies" drew staff, students, and parents under a shared and sacred cultural canopy and reconnected everyone to the long road the school had traveled to its current success.

Priests and priestesses are key members of the cultural network because they keep the deeper purposes and values of the culture front and center. They balance tradition and innovation, making sure that new ways don't stray too far from time-honored cultural roots. Woe to the new principal who enters the school as a self-proclaimed agent of change. The priest or priestess has tight connections with the school's power players, as well as parents and community leaders.

Direct confrontation is not typically part of the pastoral repertoire. All it takes to bring the new principal into line is a few strategic conversations: "Have you met the new principal yet? He seems OK, but the fact that he wants to try experimental methods with kids troubles me somewhat. But keep that under your hat." The ensuing chain of events is very predictable. School board members' telephones begin to ring. Then the school superintendent is the recipient of late-night calls. The next morning the new principal is in the superintendent's office, hearing a less than subtle word of warning: "I think you're moving a little too quickly, don't you? The new reforms are needed, but not at the expense of unneeded turmoil. See my point?"

How does one become a school priest or priestess? Anyone can qualify, and the casting process is more serendipitous than lock-step. Longevity is important, as well as a rock solid commitment to tradition and honored values. The priest of a large urban junior high school was the custodian. He could talk to anyone and vice-versa. He was not shy about counseling new teachers on how to teach the "Washington Way." He knew everyone in the community, including former students who were now parents. Parent conferences were often convened and chaired by the custodian. He was the guardian of historical roots and an everyday reminder of the school's core beliefs about young people and learning.

In an Atlanta elementary school, the secretary was the ordained priestess. The centrality of her role was confirmed by the reserved slots in the parking lot. One close to the school's main entrance was clearly marked, "Reserved for the Principal, Mr. Salazar." The parking place closer was even more noticeable: "Reserved for Mrs. Simpson, School Secretary." The delineation of the roles of chief and priestess was clearly drawn. The school was a theocracy: the principal was officially in charge, the secretary ran the school.

Storytellers are powerful and indispensable members of the cultural network. Their power and influence derives from the centrality of stories in life—at work and elsewhere. Storytellers are gifted with a knack of seeing drama in mundane happenings that others often miss. As modes of communication, stories have the capacity to tap levels of our experience that other options fail to access. As we detailed previously, stories tickle our fancy, hook our hearts, and help us deal with pathos and grief. Storytellers furnish the school with a willing and engaging source of legend and lore about the school that energizes, bonds, and inspires loyalty and commitment to cultural values and beliefs. Without stories life would be drab and mundane, lacking the color and oomph people yearn for—at home, at school, and at work.

Most people remember and respond to stories of success and accomplishment more than they do to quantitative descriptions. Although numerical depictions are useful, the crisp, personal story provides a vivid representation of what has transpired. Storytellers are often assisted in their efforts at preserving and perpetuating school lore through the unofficial grapevine, whether face-to-face or e-mail. Sometimes these stories are short reminders of the perils and pitfalls of innovation or efforts of promoting collegiality in the school; other times they are in-depth sagas providing a broad portrait of heroic efforts of others to infuse the school with renewed passion and significance.

As we discussed in Chapter Five, stories resonate deeply for staff, connecting them to the core values of the school community and re-invigorating their personal hopes and dreams. Schools have a particular advantage, since many of the most humorous or poignant stories capture the exploits of students, who have an innate capacity to produce material that stokes the imagination of a good storyteller. Shared in the teachers' lounge, at social occasions after school, or around a real or figurative campfire, once in a while stories knit people into a noble quest. Storytellers' tales breathe zest and vigor into everyday life in schools.

Gossips thrive in every organization because they provide real-time information and the scuttlebutt that everyone wants to know. There are very few, if any, organizations where secrets are kept safely in airtight vaults. This is not a gender-specific role but thrives equally among males and females. All gossips have sources, insider information on decisions, changes, staffing, and personnel. Rarely is this information shared openly in e-mails, memos, or open meetings.

The latest scuttlebutt is exchanged by the coffee station, around the water cooler, or after hours. Occasionally an animated, hushed conversation behind closed doors in glass offices tips people off that something sizzling is making the circuit. Gossips are renowned for maintaining major informal networks that circulate the latest rumors early and accurately. They get the latest out to everyone in their network. A local school council made sure that the gossips in contact with resistant staff and worried parents were filled in whenever a key decision was being considered. Information flowed freely and quickly through the networks, thus reducing carping and griping about being "in the dark."

Gossips can also transmit news of tragedy and help to stimulate the grieving process. They also are quick to transmit notice of awards, completion of degrees, presentations at a national conference, birth of a baby, or other accomplishments. These quickly disseminated messages keep the corpus of the culture informed, enlivened, and well connected.

Spies are the covert observers of what is going on. Every organization has a shadowy, clandestine underworld, where agents compete for secrets to give their sponsor advantage over others. Spies pass intelligence information to open ears. Each time key school leaders attend conferences or seminars, spies quickly acquire data on the topics, interests, and opinions of participants. Spies keep some people informed while undermining and throwing others off balance. Principals cultivate their spy networks often unaware that some of their operators are double agents working for teacher groups. A new principal is very often monitored by a well-placed mole assigned to see what agenda the new arrival has in mind. Spies and counter spies let people know what's coming down the road. They have their ear to the rail and are always ready to peddle their secrets to the highest bidder.

Heroes and heroines persevere in every school and are key to forming a strong cultural foundation for the school. To be a hero or heroine, one doesn't have to be Joan of Arc, Martin Luther King Jr., or Patton, Mother Teresa, or Cesar Chavez. One only needs to be an emblem or exemplar of core values. Heroic figures or icons are role models who inspire us to be more than we think we can be. They force us to see novel vistas and entertain new possibilities.

Heroic figures are salted throughout the culture irrespective of position or rank. One school's hero was the custodian of twenty-five years who always arrived early, had a kind word for people, and every summer painted two classrooms so they would sparkle for the new school year. By the time he retired he had painted the entire school twice. In another school the heroine was a counselor who helped distressed children with care and attention (and sometimes a needed coat) and also offered support and advice to staff. She was always professional, from the first day she came to work in the school to her last day on the job. Heroines and heroes show us what we can aspire to. They provide the culture with a concrete image of what a school values and holds most dear.

These are informal cultural roles endemic to most organizations. Informal titles are not listed in the formal directory or affixed to office doors. Still, everyone knows from behavioral cues who the cultural players are. Once in awhile, they make themselves known in more overt ways. A high school chemistry teacher had cards made with his informal role as the school's "chief of rumor control" highlighted. His job was to confirm, deny, or chase down the gossip and get back to the person inquiring. Both his telephone and e-mail numbers were listed. He claimed to receive more calls than the principal.

Beyond these generic cultural roles, schools develop their own "homegrown" types to satisfy unique symbolic needs. Some examples include

Navigators are people who, often informally, help the school steer clear of the shoals and rocks of a journey into unfamiliar territory. They can see what to avoid and suggest ways to reach a destination safely.

Nodes are like computer routers on the Internet, rapidly circulating official or timely information throughout the school. They let staff know who is doing something interesting instructionally, share articles on new techniques, and seem aware of every workshop that is worthy of staff consideration. Unlike gossips, nodes concentrate on technical rather than social issues.

Compasses remind people where True North lies. Like priests or priestesses, they hold steady on the deeper purposes of education and learning. They are philosophers or spiritual gurus, maintaining movement toward education's deepest and most profound truths.

Explorers and pioneers. Some people are perennially up-to-date and out front with new technologies or techniques—explorers who enjoy the risk and rewards of innovation. Explorers are the first to try new practices and are always searching the landscape for new ideas. Pioneers follow the explorers, taking the new ideas to a wider audience and keeping a school current.

Spirit guides. In Native American culture some individuals are often expected to occasionally go off on a spiritual search or vision quest. Spirit guides are symbolic messengers who bring ancestral wisdom from the "ether-world."

Noxious Networks

Positive schools display a supportive, nurturing complex of informal roles that reinforce and support an existentially rewarding and meaningful way of life. Toxic cultures also have a network of informal players. But their avowed mission is to perpetuate a downbeat, pessimistic status quo. This noxious, highly influential cast includes a number of roles, including the following:

Destructive spies see current information in order to squelch or blockade any effort to make things better. In an elementary school, the staff council regularly attended a voluntary leadership retreat to talk about the coming year and identify the most promising goals to pursue. Back at the ranch, a group of disgruntled social studies teachers planted a spy to report on what was being discussed and then gathered ammunition to assail and destroy the new ideas before they took root. Even before the leadership team returned from the retreat with their strategies, a coalition of saboteurs was forming and plotting their counterattack.

Saboteurs almost always find ways to incapacitate, scuttle, or trash any new ideas, innovative programs, or positive activity. They are aware of everyone's weaknesses and use them to their own advantage. Their cloak and dagger plots or heavier artillery are always ready to slay new ideas. When saboteurs are effective, they drag down enthusiasm, depress willingness to innovate, and make change a transitory illusion. They are experts at co-opting others to join their cabal.

Pessimistic taletellers spin yarns to jog memories of every failure, unresolved problem, or lost opportunity. When short on material they invent stories of past awfulness. These negative raconteurs poison the culture and dampen energy and enthusiasm. Their purpose is to assure that the school will never rise above the depressing, failing mess their stories represent. In one high school a distinctive negative legend prevailed. It was constantly revisited. It was the "Tale of the Thirty-Four Graduates of Westchester High School (a pseudonym) Who Were in Prison." This story shaped how people thought and felt about their current students, their future, and the potential of the school to make a positive difference. Everyone knew the story. It was true but has been embellished over time. But even more damaging, the story eclipsed narratives of hundreds of other successful graduates.

Keepers of the nightmare never fail to remind the staff of dreams that went awry, hopes that were dashed, and past programs that did not work out. They comb the past for disasters and cull out positive precedents. Energy to cope with present difficulties is further sapped by these individuals, who love to shatter emerging dreams.

Negaholics (Carter-Scott, 1991) find something negative, nasty, unfavorable, or pessimistic in any new idea. They are addicted to negativity. Their role drags down motivation and commitment. When negaholics dominate discussion, staff recede into their own classroom worlds and avoid innovative projects. Negaholics dominate the change agenda and make sure that any proposal is trashed before it leaves the drawing board.

Prima donnas want more than their share of attention, resources, and top students. For multiple reasons, they feel entitled. They must be center stage with the spotlight, even when they are not the main event. The quality work of others is lost in the bright lights they demand.

Space cadets have no idea what is going on but latch mindlessly on to anything new. They mouth the jargon but have no clue about what it means. Talkative space cadets can take up important time in meetings as they ramble on about nothing.

Martyrs expect people to recognize any contribution they make or time they spend as an enormous personal sacrifice. Like the prima donnas, martyrs have deep personal needs that they want the school to fulfill, and they drain energy needed elsewhere.

Rogue pirates steal ideas from everyone and never give credit for others' inventiveness and creativity they have used. They also hide their own ideas from staff for fear they will be "stolen" and applied in other classrooms. Pirating in a school fosters protectionism and damages collaboration.

Equipment and resource vultures snag any resource they can. They are the first to claim new equipment or materials and hover around the supply room waiting for deliveries. If a teacher retires or leaves they are first into the deserted classroom to seize any equipment, materials, ideas, or resources they can find. The teacher who takes over the room finds the classroom empty, devoid of all the equipment needed to adequately serve students. If these actions become acceptable practice, the school becomes a "vulture culture" where self-ishness and self-interest reign.

Deadwood, driftwood, and ballast are along for the excursion, the glory, the excitement of teaching in a good school—and the paycheck. But they refuse to do any work and seldom keep up with new ideas. Deadwood people are lifeless teachers who refuse to leave or retire. They serve as ballast that keeps the school from moving ahead. These are negative role models for passivity, lack of engagement, and avoidance. As role models, they can attract newcomers to accept similar modes of being a staff member.

Rumor mongers look for any dirt they can spread to assure that good reputations are quickly tarnished. If they can't find anything harmful, they'll make it up. They flit from person to person like a bee collecting pollen. They take new tidbits away, leaving the latest tittle-tattle behind. Eventually, the negative rumors become the norm and positive stories are ignored or rewritten.

Anti-heroes and devils are negative role models; they encourage others to act in ways opposite the core values of the positive culture. Some of these characters are benign, exemplifying disengagement, tuning out, and just going through the motions. For example, in the movie *Teachers*, one teacher nicknamed "Dr. Ditto" copies hundreds of pages of worksheets for his high school students to fill in. He doesn't teach, but rather reads the paper and sleeps. These anti-heroes can become destructive or even devils if less-dedicated staff start to see evasion of work and effort as the normative model for teaching.

Devils, on the other hand, are downright evil. They take delight in undercutting colleagues, leaking negative information to parents and the community, and undermining the confidence and self-worth of students. A large high school's league of Lucifers banded together in a "Turkey Club." They took great pleasure in being turkeys and getting together reinforced their commitment to mediocre teaching. They belittled students, chided colleagues for their caring and enthusiasm, and took every opportunity to derail the new principal. In their meetings, they told stories of devising exams impossible to pass and giving overloads of meaningless homework. Grades for their classes were always well below the school's average. Their only redeeming quality was providing an explanation for anything that went wrong in the school. Their mere presence drew others together in a tight oppositional coalition. But this prevented the school from developing positive symbols to rally behind.

As a collection, characters of the negative network create and maintain a school committed to mediocrity and ineffectiveness. Just as a positive culture helps people aspire to great things, a negative culture traps people in a powerful pocket of incompetence. Negative symbols hold a group together as tightly as a culture of virtue.

Whatever its valence, the informal cultural network is a crucial component of a school. Leaders nurture and support the positive players of the network and reduce the impact of the negative side of the network. Specifically, school leaders should know who resides in the central roles of the network, consult priests or priestesses at critical junctures (especially before launching major changes), provide stages for storytellers, anoint heroes and heroines whenever possible, use gossips to pass information, reinforce the compasses, nurture the nodes, listen to your navigators, and find spirit guides for support and direction.

The woof and warp of the various actions of cultural players plus the interweaving of others spins the social tapestry of a school. We look more closely at this weaving process in the next chapter.

Part II

The Symbolic Role
of School Leaders

9

Weaving the Cultural Tapestry

Seven Schools

Knitting the elements of culture into an artistic tapestry is like creating a word from the letters of the alphabet or stringing words together to create a sentence. Juxtaposed with one another the letters or words form a meaningful expression, just as combining the elements of culture create a cohesive school identity. Too often, principals intent on shaping a culture become plagiarists, copying an admired school or following a "how to" recipe from a book or magazine. Although such strategies may provide some comfort and reassurance, they rarely ever pan out. Thriving school cultures are cobbled together by using local materials and shaped in accordance with community ideals and expectations. Weaving separate strands into a significant tapestry that incorporates all local ethnic groups and subcultures is a formidable challenge for even the most talented leader and knowledgeable staff. But it can be done with a measure of cultural awareness and sensitivity and a large dose of courage and optimism. The pathway is fraught with barriers and littered with things tried that didn't pan out. But it can be done.

In this chapter, we explore how three principals, working alongside others, formed a strong school culture from indigenous symbolic elements: purpose and values, ritual and ceremony, history and stories, architecture and artifacts. Because each set of local challenges and beliefs about education is different, each cultural profile is unique. But the general principles and lessons to be learned are remarkably similar.[1]

Charles Baker, Wheaton Warrenville South High School

Charles Baker was the principal of Wheaton Warrenville South High School—a large, public secondary school located in a middle-class suburb west of Chicago. The school serves students from two different communities: those from well-educated and affluent homes and those from blue-collar families. A relatively new school (built in 1993), Wheaton Warrenville South replaced Wheaton Central, which had served the two communities for almost a century. The way Baker handled the closing of a venerable old institution and the move to a renovated building provides a good example of how a leader makes extensive use of ceremonies, rituals, traditions, and symbols to create a shared hybrid template of values and beliefs (Vydra, 1998).

Wheaton Central High School was closed when it became obvious that needed renovations were too expensive to be pulled off. The closing of a high school is never easy, but Baker portrayed the move as one necessary when a family that had outgrown its house needs a larger one. But sensitive to the symbolic pitfalls of transition, he worked with teachers and students to determine what artifacts should be moved from the old school to the new home. At the final graduation at the old school, Baker distributed personal notes he had written on orange cardstock (school colors are orange and black) to the four hundred graduating seniors. The notes asked that the students join him at graduation in singing a special song. There was not a dry eye in the house as the seniors joined Baker in singing "Auld Lang Syne," a fitting tribute and closure to the end of an era.

[1] These first three cases were adapted from Vydra (1998), used with permission.

Baker helped students make certain that Wheaton Central traditions became part of the new way of doing things at Wheaton Warrenville South. After the move, the students helped decide the best ways to incorporate the old school's seal and motto: "Scholarship, Commitment, Tradition, and Integrity." At the old school each of the four main hallways had been named for one of the words engraved on the school seal. This created a problem in the new school; there were only three hallways. Students solved the problem by suggesting that the hallways should be named for the first three values because Integrity should be part of the school's foundation.

When the school board pushed Baker and the students to accept new colors and start afresh with new traditions, symbols, and icons, students refused to budge. With Baker's support they insisted that only the Tigers, the motto "Sempre Tigris," and the colors orange and black could represent the proud traditions and heritage of their school. Nothing else could or would do.

Students and faculty sorted through more than one hundred years of Wheaton Central memorabilia to determine what artifacts should be displayed in the new Tradition Hall. Among the most treasured items now on display are those donated by the widow of the "Galloping Ghost," Wheaton's football hero, Red Grange. Students had kept in close touch with Grange's widow until her death.

School history now comes to life in a walk through Tradition Hall. Memories live on through the Principal's Pin, which is a duplicate of the old school seal and is given by principals to students who distinguish themselves at the school, community, district, state, or national level.

Through storytelling, Baker underscored the importance of ritual, history, traditions, and celebrations. Once each year at the homecoming assembly, Baker brought out a new chapter in the story of "Tom the Tiger" and read it to the enthralled students. Several years ago the story related how Tom called on his old friends, the Blues Brothers, to help him defeat the homecoming opponents and crown the homecoming queen. As the story goes, Tom the Tiger got to know the Blues Brothers through John Belushi, himself a Wheaton graduate. Adding drama, a local pair of actors who regularly performed at Chicago Bulls basketball games joined Baker at the microphone. The Blues Brothers' antics and music had all of the school's students and teachers revved up and dancing in the aisles. Although Baker is the one who wrote and read the exploits of Tom the Tiger, he also played other dramatic roles at pep assemblies. One year he dressed in tiger garb complete with a tiger head and orange tights. In costume, he danced down the bleachers to the song "Bad to the Bone." The students rose to a fever pitch when he took off the tiger head and revealed that the dancing tiger was their much-loved principal. The very next year he brought a live tiger cub to a schoolwide homecoming assembly. As a mascot the Wheaton Warrenville South's tiger influence is widely felt. Baker's office was filled with tiger memorabilia, and his clothing was always resplendent with a tiger-paw pin, a tiger-embroidered emblem, or some form of tiger pride. "Sempre Tigris" is a motto with deep meaning. Baker wanted to make certain that each graduate left the school knowing the Tigers are always with him or her.

A number of years ago a nationally recruited senior football player came down with encephalitis during a spring vacation in Florida with his family and became gravely ill. The next fall the football team dedicated their season to the former Tiger. The entire student body paid tribute to him in an all-school assembly—a reminder to everyone that Tigers are bonded forever. The football team won the state championship that year, and his parents credited his subsequent progress to the support he received.

Baker regularly gave Tiger Paw pins (done in different colors and shapes each year) to those teachers, staff members, parents, and community members who helped the high school reach its goals. A local store owner who donated supplies to the speech team or a teacher who gave dozens of hours to a committee might walk away with a Tiger Paw pin and a note of gratitude from the principal. Many faculty members proudly display years of accumulated Tiger Paws in their classrooms.

Tiger posters are auctioned off periodically to faculty members who can answer questions publicly about the school and about real Siberian tigers. Baker accomplished two symbolic purposes with these auctions. He made certain that all faculty members knew that tigers are near extinction and encouraged them to support efforts to save the species. He also got Tiger memorabilia distributed into more of the classrooms.

Knowing that not all students are motivated by athletics, Baker used the tiger to support other values, such as environmental responsibility. The tiger cub that appeared at the homecoming assembly had been adopted by students, who raised the more than $2,000 needed for its annual care and feeding at an Arkansas refuge. The South Tigers rejoiced in their adoptee's spirit and willfulness, even though the grown animal wasn't allowed to visit the school. Other students collected money to support tigers in the wild in India and Siberia. Still other students were involved in preserving local habitats that surround the school and mounted a large Prairie Project that protects the natural ecology of a nearby forest preserve.

Students were continually challenged by the principal to be the best they could possibly be. A published playwright, Baker knew how to use drama to entice and enthrall. His speeches were always memorable, whether to the National Honor Society or to the volleyball team. One year he asked National Honor Society students what they would choose if stacks of *Schindler's List* videotapes or Snoop, Doggie, Dog CDs were their alternatives. He went on to challenge the students' choices by encouraging them to make a difference with their lives—to be a Schindler rather than one of the masses simply listening to popular music. Another year, Baker showed incoming freshmen the grade book for the class of 1902, which he had taken from the school archives. He recalled the story of how one of the Wheaton students from 1902 discussed her courses and her grades. Baker noted a section at the bottom of the student's report card called "deportment" and mentioned that this might be an unfamiliar word. He went on to explain why deportment was just as important in 2002 as it was in 1902. It is part of the school's cultural heritage.

Although Baker moved on to other roles in the district, the culture of the school has continued as new principals have joined the school. The core values remain, and the legacy of Baker's symbolic leadership lives on in stories and history.

Rick DuFour, Adlai E. Stevenson High School

When Rick DuFour accepted the principalship of Adlai Stevenson High in 1983, he inherited a suburban Illinois secondary school with a structure and culture reflecting a traditional commitment to sorting and selecting students into watertight categories (Vydra, 1998). Incoming students were ranked from highest to lowest on their performance on a single, nationally normed test. On the basis of that ranking, they were assigned to one of five ability levels. Strict caps and quotas ensured that each incoming class was distributed among the five levels, according to a bell-shaped curve. School personnel spent a great deal of time dealing with students and parents who aspired to placement in a higher-ability group. Students who had difficulty in classes were recommended by teachers for a less rigorous level. As a result, hundreds of downward-level transfers were initiated each semester. Teachers often defined their job as presenting information clearly, assessing a student's aptitude and work ethic, and promoting academic success by placing students at the appropriate ability level.

DuFour began by engaging faculty, parents, staff, and students in extended discussions regarding the kind of school they hoped Stevenson might become. Throughout the dialogue he made a conscious effort to provide participants with information they needed to arrive at informed decisions about future directions. He shared research on effective schools, gathered information on the academic performance of top schools in the state, compiled data on Stevenson students, and presented countless examples of how the school fared in comparison with others. Gradually, consensus emerged as to what Stevenson High School might become. A vision statement was written, endorsed by all parties, and adopted as board policy.

The vision statement provided a blueprint for the school's improvement efforts. Although it sketched a general direction for improvement, DuFour attempted to sharpen the focus by engaging the faculty in a series of questions. He asked the faculty to move beyond the affirmation of the belief that "all children can learn" to address such questions as, what do we expect all students to learn in each of our courses? How will we respond to students who do not initially achieve the intended learning? How can we provide these students with more time and support for their learning? What collective commitments must each of us make to ensure that all our students learn? What criteria do we use in assessing students' work? What are our strategies for improving upon the results we are getting?

As the faculty discussed these questions, discrepancies between the school they envisioned and the actual conditions at Stevenson became more apparent. Structural changes were initiated to assign students to courses on the basis of proficiencies rather than quotas. Remedial programs that perpetuated low performance were eliminated, and support systems were put in place to provide additional time and assistance for students in need of help. Grading systems were modified to provide students with more timely feedback. Courses that had been reserved for the select few were opened to all. Task forces were created to address specific areas of the school's operation and to identify strategies for improvement. Teacher-leaders became active participants in the restructuring. The school became the model of a professional learning community.

Although structural changes posed significant challenges, shaping the culture of the school to support its new direction was far more complex. Traditional beliefs, expectations, and assumptions that had previously guided the school were no longer appropriate to finding new ways to help all students meet high academic standards. Now the school hired only teachers who had a clear sense of what they were trying to accomplish, who connected their purpose with the experiences and interests of their students, and who motivated and inspired students to believe in themselves and their ability to be successful. Above all else, a school truly committed to every student's success needed teachers who were willing to accept responsibility for students' learning.

At every faculty meeting DuFour began to relate stories of teachers or instructional teams who were reaching above and beyond the call of duty to help students achieve high academic standards. He shared stories about, for example, a social studies teacher who suggested that sophomores be admitted to an Advanced Placement course. He then went to extraordinary lengths to ensure that all of the students qualified for college credit by earning a high score on the College Board exam. DuFour told stories of teachers in the math, English, science, and social studies departments who developed an experimental two-year interdisciplinary program and what they had learned as a result. He recounted the English department's effort to eliminate remedial courses by developing a writing center to assist students experiencing difficulty in their classes. He described a teacher who went to the home of a student to confront him about his absences from school. As he narrated each story, he presented the teacher being recognized with a small plaque—a "Super Pat," for Super Patriot (the school's nickname). Initially teachers were uncomfortable with public recognition of individuals because it was a departure from the culturally acceptable rule of general praise: "You are the best faculty in the state—everyone is equal."

DuFour stressed that the school had to identify and celebrate examples of commitment to its vision statement. He invited all staff members to nominate colleagues for Super Pats and share their stories of extraordinary efforts. Gradually teachers began to come forward with nominations and soon became informal hosts of the celebrations. Part of every faculty meeting was devoted to the presentation of Super Pats. In the eight years of DuFour's principalship, over five hundred Super Pats were presented to members of the Stevenson staff.

Stories of collective achievement became another standard feature of Stevenson's faculty meetings under DuFour's leadership. He searched constantly for evidence of progress—in grade distributions, reduced failure rates, improved attendance, higher levels of student or parent satisfaction. He looked for gains on standardized achievement tests, increases in the number of students exceeding state standards on state tests, reductions in suspensions, and so on. With the passage of time his reports to the faculty offered longitudinal data and trends to demonstrate that the hard work of the staff was making a difference.

Parents and students served as additional sources for stories paying tribute to staff members. He asked parents to notify him whenever a teacher went to great lengths to help a student succeed. Each year he surveyed seniors to identify teachers who had the greatest impact on their lives. Four times each year he published excerpts from these parent and student tributes in an internal "Kudos Memorandum" to remind teachers of the significant impact they were having.

Celebrations and traditions also shaped the unique Stevenson culture. Each school year began with a "Happy New Year Party" planned and orchestrated by the faculty leaders. Accomplishments and milestones (weddings, births, graduate degrees, and special times) of staff members were publicly acknowledged and applauded. New staff were introduced, presented with their official staff T-shirts, and then led in a recitation of a humorous "faculty pledge." Orientation time was devoted to a review of the school's history, vision, and priorities rather than administrative trivia. The board of education hosted a back-to-school dinner dance for all staff to extend their wishes for a great school year. A "Quarter Century Club" was established to honor those who had served the school district for twenty-five years, and longevity pins were presented to staff for every five years of service. The school hosted an annual formal dinner party for teachers appointed to tenure. An annual appreciation luncheon was inaugurated to honor staff members who had volunteered their time to work on school improvement task forces or to serve as a mentor to a new colleague. Special ceremonies were created to pay tribute to retiring staff members.

What was the result of these efforts? In the year prior to DuFour's arrival, the local community had defeated a badly needed referendum, a major section of the community had started a petition drive to annex itself to another district, and the state had refused to forward the school's application for the United States Department of Education's (USDE) Excellence in Education Award. During the eight years of DuFour's tenure the community passed two referenda. Stevenson became the first in the county to receive the USDE award and the first in the state to receive the award a second time. Although DuFour left the principalship in 1991 to become superintendent of the Stevenson district, the stories, Super Pats, Kudos Memoranda, celebrations, and traditions have continued under the leadership of many people. Since 1991 Stevenson has been cited as one of America's best high schools on five occasions by national magazines and has become one of ten schools in the nation to receive the USDE award for a third time. In addition to becoming superintendent, DuFour went on to become a nationally known consultant. Subsequent principals and teacher-leaders have continued to nurture, enhance, and deepen the professional culture of the school.

Hawthorne Elementary School

Joan Vydra became principal of Hawthorne School at the same time the boundaries changed and it welcomed a sizeable increase of low-income students. This was the first time in its almost forty-year existence that Hawthorne was faced with a diverse clientele. The clash of cultures loomed close on the horizon: neighborhood families with conservative values and the "bus" students seen as not fitting the neighborhood standard. Vydra had to move fast to establish common ground to bring the two groups together Throughout her first year she worked with parents and staff to transform older, established ways to benefit students of different ethnic and economic backgrounds (Vydra, 1998).

Influenced by the work of Nel Noddings, she felt that caring and compassion could provide the cultural glue initially to knit the school together. Her strategy paid off. At the end of her first year, a parent wrote a note expressing her thanks for all the good that was done by "the little school with the big heart." Vydra seized that promising theme as the centerpiece of Hawthorne's culture.

Care Week became the school's fall tradition. During the first day of Care Week, students learned how important it was to care for themselves. On Tuesdays, students showed they cared for their families by writing thank-you notes to their parents. On Wednesdays, classrooms were celebrated as students figured out ways they could show that they cared for each other. On this day each student had his or her picture taken with the classroom teacher, who wrote a personal note to each student. Thursday found the students cleaning up and caring for the school. On Friday the focus went more global, as each year the students decided on a different charity to support—a local food pantry, homeless shelter, or an orphanage. In the spring the school worked with parents to create an all-school planting day. Each student brought a plant from home (or received one at school) and went outside at a predetermined time to plant the annuals or perennials in new flowerbeds surrounding the school. Different families then signed up to care for the flowerbeds throughout the summer. Hawthorne students who used to regularly trudge through the landscaping became protectors of the grounds because they had helped to plant and care for them. Caring was becoming a way of life at Hawthorne.

Within two years the school had successfully given parent volunteers a role far beyond that of the traditional baking for parties or chaperoning field trips. Every classroom had a head liaison parent who worked with other parent volunteers. Parents took on many responsibilities. For example, parent "publishers" helped distribute student writing and parent "sunshine providers" organized meals when families experienced tragedies. In addition, the principal and staff worked with several families to "adopt" other families in which parents had never felt any personal success in school. These were the disenfranchised parents who typically did not support school activities, failed to bring their children to programs or to parties, and who seemed not to care.

The school reinforced the value of student success by ensuring that every decision made by faculty and parents was linked to student accomplishments in the classroom or in life. Teachers learned to make plans and purchases as steps to improve achievement. The principal worked with teachers and parents to make certain they shared the vision of universal success. When the first-year evaluation revealed that new arrivals were the only students who did not achieve standards, Vydra used the results to celebrate the school's overall success while simultaneously calling attention to what needed to be done to make certain new students were given resources necessary for achievement on a par with others.

Parents received a newsletter each week featuring current events and activities, as well as suggesting how parents could do their part in improving achievement, building students' self-esteem, and contributing to the school's overall success. The school routinely included stories of student success and achievement in the newsletter. The principal used the medium to explain to parents that the

"Hawthorne Way" of doing things was similar to the Golden Rule. This was something stressed with students at each assembly, as they boarded the buses, or got ready to walk home. These efforts started to bear fruit. When a substitute teacher began to tell second-grade students about the behavior she expected to see at an assembly later that afternoon, she was interrupted by a student who told her that students would never misbehave at an assembly because "that was not the Hawthorne way of doing things."

Vydra promised the teaching staff that she would do whatever she could to make sure there was nowhere in the world teachers would rather teach than at Hawthorne. She shared her fervent belief that there was no greater calling than teaching and worked hard to put the best teachers into Hawthorne's classrooms. She made certain that school culture was an important part of the interview process when a team looked for a new teacher. Applicants were peppered with questions such as: What is one nonnegotiable value for your classroom? Who is one of your curriculum heroes and why? How do your students know you care about them each and every day? How would you describe the school and classroom in which you most want to teach? Teams were looking for teachers who understood the importance of their role in building a unified school culture, as well as a compassionate, inspiring classroom.

Teacher-leadership was widespread. Every Hawthorne teacher chaired at least one all-school event and served on at least two other committees. Committees planned events such as Care Week, Literacy Week, Earth Week, Family Math Night, Family Sciences Night, Curriculum Night, Field Day, All-School Song Fest, and the Year-End Celebration. All events were planned to bring the entire school community together in ways that enhanced the curriculum, helped parents become partners in the learning process, or celebrated student success and achievement.

Teachers worked together easily. They learned to appreciate different gifts that each of them brought to the table. The principal encouraged staff to visit other teachers' classrooms. At one faculty meeting teachers were surprised that in lieu of a regular agenda, they had a treasure hunt to find a specified list of items. Teams searched every nook and cranny of the school to find the special and unique things that each teacher had done within his or her room. On another occasion, teachers were given a week's notice that they were not to plan any instruction for a Thursday afternoon. The teachers returned from an all-school field trip taken that morning, during which they had seen The Wizard of Oz performed at a local high school. Upon their return, each teacher found a bag of straw, a notepad of hearts, and a roll of tinfoil in the classroom. These were the props with which they were to plan with their students and then carry out the afternoon's lesson. The creative ritual was formally discussed at the next faculty meeting and then informally celebrated for weeks to come.

Celebrations and play were a very regular part of Hawthorne. Faculty meetings became times of celebration of teacher success, as stories were shared and teachers recognized. At other meetings risk-taking teachers were frequently acknowledged by having candy tossed their way. Vydra used playful ways to celebrate the hard work of teachers. For instance, when teachers completed student progress reports they found a pack of Extra gum in their mailboxes to thank them for the extra time they had to spend completing the task. On another occasion teachers found Lifesavers in their mailboxes with a note thanking them for all the lifesaving work they did for students day in and day out. Snickers bars were the reward when there was something that it would be better to laugh at than to cry about. Teachers were given squirt guns on a hot spring day and bubbles on another occasion. End-of-year celebrations were especially memorable. By the end of her fifth year at Hawthorne, Vydra had convinced 100 percent of the teachers, office staff, and instructional aides to entertain the students. Slides celebrated the accomplishments of students throughout the year with songs sung by each grade level, providing a year's walk down memory lane. The culminating event was a compendium of skits and songs performed by the staff members. Parents and students grew to love and look forward to this closing ritual.

Leadership transformed the culture of Hawthorne. With new school leadership when Vydra retired, the culture continued to focus on student achievement, use of data, and celebrating successes.

Three Schools, Three Cultures

Three schools, three different challenges, three unique cases of cultural and academic accomplishment—each principal focused on the elements of culture that made the most sense, given the situation. Baker and his staff capitalized on tradition, stories, and a mascot that reinforce school spirit. DuFour and his informal leaders emphasized developing a shared belief that all students can succeed and on stories, recognition rituals for teachers, and all-school ceremonies of various types. Vydra and her staff brought a divided community together by emphasizing the values of caring and universal success, as well as by telling stories and using playful rituals and ceremonies.

In addition to showing how the elements of culture can be interwoven to enhance or improve life in schools, these three principals exemplify the virtues of symbolic leadership. These roles will be elaborated in the next chapter. The rest of this chapter examines the conditions that set the stage for cultural development and describes various routes four schools took toward cultural improvement.

Pathways to Successful Cultures

Unrelenting reform, rapid change, or benign neglect can quickly undermine cultural focus and cohesion. The result: a sterile school that people tolerate because it does no harm. Neither does it do much good. Or a school can grow toxic. The result: motivation, commitment, and loyalty are destroyed across the board for students, staff, parents, and administrators. We speak more of this later in our discussion of toxic cultures.

How does a sterile or toxic school reestablish its symbolic buoyancy and become a healthy, vibrant place of teaching and learning? Burton Clark (1972) has argued that new cultural forms emerge under one of three conditions: (1) when a new organization is launched, (2) when an existing organization is open to cultural evolution, or (3) when a crisis forces an organization to reexamine its traditional ways.

We examine four schools that exemplify one of these three pathways to shaping a flourishing culture. New York's Central Park East Secondary, launched in 1985, is an example of a school that began with a blank slate. Hollibrook Elementary in Spring Branch, Texas, and Joyce Elementary in Detroit are examples of cultural metamorphosis—schools that emerged from toxic crises to become highly successful. Dibert Elementary in New Orleans demonstrates how a school can fine-tune itself over time, evolving through the leadership of four principals into a model enterprise. Together, the four cases show three interesting pathways for cultural development or change: pioneering, overhauling, and evolving or tweaking.

Central Park East Secondary School, New York City

Central Park East Secondary School was established by Deborah Meier and others in 1985. They started the school in response to the poor performance of the local traditional high school. Meier, a former kindergarten teacher, worked to develop a new kind of school. She had a clear vision for what makes a good school: "We wanted a place where young people and their teachers could work in shared ways around topics and materials they were inclined to enjoy, for long stretches of time, and without too many preconceived structures.... We wanted settings in which people knew each other through each other's works, through close observation of practice" (Meier & Schwartz, 1995).

The organizers wanted a school that remained small, multi-aged, intimate, and interesting; developed "strong habits of mind" in students; offered teachers "responsible control" over their professional lives; used performance-based assessments and held students to high standards; nurtured a strong professional community where discussion, dialogue, and innovation were highly valued; and promoted staff and student inquiry and investigation into pressing contemporary problems.

These original guiding principles are enacted now in everyday practice. Small classes symbolize the commitment to personalization. Time is available for staff to discuss problems, plan new curricula, and make schoolwide decisions. Passionate professionalism is bolstered through peer observations and extensive collegial feedback. During assessment, the role of "critical friend" is applied to both students and staff. Appropriate habits of mind are mirrored constantly through discussions, problem-solving retreats, and student assessments. The interweaving of these underlying beliefs and principles solidifies the culture and encourages in everyone a deep identification with the school's abiding purpose.

Leaders at Central Park East are not out of sight and out of touch. They are visible symbols of what the school values and cherishes. The way they spend their time, what they attend to, and how they direct their efforts all serve to communicate the school's values and model its principles.

Rituals and traditions in the school build on shared values. Staff stop formal instruction and create ritualistic space to deal with crises, discuss challenges, and deal with personal loss. The final performance assessment has become a powerful tradition that reinforces the collaborative nature of learning and the high standards of the school. As new staff come on board, stories of the early days, of the development of new instructional planning, and of the constant flow of visitors convey to newcomers that they are signing on to something unique.

Meier also had the foresight to link up with the Coalition of Essential Schools, thus providing Central Park East with heightened legitimacy, additional resources, and external expertise. The school, started from scratch, has shown how a positive culture can be molded in secondary education (Meier, 1995).

The high school continues to offer distinctive educational experiences in New York City, sending a large percentage of students to college and maintaining its early commitment to unique cultural ways and practices. In addition, it has helped launch other high schools with similar values and purposes.

Hollibrook Elementary, Spring Branch, Texas

Suzanne Still, as the new principal of Hollibrook Elementary, did not enjoy the luxury of starting afresh—it seemed more like starting afoul. Hollibrook was considered one of the school district's worst places for staff to work and teachers to teach. North of a major freeway and squeezed between abandoned businesses and apartment buildings in disrepair, the school was home to a mix of students from a variety of foreign countries. Ninety percent of the student body qualified for free or reduced-cost lunch programs. Eighty-five percent were Hispanic, claiming Spanish as their primary language. Students' achievement scores ranked at the bottom of the district's distribution. Parents felt disenfranchised. The school's physical plant itself was in poor repair and staff morale was abysmal (Johnson, 1995; Hopfenberg, Levin, & Associates, 1993).

Like Meier at Central Park East, Still had the foresight to link up with an external program. Her choice was the Accelerated Schools Model, founded by Henry Levin, a Stanford professor (Johnson, 1995; Driver & Levin, 1997). Rather than outlining a lock-step recipe for schools to follow, the Accelerated School

Program focuses attention on inner resources and potential (Driver & Levin, 1997):

> A school is its own center of expertise, equity, community, risk taking, experimentation, reflection, participation, thrust, and communication.

> A school focuses on the strengths it has, its inner power, vision, capabilities, and sources of solidarity.

> A school has an obligation to provide all students the best education possible, to value equality of opportunity.

> A school should provide equitable outcomes for students as well as equal choices for parents' participation.

> A school is not a balkanized conglomerate of interest groups; it is a community.

> Life experiences of students should be acknowledged and incorporated into instructional activities.

> Achieving such noble ends will require a school to enhance experimentation, reflection, trust, and communication.

This flexible, philosophical base undergirded Hollibrook's new belief system and guided the school's cultural renaissance. The school's emergent culture supported the following ideas (Hopfenberg, Levin, & Associates, 1993; Johnson, 1995):

> If the existing curriculum and instructors' techniques are not working, new ones should be found. We can find the right ones.

> We should seek new ways from research, experts, or best practices.

> Students learn best when instruction fits their interests and engages them as active partners.

Skills and knowledge should be integrated, not fragmented into isolated parts.

We may have our differences, but in times of crisis we pull together.

As a school we share responsibility for student learning. If students aren't learning, we have to do something about it.

Parents are our friends and colleagues, integral to our success.

We can be successful with all children.

Interaction with other professionals helps build my skills as a teacher. I can learn by talking about my craft. I want to learn.

Teaching and learning involve the whole school. As a teacher, I am valuable as a decision maker, planner, and collegial trainer.

We believe Hollibrook can become an exemplar of quality learning—for all schools.

Hollibrook's positive, emerging beliefs were reflected and reinforced in new cultural traditions, such as the following (Hopfenberg, Levin, & Associates, 1993):

- Faculty meetings became hotbeds of professional discussion. Once morgue-like and dominated with administrative trivia, the weekly rituals became lush with Socratic dialogue focusing on instruction, student learning, and the deeper meaning of teaching. A common ritual during faculty meetings was a discussion of a research article selected by the principal.

- Fabulous Friday was a creative new program offering four weeks of minicourses for students. This innovative curriculum idea provided students with a wide assortment of courses in which they could explore new content, activities, and topics.

- A parent center—"Parent University"—provided courses on parenting and other educational issues, fostered a heightened parental involvement, and created a strong bond of trust between parents and staff. Parents were highly valued and their contributions regularly celebrated.

- Small discussion groups were held in parents' homes through a program called "Gente a Gente." This provided an additional opportunity to break down barriers between parents and teachers.

- A shared governance council provided a symbolic arena for community problem solving and planning. As a ritual it brought everyone together around the school's premier purpose.

- Student tour guides showed the school's many visitors around the campus. They explained the Hollibrook program and radiated pride in their new shared enterprise.

Once at the bottom, Hollibrook now revels in being at the top of the district's schools. The school is widely recognized beyond the local community for its excellent educational program.

Anna M. Joyce Elementary School, Detroit

Joyce Elementary demonstrates how a positive school culture can evolve over time. The school building was built in 1914 and, for a time, served as the community city hall. As the local government was absorbed into the city municipality, the building became a high school and later an elementary school. Today Joyce Elementary sits in a largely African American neighborhood on Detroit's east side, adjacent to Indian Village—a designated historic community (Peterson & Bamburg, 1993).

Inside the school a visitor quickly senses that Joyce Elementary School is a special place. The school mission statement is enlarged to poster size and faces anyone who walks up the steps to the main office. The wide halls and high ceilings built in the early 1900s convey a feeling of spaciousness, even of grandeur.

However, it is the obvious cleanliness, warmth, and attractiveness of the newly painted interior that commands attention. It conveys the sense that Joyce Elementary is a loving place, carefully tended to by those who call the school home. The walls and lockers are freshly painted in bright, attractive colors. Walls and stairwells are decorated with an up-to-date graphic design. The floors are clean; there are few broken or cracked windows. The hall has display cases full of examples of student work; outstanding student performances are recognized in a variety of arenas. Lockers, running the length of the hall, are topped with carefully maintained potted plants. A designated community member carefully waters each plant. Despite its age—it's more than eighty years old—Joyce is a school obviously full of vitality and life.

A prior principal, Leslie Brown, Jr., was principal for twenty years. His demeanor, like that of the school itself, was a blend of seriousness and caring, fun and hard work. Always dressed professionally, Brown is a tall African American man with graying hair and a broad smile. For twenty years he worked with staff and community to build a highly successful school culture.

The school's classrooms are well organized and focused on learning. Although the classrooms are old, the equipment is not. A profusion of materials and equipment is available for student use. Children are attentive to their work, and teachers engage in a multitude of instructional activities. Energy and caring are obvious everywhere. During recess and lunch the school is full of the usual chatter and fidgeting to be expected in children. Also obvious is a clear understanding about appropriate behavior, reinforced with gentle reminders from teachers.

When Brown was principal the office was a center of activity. The office often looked like this: the school day has not begun, yet the secretary and office aides busily juggle their too-many tasks while the principal focuses on several issues that need immediate attention. Everyone in the office is busy until the morning bell sounds. Then their attention focuses on classrooms and learning.

Joyce Elementary's growth into an exemplary school didn't occur overnight. It evolved over three periods. Prior to the arrival of Brown, Joyce was an urban elementary school with a traditional staff, a principal renowned for his laissez-faire leadership, classrooms that were filled with traditional methods of instruction, and few special programs. The school's metamorphosis began in 1979 with the appointment of Brown as principal.

Following his appointment, Brown and a new assistant princi-pal initiated a series of key changes that laid the foundation for transforming the school. These initiatives included the formulation and articulation of a clear, student-focused mission; a program to clean up and landscape the outside of the school; the transfer or retirement of some who did not believe in students or embrace improvement; the design of initial programs to increase partici-pation of parents and staff in planning; and the launching of an extensive after-school program to expand the learning experiences of students.

These early initiatives focused attention on the needs of students, communicated that change and improvement were important, and garnered momentum for other initiatives. They were followed by careful attention to building a school that stu-dents could feel proud to attend and come to happily, where they could become successful and try something new. Staff were sought who wanted to work toward this mission, and parents were snared to help out.

As retirements and vacancies occurred, Brown sought staff who had a commitment to change, believed that all students could learn, and were willing to work together for the good of the school. The culture of the school began to change slowly as new staff arrived, parents developed renewed trust in the school, and programs became institutionalized traditions.

The last period in Joyce's evolution saw the school gain greater flexibility through the district's site-based decision-making program. As the school became more successful and staff more committed, there was increased interest on the part of staff and the principal to gain further independence from a highly centralized bureaucracy. Through a new program in the district, Joyce Elementary became one of Detroit's "Empowered Schools," with discretion over the budget and many of its programs.

Shared decision making evolved at Joyce. Beginning in 1990 the principal began involving parents, students, staff, and community in a school improvement planning process. In November 1992, the staff voted (87 percent were in favor) to submit an application to become an Empowered School, thus gaining further autonomy.

As an Empowered School with control over its own budget, the school became more responsible for ensuring that resources were used to support its mission. This flexibility has made it possible to outfit a computer lab and place four computers in each classroom. Also made possible were a local area network, an increase in staff development opportunities, improvement in the appearance of the hallways and classrooms, and extensive after-school opportunities for children. By 1997 students were performing at the 75th percentile on standardized tests, fewer students were retained, attendance of both the staff and students reached 96 percent, and the school was selected as a National School of Excellence.

Core features of the Joyce culture are shared beliefs that emphasize high expectations, quality teaching, and concern for children. These features include the following:

Make student achievement and development a core mission.

Believe that all children can learn if given a chance.

Provide students with varied experiences that are fun.

Honor and recognize those who work hard and succeed.

Make the school a community center where everyone is welcome and everyone becomes a learner.

Develop independence from the district to tailor programs to serve the local clientele.

Seek out funds to increase learning opportunities.

Make the school building an enjoyable place to work in and visit.

This set of elements fosters a rich school experience, recognition and awards for effort and achievement, a deep support and belief that students can learn, a positive connection to parents and community, a proactive approach to getting things done, and an attention to purpose that keeps everyone focused on what is important and valued. Over time, school leaders developed a shared set of beliefs that are condensed in the school's mission statement.

The Joyce Elementary school staff and community are committed to

Providing a productive learning environment

Developing positive student self-esteem

Motivating students to achieve their educational goals thus preparing students for the future.

The school's mission statement is reflected and reinforced in other traditions and ceremonies. One element of the school's purpose is to make school a place that is fun and offers children special chances to enrich their lives. To do this the school started after-school programs in golf, tennis, softball, aerobics, drill team, "Academic Games," and "Future Problem Solvers."

The school also found powerful ways to bring the community together to celebrate student success. For example, the Honors

Dinner, held since the early 1980s, offered a way to celebrate students who maintain a high GPA. The dinner began with 175 attendees, including students, staff, and parents. Currently, several hundred attend. Now there are so many at the ceremony that they must televise the ceremonial event to an overflow crowd via closed-circuit television. During the occasion teachers individually let each child know what a wonderful job he or she has done that year and present all of them with a special medallion and T-shirt displaying the names of all those on the honor roll.

Another ritual is the "Clapout," an indoor parade. When something of significance happens, the staff organizes students in the hallways, and the honorees walk through the hall regaled with the applause of their fellow students. As an example, when 140 students posted perfect attendance during a ten-week period, it was an accomplishment deserving of a Clapout parade. Those with perfect attendance marched through the halls as other students clapped and cheered. Recognition, celebration, and fun characterize frequent cultural ceremonies at Joyce.

Parents are not simply welcomed to ceremonial occasions; they are integral contributors. They have their own workshops on a variety of topics; they also help in classes and participate in making key decisions. Through these efforts the school has been able to actively engage parents in the education of their children, improve the quality of life at home, and help parents address some of their personal needs.

At Joyce the culture supports continuous personal and professional learning. Staff are encouraged to attend staff development workshops and seminars and to bring the ideas back to the school. Parents are provided programs for their own education. And the new principal regularly seeks workshops and seminars that provide opportunities for her to learn new ideas and reflect on her leadership.

Brown's values came out when he spoke of what he thought ought to occur at a good school:

> A positive self-concept of all "stakeholders" must be promoted. Encouragement, celebration, affirmation, and understanding should permeate the school. For example, students should have access to technology, library books, field trips, [have their] work displayed, counseling, "I caught *you* being good" awards, to name a few positive building blocks. Parents ought to feel welcome at school, volunteer, support at-home projects, prepare children for school daily, know the school's mission, policies, procedures, and calendar for maximum support. Teachers must move toward grade-level instruction, utilize technology, involve students in the design of the classroom, promote student success, involve parents and community meaningfully, and pursue staff development. The principal, the team leader, must work to keep the vision *alive*, seek and provide resources, encourage and further staff and parent development, "go the last mile," and constantly model success and positiveness. (L. Brown Jr., personal communication)

Leslie Brown Jr. managed the everyday complexities of the school while providing symbolic leadership that has helped the school evolve into a real treasure. Brown retired and left the school to new leadership, but the school has continued to thrive, winning awards from foundations for its accomplishments. Sallie Morton took over as principal, continuing the cultural ways and traditions but adding her stamp to the culture. She knows the ins and outs of the school and spearheads its continued evolution.

Dibert Elementary, New Orleans

One of the best examples of the growth of a school culture over time can be seen in the John Dibert Elementary School's evolution before Hurricane Katrina (Boyd-Dimock & Hord, 1994–1995). Over the course of many years and under the leadership of four principals, a deep and positive culture of learning, caring, and innovation emerged.

Located on the outskirts of New Orleans in a seventy-year-old building, Dibert was a K–6 school enrolling four hundred students, the majority from low-income families. In the early 1970s Dibert was highly bureaucratic and rigidly structured, dominated by a rigid, authoritarian principal. The school subsequently recreated itself through the leadership of four principals and the school's other leaders. It became an excellent example of a "learning community" where staff feel connected to each other and collectively encourage creativity and productivity. The school's culture in the 1990s encouraged communal attention to student learning, high levels of staff collaboration, creativity, and supportive relationships through shared norms and values (Boyd-Dimock & Hord, 1994–1995).

It was not always that way. In the early 1970s, the school started losing students. At one point the New Orleans school board discussed closing the school permanently. But parents banded together to keep it open as an open-enrollment magnet school. This began the "re-creation" of Dibert.

The first principal of the new magnet school was Lucianne (Lucy) Carmichael, a creative and caring administrator, who is also a ceramic artist. She arrived with a vision. Her vision for the school included providing opportunities to develop artistic creativity, viewing the staff as the school's most important resource, and focusing on the unremitting expansion of faculty skills and knowledge.

Under Carmichael's leadership, learning became a tradition at Dibert. The first summer, she gathered teachers for a week-long session to review the instructional program and begin to build a sense of community. Later she helped institute "Faculty Study" on Thursdays so teachers could talk about curriculum, instruction, and ways to implement a child-centered approach in classes. Staff visited other schools. Some traveled to England to visit schools implementing creative instructional approaches. Quality teaching and learning became a part of the school's values and traditions for both teachers and students.

Celebration and sharing became a central part of the way of life at Dibert. Each day the school community gathered in the basement to swap stories and recognize student and staff accomplishments. Out of this, a real sense of family grew and flourished.

Carmichael's departure had people wondering whether the same spirit would continue. Sometimes a new principal means the end of old ways. But Dibert's cultural traditions and ways survived the transition. Clif St. Germain, the new principal, had been a guidance counselor and assistant principal. He wanted to build on the foundation Carmichael helped foster. To the spirit of Dibert, St. Germain added heart, making the school a happy place where children learn and grow in an atmosphere of kindness and sharing (Boyd-Dimock & Hord, 1994–1995).

The school took advantage of the new leader's arrival to address some gnawing issues that needed attention: classroom overcrowding, more time for planning, student discipline, and building trust among staff. Time and energy were spent cleaning up and decorating the dingy facility. But extra effort was poured into ritual and ceremony. The rituals of Morning Meetings and Faculty Study continued to reinforce the values of learning and connectedness. Thursday volleyball games with staff broke down barriers. Friday gatherings at local restaurants built ties, reduced tension, and cemented trust among staff. Dibert's culture became even more personal and cohesive under St. Germain's leadership.

Before St. Germain moved on, he went to great lengths to ensure that Dibert would have a new principal who would build and reinforce the school's values and traditions. He succeeded. Nancy Picard took over as principal, believing it was her central task to continue the school's direction and focus. She added other positive touches. Through her leadership, staff sought out grants to start an Arts Connection Program. Their efforts paid off with a new arts program. Parents increased their involvement in the school through projects, time, and support. Students learned about democracy through experiences in a student council. New report cards were designed to reflect the school's values. Faculty Study was refined to focus more on professional development needs. Administrative procedures that distracted from instructional time were discontinued. Dibert's focus on professional improvement, which was deeply embedded in the culture, gained momentum.

When Picard left, the Dibert culture faced another transition. Again, it was made smoothly; the beat continued. The new principal, Wiley Ates, was as committed as his predecessors to cultural continuity and the evolution of instruction. Under his and staff leadership, the school reviewed the mission statement and core operating principles. Reflective dialogue on the curriculum fueled the energies of staff and helped address openly and honestly other issues, such as conflicts that had arisen after a strike. The continuing ritual of Morning Meetings cemented the deep bonds of students, staff, and parents. The school's symbol of the rainbow perpetuated the multicultural values of the school.

Over time the culture of Dibert Elementary School integrated continuity and change. It became a cohesive culture that valued universal learning opportunities; promoted a sense of togetherness and caring; supported the empowerment of staff, students, and parents; nurtured change and improvement; and provided rituals and traditions that supported and illuminated values and accomplishments.

At Dibert, school leaders built upon the previous culture, each leader adding new layers onto the original foundation, until the tragedy of Hurricane Katrina that severely damaged the school.

The school has been reopened with a new principal, new staff, and new students. It is trying to reconnect to its history but faces great challenges.

Passages to Successful Cultures

Each of these seven schools found their path to a successful way of life along complex organizational passages. All chose a different route by interweaving the elements of culture—values and beliefs, ritual and ceremonies, heroes and stories—into a unique tapestry custom made to fit local challenges and circumstances. The lesson here is simple and straightforward: each school will find its own path if school leadership can help people discover the right direction. The voyage is never easy and is perennially littered with false starts and stops, dead ends, and colossal blunders. It takes leaders who understand the role symbols play in human experience, have the courage to take risks, and provide hope and faith along the way.

In the next chapter, we look at what happens when things go sour, when a school becomes septic. But as Studs Terkel wrote, "Hope dies last." There is always the chance that an effective leader can launch an effort to transform "a silk purse from a sow's ear."

10

Transforming Toxic Cultures
Renewal Strategies

*Sometimes it got so bad I didn't want to come to
school, go to meetings, or talk to anyone—everything
was negative or hostile.*

Think about a promising new teacher filled with enthusiasm who becomes trapped in such a negative situation. It is a troubling reflection, since the teacher's mood will undoubtedly rub off on students. Unfortunately, it is an all too familiar scenario in today's schools. For a variety of reasons, the culture of many schools has become sterile or toxic. This creates an unhealthy septic situation in organizations entrusted with one of society's primary purposes—the grooming of the next generation.

Jefferson High School (a pseudonym) is the oldest school in a California urban district. At one time, it served a population of high-achieving, wealthy students—nearly all headed for top-ranked universities or prestigious colleges. Within a relatively short period, the neighborhoods surrounding the high school went through a dramatic demographic metamorphosis; many of the students after the change were low-income and recent immigrants. Interest in postsecondary education was low, but the students, deep down, had the spark to learn if teaching was engaging. But more than a few students found a sense of connection through membership in a gang. Most parents cared but were often working multiple jobs just trying to make ends meet.

Rather than changing to meet the educational needs of their new clientele, Jefferson teachers and administrators took refuge in the perceived glory of the past. Negativity replaced optimism and the staff culture took on a strikingly negative tone. Teachers berated students and lowered expectations. Dropout rates skyrocketed and academic performance dropped dramatically. Teachers often left if they could find other positions.

The principal began to think that his chief function was now maintaining order and keeping angry parents at bay. His dream of becoming an instructional leader had long since evaporated. Until early retirement his role would remain head flak catcher, taking it from all sides. Negative teachers ruled the roost. Staff regularly leaked negative information to parents and the press. Stories of anything that might be going well were squelched. Teachers who believed students could succeed were ostracized. A group of self-labeled "incompetent" teachers formed a "Turkey Club." Meetings held once a week after school in a local bar focused on making fun of students, plotting against the administration, and trying to recruit other colleagues into their private guild of negative thoughts and deeds. One group even kept a notebook chronicling things that went awry and shared it with other disgruntled staff. They especially targeted newly minted teachers and tried to convince them to leave teaching for other occupations.

Conflict between various factions was handled behind the scenes, with the foremost intent to harm and undermine others. Complaining and griping in the coffee room before and after school became a pervasive ritual and promulgated even more negativity. Complaining and bickering never led to sharing or problem solving. If you tried to suggest ways to engage students you were silenced with comments about "that will never work" (even if it had worked in your classroom), rolling of the eyes, or "you'll learn." There was an abiding distrust among the staff for each other and especially toward the administration.

It was almost impossible to find a teacher with a positive attitude—or even one who would admit to having any hope. To be seen as upbeat and committed to students and learning invited certain ridicule, scorn, and mockery of your optimism. It was clearly better to feel jaded than joyful. Any sense that teachers or anyone could collaboratively address the new challenges was quickly shattered and disparaged as ridiculous. Carping replaced caring in the nomenclature of the staff.

The principal spent a large amount of time hiding in his office or in meetings at the district office (or so the staff was told). He was a constant target of criticism and disdain. He was seen as an obstacle, and opposing him was one of the few things that held a divided faculty together. In sum, Jefferson was a school culture in toxic free fall, a descending spiral that was neither healthy nor productive for anyone.

The Negative Side of School Culture

By looking at schools like Jefferson, we can learn about these negative situations and discover how to change them. Many principals in today's punitive environment of standards and high-stakes testing preside over or inherit messes and are forced to deal directly with toxic cultures and subcultures. Although the Jefferson portrait is an extreme case, toxic features exist in many schools across the country. They can be found in middle-class suburbs, small towns, and big cities.

In this chapter we examine school cultures that range from negative to noxious, from mean-spirited to downright hostile, from deeply divided war zones to disconnected silos. It is important to emphasize that negative, isolating, and hostile cultures sap the energy, motivation, and commitment of staff and students alike. These are negative places to teach in and difficult places in which to learn. We describe the forms that septic cultures take and highlight their key features. In addition, we describe the etiology of unhealthy patterns, why they flourish, and the ways school leaders have transformed noxious situations into positive, rewarding, and nurturing places.

Characteristics of Toxic Cultures

Toxic school cultures possess the same elements as positive cultures—values, rituals, stories, and traditions, and a network of cultural players. But these features take on a negative valence. Rather than being positive and uplifting, they have become downbeat and debilitating. The following characteristics are common in toxic cultures:

Schools become focused on negative values or parochial self-interests. They make work off-putting for adults, which transfers directly to students; teachers conduct routine, boring classes that "follow the rules" and go through the motions; they serve only a small group of elite students and spurn others who also deserve to learn; they focus on primarily achieving outcomes that are unimportant (football championships), too low (basic skills), or undemocratic (hierarchical control displaces collegiality). These misdirected values are often deeply held and transferred to new hires like a contagious disease, thus perpetuating unconstructive, harmful actions and results.

Schools become fragmented silos; meaning is derived from subculture membership, anti-student sentiments, or life outside work. No real, positive, symbolic glue holds people together in toxic schools. Schools are like isolated cells or tubes that people enter in the morning and leave at night. Separate, powerful departmental or grade-level fiefdoms replace collaboration and community. Divided along racial or ethnic lines, people organize into often warring or antagonistic camps. Small cohorts of veterans pander to worn-out educational philosophies and perpetuate negative attitudes toward work and students. Or staff is deeply committed to life away from work—outside interests are their real passions.

All schools have subcultures, but significant fragmentation in toxic settings increases friction and often leads to sabotage and outright warfare. Division decreases the sense of shared mission and purpose. Staff members, like teachers, go through the motions. Cooperation is nonexistent. Students pick up on the fragmented sense of purpose and become disengaged themselves.

Schools become hostile and destructive. Faculty meetings become Sarajevo firefights, with everyone "sniping" and "attacking" each other. Landmines of prior gripes and grudges are buried still active in the school's soil, ready to blow up in the face of the unwary. Cabals and guerrilla groups of "negaholics" harass and attack anyone trying to improve the situation. Mistrust and revenge abound, damaging any emerging signs of collaboration or impeding sharing of information or ideas among staff (Tschannen-Moran, 2004). Aggression is met with aggression and escalates quickly.

The informal network is filled with hostile people. If the most powerful members of the informal network are negaholics (Carter-Scott, 1991), pessimists, or intensely self-interested, cultural transactions take on a negative cast. The social space fills up with disparaging remarks, downbeat stories, and caustic messages. Communication becomes septic. Negative "priests and priestesses" undermine positive efforts of teachers or administrators. They constantly refer to the "good old days" and try to convert new initiates to well-worn, ineffective ways. Gossips fill the grapevine with innuendo and the latest dirt. Their tittle-tattle frequently moves outside, leaving parents to fret and assail the school. More positive or pleasant staff are driven out, thus draining the school of positive talent. Although there are always tension and disagreements among professionals about aspects of work and teaching practices, in toxic schools hostility depletes energy, tamps down productive discussions, and depresses problem solving.

Exemplars of the school are anti-heroes or villains, valued for their opposition or lack of commitment and drive. Schools, like other social organizations, need heroes and heroines to define what is possible, to provide an ideal to reach for. In toxic schools, villains put a negative spin on possibilities and what is prized. In one school, the main anti-hero was a teacher who hadn't changed his instructional approach for twenty-three years. It was, to him, a badge of honor. He actively resisted pressure from staff and administration to do something more educationally relevant and creative. He refused to go along with change and championed stubbornness as a virtue, reinforcing similar unconstructive stances in others. Without authentic heroes a culture loses positive role models and the lowest common denominator becomes the standard. In schools with anti-heroes, energy, focus, and commitment are misdirected.

In toxic schools students are viewed as superfluous or as burdens. In these downbeat settings, staff and administrators dislike their clientele and generally foster pessimistic, jaded mindsets about students. If anything, students become test scores, but without other talents or needs. Teachers and staff spend their energies protecting themselves, hiding out, or withholding participation. Many hope students do not attend school. With a lack of real commitment to the needs of students, few attempts are made to change practice, reach students who are disengaged, or connect with the true meaning of education.

Septic schools are frequently spiritually fractured. In such schools there is often a lack of élan or sense of enthusiasm or passion. Most people display a sense of anomie, hopelessness, narcissism, or "undeadness" (a condition, as the poet e. e. cummings suggests, that lies somewhere between being alive and being dead). Under these conditions, teachers meander into school just before the first bell and leave immediately after classes are dismissed. In between, there is little energy, excitement, or emotional connection to students.

Most faculty are educationally "clinically depressed," suffering from rampant disengagement. These conditions dampen any possibility for working together, reduce energy needed to inspire students, and diminish the motivation required to infuse the school with meaning and hope.

Toxic schools have few positive rituals or ceremonies that bring people together. There is a decided lack of ritual and ceremony that can help staff maintain focus during tough times. Or rituals are negative (some toxic schools have a ritual of starting the day with a complaint about students). In such schools there are few opportunities to celebrate accomplishments, develop appreciation for the hard work of one's colleagues, or connect everyone with the deeper purposes of education. Lack of rituals and ceremonies produces a vacuum in the spirit and soul of the school.

Stories in toxic schools highlight incompetence, low expectations, and apathy. Toxicity breeds stories of incompetent, uncaring teachers, students with poor academic skills and limited futures, and parents who are apathetic and disinterested. Negative stories about teachers flow freely among students and parents. Teachers relish off-putting narratives regarding students and parents. Positive tales are quickly quashed by most anyone. These negative stories become reality in the minds of staff and students alike.

Toxic cultures are hard to change because people find meaning in negativity. Villains unite people just as well as heroes. Unfortunately, grumbling and whining offer the same ritualistic bonds as positive rites. Hopelessness provides a ready excuse for not putting your heart into what you do. Pessimism is just as contagious as optimism. When a school is mired in a noxious past and dysfunctional present it is hard to envision a more promising future.

How Toxic Cultures Develop

How do school become toxic? Why do school cultures descend into unconstructiveness and lack of enthusiasm? Positive cultures take time and energy to nurture and maintain, but schools can become toxic relatively quickly—sometimes in only a few months. There are many pathways that can slide a school into decline. This can occur through direct actions or inactions on the part of principals and teacher-leaders, but it can also occur over time as the beliefs and attitudes of the staff shift. There are many cases of schools with affirmative cultures where staff once worked together toward common goals, collaborated in making decisions, and celebrated accomplishments that literally fall into a rapid and deep decline in a very short time. Sometimes key people leave. Other times demographics of the local community shift and rather than embracing the new students, staff become hostile to them. On still other occasions, top-down reform pressures for standards and testing shove a school in a different direction and undercut existing cultural patterns and practices. For example:

- In a southern school a new principal took over and proceeded to wreak havoc by ending faculty discussions at faculty meetings, controlling agenda, and criticizing the "frivolous" practice of recognizing small but meaningful accomplishments. The faculty initially pressed for a continuation of discussions and advocated open participation in choosing topics, but to little avail. The school entered a downward spiral into self-interest, disengagement, and isolation.

- In a large high school the situation deteriorated when a small yet vocal negative faculty subculture was not confronted. Over the years the principal overlooked the negativity, allowed mean-spirited comments in faculty meetings, and permitted sporadic attendance at professional development activities. Over time, nay-sayers took control and their unconstructive behavior became the norm. Productive staff either left or retreated into their cubicles or classrooms.

- One school with a deep sense of mission and purpose
  reinforced in words and actions by the original
  principal was sideswiped into a downhill spin by a
  new principal who seldom talked about the historical
  mission of serving children. He emphasized rules,
  procedures, testing, and data. The school soon lost its
  deeper sense of meaning. Key people either retired or
  moved on to other positions.

Pathways to Negativity

Leaders can unravel a culture in two ways: (1) by commission—
pronouncing new values or damaging or destroying key symbols or
rituals and (2) by omission—neglecting core values, letting important rituals and ceremonies wither and ossify, allowing negativity
to grow, or focusing exclusively on standards, rules, and test scores.

Perhaps the most common pathway to cultural decline starts
when a new leader becomes principal and fails to read the existing
ritual order, does not understand the historical evolution of values,
or doesn't respect beliefs and ceremonies that are deeply rooted
in the community. They may champion complex managerial procedures at the expense of subtle intangibles that have historically
made the school tick.

A few examples help illustrate these pathways:

Dropping cultural customs can begin a deterioration of core
values. One new middle school principal stopped staff learning activities during faculty meetings, activities that were
emblematic of enhancement and craft knowledge. Without these communal events the culture began to wither,
eventually fragmenting into separate enclaves.

Closing out opportunities to build trusting relationships. Cultures
are sustained by the positive interaction of staff. If staff
have little time to talk and share ideas, trust and collegiality

suffer. A high school principal changed the master schedule, eliminating department members' shared planning times. Their once cohesive teams bolstered by planning discussions slowly deteriorated. In another school the principal simply forgot to build in time to share, talk, and problem solve during faculty meetings—this practice and the collegiality that had once been a hallmark of the school wasted away.

Terminating valued rituals and ceremonies. Little things matter symbolically. A principal moved the copy machine out of the main office to the teacher room in the basement. The morning ritual of coffee, copying, and communication ended as a fragmented staff drifted to unfamiliar surroundings. In another school the new principal spent so much time on new rules and procedures that she forgot to recount the history of the school for the new staff—that tradition was lost forever after that moment. In one small, rural elementary school the ritual "breaking of bread" every Friday (actually wonderful home-baked cookies, cakes, and rolls brought by staff) was lost when no one organized the schedule. A key time to come together vanished and new teachers lost a chance to become socialized into the profession.

Ignoring or changing core symbols. A new principal decided independently to have the school logo redesigned because the old one was too "unprofessional." The logo had been designed by the students and voted on by staff, community, and students. Changing it severed the symbolic ties that held the school together. In another school the school mission statement was allowed to become worn and tattered in the front hall—to many staff and students it represented the vanishing of the school's purpose.

Neglecting and forsaking the core story and core mission of the school. Even the strongest cultures need nurturance or the symbolic glue that bonds people together will lose its cohesion.

If school leaders—principals and staff—stop reinforcing, supporting, and modeling the mission, it will lose its influence and punch. A principal new to a school simply stopped talking about the mission and values that had for decades been the underpinning for action. Eventually, following rules supplanted the traditional mission and teaching depreciated from a noble calling to just another job. In a small elementary school located in a midsized city, the staff slowly forgot its symbolic dedication through gradual decline as the storyteller, historian, and local heroine retired and no one filled their shoes. It was almost as though their soul and spirit had vanished—the social energy that once filled the building was gone.

Schools, like all organizations, experience times of difficulty and failure. It is how the culture deals with those difficult times that largely determines whether optimism or pessimism will prevail. It is up to formal and informal leaders to meet current challenges head-on before cynicism eats away at the core story of the school. For example, in a hard-working semi-urban school, student performance started to slip as the community was facing new economic challenges. A small group of downbeat staff started to poison the wellspring of good feelings. These venomous people had been lurking in the background when things were going well, but they were quick to surface when things started to decline. They brought up old stories of curricular breakdowns, ideas that didn't work, and kids whom they never reached. The principal never countered these tales with narratives of hope and possibility, problem solving, and new plans. Eventually, the more optimistic teachers left, and their replacements bought into the negative stories. Achievement continued to tumble as teachers spent less and less time building colleagueship and developing more effective and positive teaching practices.

Contrast this example with what happened in a large urban elementary school. The school had been improving student learning year after year through new teaching techniques, professional development, and a culture that engaged students in their learning. But the district changed its accountability process and the school was labeled on "probation" even when it was improving. For two months after the negative label was published in the paper the staff became disheartened, emotionally down, and dispirited. Rather than settle in the funk, the principal and the school's "Keepers of the Dream" met to plan a way to focus on what they had accomplished, to voice frustration at the new accountability system, and to reconnect to their core values during a "We Will Succeed" party at the home of a veteran staff member. Their positive culture rebounded and thrived; students continued to improve.

Schools can descend into negativity so slowly that it is hardly noticeable, but deterioration can also be rapid, as we describe in the business examples below.

Quick Descent or Slow Downward Spiral?

Sometimes cultures fall from grace very quickly. Other times, cultures drift away from valued patterns and practices over an extended epoch. Two well-known businesses demonstrate each possibility: 3M and IBM.

3M is an American company widely known for its innovation. Its history includes the breakthrough products Scotch Tape and Post-it® Notes. In 2001, James McNerney from GE was brought in to pump some new energy into a company losing its edge. He brought with him Six Sigma, a highly rational management process of metrics, measurement, and analytical methods. The process was highly successful at GE and worked for awhile at 3M. But very quickly innovation slowed to a trickle and the situation slid toward toxicity. McNerney moved on, but the cultural damage was rampant. One of 3M's executives remarked, "It is remarkable how fast a culture can be torn apart. McNerney didn't kill it but it was because he wasn't here long enough. But if he had been here much longer, he would have" (Hindo, 2007, p. 9).

The situation at IBM in the 2000s was very different. For many years it had been the most admired company in the world. But over time the symptoms of toxic etiology began to appear, and before long the company was in trouble. Louis Gerstner, from RJR Nabisco, was brought in as the new CEO. Initially he and others assumed that he would bring new cultural practices to the foundering giant. But he quickly realized that the company didn't need a complete overhaul. It needed to get back in touch with its original values and cultural ways. IBM's founders, William Patterson and Thomas Watson, had it right. But over the years the company had drifted from its early moorings. Gerstner's job became one of reviving the old culture, not initiating a new one. He concluded that in business "culture is not part of the game, it is the game"(Gerstner, 2002, p. 182).

Principals, like some corporate CEOs, have been known to damage well-established cultures in short order. In a midwestern middle school, a new principal took over in September. Staff meetings by Thanksgiving had become sterile and principal-dominated. Conversations about teaching had been stifled, and the teachers lounge, once a place of animated conversations and active sharing, was a dreary place of whining and destructive gossip. Staff had begun to withdraw socially and emotionally from the school. Although they continued to teach well in their private domains, their commitment to the school had deteriorated to the point of nearly complete detachment.

In other settings, schools drift slowly but surely away from a state of grace until teaching and learning has been replaced by lock-step conformity to external mandates. Some schools over time didn't face up to problems, avoided confronting a hostile or constantly critical colleague, or began to believe "the bad press," thus losing all sense of efficacy and hope. Eventually, talented staff leave, problems intensify, and teachers who remain retreat into their classrooms to avoid contact with the toxins.

Overall, the descent into a toxic situation can be fast or slow, but these misguided actions eventually fragment cohesion, put an end to collegiality, and erode meaning and hope.

The Negative Network in Toxic Schools

Positive schools have a supportive, nurturing complex of informal roles that reinforce and support the existing way of life. Toxic cultures also have a network of informal players. Their avowed mission is to perpetuate the downbeat, pessimistic status quo. This noxious, highly influential cast includes a number of roles:

Saboteurs

Pessimistic tale-tellers

"Keepers of the nightmare"

Negaholics

Prima donnas

Space cadets

Martyrs

Rogue pirates

Equipment and resource vultures

Deadwood, driftwood, and ballast

Rumor mongers

Anti-heroes and anti-heroines

School leaders should identify which of these roles exist and know how influential they are in the school. It is also important to understand the impact of these roles on staff and students alike. Finally, leaders need to work to neutralize the impact of these individuals and to end their reign of terror.

Toxicity Transformed: Revisiting Jefferson High

In the late 1990s and beyond, the popular remedy for dealing with downbeat school environments was reconstitution—sort of a neutron bomb approach to school reform. Take out the people, leave the building intact, and start afresh with a new cast of characters. This may occasionally prove to be a viable solution. But cultural scripts and types are carried in people's heads, and cultural histories have a way of creeping back into a newly launched initiative. Remember that architecture, artifacts, alumni, and lingering cultural baggage can do a number on even the best-intended reconstitution efforts.

Even though there is no tried-and-true formula for turning a negative situation around, school leaders might consider some lessons. Jefferson High, the highly toxic place at the chapter's beginning, offers a dramatic example of how a school can transform itself. It's hard to imagine a worse starting point.

Searching for something that might help the school improve, the principal and a steering group of teachers and staff called upon a nearby consultant. They asked him to visit the school, promising a preliminary meeting with no more than twenty teachers and staff. The consultant arrived to find himself face to face with all seventy faculty members, who had been required to attend. As the consultant began to outline a possible change strategy, one older teacher, well known for his frontal attacks on others, stood up and asked the consultant to leave. The consultant replied that he felt lucky to have that luxury. Everyone else in the room was stuck in a less than desirable mess. Another teacher said, "Well you're being paid. At least stick around and earn your fee."

For the rest of the morning and afternoon the consultant held court, listened to concerns, and heard people blame everyone else as the cause of the problem. The school's tale-teller recounted all the negative events in detail. One older teacher, a school anti-heroine, lent the consultant a card. It read, "There is no Santa Claus."

At the end of the day, the steering committee agreed to take a second step. They decided to have a colleague of the consultant's interview every member of the faculty, staff, and administration, as well as the students, to gain a sense of the culture. Her one-on-one sessions made it possible for people to vent their frustrations, share their fears of the negativism continuing, and describe the few hopes and dreams a handful still held onto.

After the interviews were examined, the consultants presented to the faculty the rather grim composite picture they had assembled from the interviews. As she began to outline the litany of negative themes, the same angry teacher who disrupted the first session again attacked the female consultant. The other consultant intervened and waved his airline boarding pass for everyone to see: "I have a ticket out of here. None of you does." The group became silent.

After a few moments, the school's cultural priest stood up and said with uncharacteristic passion, "I'm not even sure I understand what these people want us to do—but I'm all for it. You people have done nothing but complain, moan, and attack everything in sight for the past fifteen years." Other people offered their support. The meeting continued and people tried to see opportunities to overcome their hopelessness. After lunch, the group agreed on several concrete steps. First, four of the most negative faculty were asked by their colleagues not to join in meetings if they were going to continue to carp and complain. Then during the summer, teachers met and brainstormed strategies for the coming school year. Students were asked to join the meetings, many of which were held in teachers' homes.

In November of the next year, the consultants received an invitation to revisit the school. Upon their arrival it was hard to believe that this was the same place. Students were well behaved and excited about learning. The dropout rate had been cut considerably. Daily attendance was at an all-time high. Students wanted to come to school. Teachers were more positive and enthusiastic about their teaching. The principal was actively involved in instruction and reaching out to parents. Finally, in a reality check, the consultants sought out the former negaholic. He was surprisingly and decidedly upbeat about the school's prognosis: "We were sinking. You tossed us some flotsam and jetsam. It's now our ship, and we're on our way. We pulled the stuff that was bobbing in the water together and built a raft."

After lunch that day, the faculty presented their first locally created in-service production, "Putting Magic Back into the Classroom." The master of ceremonies was the school's priest, himself an accomplished magician. The sessions, many of them led by some of the schools previous "deadwood," were state of the art. The day ended with a party at an assistant principal's home. A veteran faculty member toasted the consultants: "We're not sure what happened here, but we sure like it. We have a whole new lease on life. We thank you for your involvement. We're not sure what you did. But we want you to know that the end result is ours. We did it on our own."

What happened at Jefferson is still something of a mystery. The key ingredients of the transformation were bringing toxicity to the surface, giving people a chance to vent, providing a chance to believe things could be better, and, finally, offering a more positive path and a large dose of hope. Sometimes, creating a crisis can provide the first step to cultural renewal. But in order to deal with toxicity, school leaders will have to risk the potential side effects of some very powerful interventions.

Antidotes for Negativism

There are no easy cures for negativism, no silver bullet. But there are ways to combat toxic situations. Two extreme possibilities to deal with toxic settings are funerals and exorcisms. Funerals help people let go of a loved one and move on. In schools it is easy for people to become attached to a negative past. To lose that attachment would threaten their identity and cohesion. The ritual of a burial, a mourning period, and a commemoration of the past can help a school cut loose a toxic culture.

This idea caught the attention of a middle school principal. He became acutely aware that his school had a long and strong symbolic attachment to ignorance: teachers, students, parents—the entire school community. He met with his administrative team and a decision was made. The principal borrowed a casket from the local funeral home. He scheduled a schoolwide meeting, including parents. When people arrived at the multiple-purpose room, they were shocked. In the middle of the room was a coffin. The group was seated and the principal began: "I have some bad news. Last night ignorance died and we are gathered here to send him to his resting place. Because of the special role that ignorance has played in this school, I've asked our local pastor to say a few words."

The pastor gave a tongue-in-cheek eulogy extolling the virtues of ignorance. The principal then invited everyone to pass by the casket and say farewell to ignorance. As each person peered into the casket, there was a mirror on the bottom. The casket was then closed and ignorance was carried to an awaiting hearse accompanied by a New Orleans style dirge band. That was the beginning of a new cultural beginning without the influence of ignorance.

The problem was somewhat different for a new high school principal. She inherited a school where whining, complaining, and moaning about all aspects of the school was the norm. Everyone blamed someone else for the problem. Her solution was to invite the entire faculty to a late afternoon beach party. When people arrived, they were given a wooden plank with a marking pen. She asked them to write on their boards all the negative things about the school. While they were writing, she was building a bonfire. She then asked each person to read what was on his or her plank, think about giving up negativity, and then throw it into the fire. The exorcism worked. The next day the school had a palpably different feeling and a new culture began taking root.

It seems strange and risky to think about funerals and exorcisms in relation to schools. But the time-worn strategies we keep trying aren't working. Too many schools are toxic places that arrest good teaching and stifle learning. Now is a time when creativity and a willingness to take risks must top a leader's agenda.

To overcome cultural negativism is no easy task. It is often easier to continue to rely on the negative, pessimistic side of schools than to defend the positive or search for new possibilities. To transform negative cultures, school leaders must sometimes resort to other extreme measures. They may need to take the following steps:

Confront the negativity head on; give people a chance to vent their venom in a public forum. Listen, challenge, and wait patiently for more positive sentiments to emerge. Venting must always be followed with actions to correct the problem. Bad sentiments without conscious correction can only poison the culture more.

Shield and support positive cultural elements and staff. In some schools staff that believe in students, collaborate in the face of adversity, and fight for change are provided sanctuary, support, and encouragement. New staff need to be nurtured and buffered from negative staff. Helpful senior staff who still deep down value professionalism and student learning should be supported and encouraged to become informal leaders for the culture.

Focus energy on the recruitment, selection, and retention of effective, positive staff. Replacing chronic negaholics who'll never embark on a more positive course may take time, but eventually the balance between hope and cynicism will change, giving rise to more interesting possibilities. The positive staff will be overjoyed when new positive staff join the school; celebrating these new hires is important as well.

Rabidly celebrate the positive and the possible. Rebuild around new values and beliefs that are regularly and publicly recognized. Tell stories of small successes, celebrate collaboration and collegiality, share humorous events, and appreciate the small moments that serve students. Establish ongoing ceremonies and celebrations that bring everyone together to communally honor and memorialize accomplishments.

Consciously and directly focus on eradicating the negative and rebuilding around positive customs and beliefs. Ask staff to discuss what they want to bury—what negative, nasty values they want to give up. Speak honestly and directly with the saboteurs, nay-sayers, and rumor mongers about what they are doing and coach them on how to stop. If coaching doesn't work, move to other means. Then, during retreats, faculty meetings, and informal discussions, keep the focus on the positive possibilities.

Develop new stories of success, renewal, and accomplishment. Find the small accomplishments and large initiatives that are beginning to emerge. Let everyone know what progress is being made. Eventually staff will start to believe in themselves and in the values that brought them to education. Toxic cultures are destructive and demoralizing. Leaders, including administrators, teachers, and parents, can triumph over the negative if they are willing to join the fray with integrity and positive stories.

Help staff find other places to work. If staff or administrators are more comfortable somewhere else, then they should be supported in finding a better place for themselves. Students and professional colleagues should not have to put up with the sustained negativity of poisonous people who may flourish in another environment. School leaders can help these people find other places to work, even if it means outside of education.

Transforming a toxic culture is a risky and scary undertaking. Many teachers and administrators have tried and failed; still others succeed without ever knowing why. It's not a job for the faint-hearted or for those who need universal approval in the short term. The process is akin to the metamorphosis of a butterfly. The caterpillar enters a cocoon. We call it the ritual process of liminality, in which an intense experience produces a dramatically different form—one that can soar to new places. The process occurs inside a school, sometimes assisted by outsiders, but is always led by those who have a vested interest in a new beginning. Like a butterfly, a school must be nurtured by its inner energy in order to thrive. In the next chapter we see how schools take this inner energy and connect with their community culture.

11

Building Trust
Connecting to Parents and Communities

Schools have a unique relationship with parents, local communities, and the wider society. Parents are "suppliers" who send their homegrown "raw material" to be transformed into well-educated, productive adults. But parents, along with local communities and the society at large, are also "consumers" of the "products" of schools. We are dependent on the next generation for the perpetuation of the American way of life.

Good businesses are very aware of their dependency on suppliers to deliver high-quality materials, free of defects, and on an intimate sense of what customers want and need. Saturn, for example, goes to great lengths to work closely with suppliers and is equally intimately attuned to the company's customer base. These important lessons of the need to nurture a close relationship with suppliers and the ultimate customers are no stranger to effective schools. One of the most consistent findings in school effectiveness research is that the involvement of parents makes a significant difference for students and staff. But Smrekar (1996) identifies some issues that drive a divisive wedge between close relationships of parents and schools. In her study of parent-school relationships in northern California's inner-city schools, Claire Smrekar found a troubling pattern in some schools. Often administrators and teachers held error-ridden stereotypes of parents—stereotypes that broke the bond between school and parents. The educators' assumptions were that parents don't become involved because they are either apathetic about their children's education, too lazy to get involved, or both. Parents didn't see it the same way. Compare those observations with some of the comments of parents in her study.

Parents valued education. They reported: "Well, nowadays you have to have a good education to do anything in life. You even have to have a degree to dig ditches. Back then, you didn't really have to have a good education, just a good backbone to do anything. School is important because you gotta live, and to live you gotta work, unless you get into that selling dope like those other people that line the streets" (Smrekar, 1991, p. 14).

Parents wanted to help their children with school. They said: "My job is sending my kids to school. I can't help them with their homework because I have had little schooling myself. I ask my children how they are doing, what homework they have, and have they done it. My job is to find out if they have any notes from school, and to keep on top of what is happening there" (p. 20).

Parents wanted to assist in schools. They stated: "Mostly parent involvement is giving money because if you go up there and say a lot of things, then the teachers feel like you're trying to take over their jobs" (p. 26).

Parents wanted to feel comfortable at school activities. They said: "Okay, when you go to school for a school meeting, you feel like, it's uncomfortable. When you're in a room with everybody around you, or sitting in a straight row—you're uncomfortable, and you can't really say what you want to say. You feel tense, like the army or something. Make us feel like we're a part of something" (p. 27).

Rather than being the disinterested, apathetic people that school leaders sometimes imagine, parents are vitally interested in their children's education. They are unsure of what they are supposed to do, but pretty sure that they're not always wanted, welcomed, or listened to.

Contrast this pattern to Carlton School, a northern California magnet school serving a mixed-ethnic population with a large number of single-parent families (Smrekar, 1996). At Carlton, parents are deeply involved in the school, and the school is deeply involved with parents.

> Parents sign a contract with teachers and students specifying respective responsibilities and mutual expectations.
>
> A telephone chain alerts parents of school events. Notes sent home must be returned with a parent signature the next day. Otherwise, the students have several minutes subtracted from recess.
>
> Weekly reports go home with each student, detailing the week's performance.
>
> Parents are encouraged to visit the school any time. They are comfortable stopping in whenever their schedule permits.
>
> Parent or student conferences last at least thirty minutes.
>
> Parents must give forty hours a year to attend school events: fundraisers, meetings, and social get-togethers. But they gladly do it.

A mutually created, shared social tapestry bonds Carlton parents, teachers, and students together. There are shared expectations, meaningful interactions, rituals of involvement, and celebrations of accomplishment. Educators and community relationships thrive in a jointly controlled, emotionally satisfying, spiritually uplifting educational community. As they describe it: "The teachers and the children and the parents. It belongs to us. It's ours. You ask the teachers around here. This is like family to us" (Smrekar, 1996, p. 11).

Many schools put in place some of the same kinds of efforts to involve parents: parent handbooks, back-to-school nights, lunches, principal chats, assemblies, newsletters, school advisory committees, fundraisers, parent centers. But too often these are the more mechanical, go-through-the-motions initiatives. They are devoid of shared meaning and the more organic, communal values that truly bring people together for a shared purpose. An overly mechanical approach is incapable of drawing parents into an organic relationship with the school. Part of the school culture must reach out and connect with parents.

Particularly when the school community consists of diverse cultures, something special must be done to lay the groundwork for a common mission and to build an inclusive, cohesive community. These outreach efforts need not be extravagant. Simple things can go a long way.

School Culture, Internal and External

It is easy for cohesive school cultures to become exclusionary, distant, walled off from the community. In some schools the culture encourages staff to draw together and shut out parents. Different languages, interaction styles, and educational beliefs too often create a sharp divide between professionals working inside schools and parents waiting outside. Building a cohesive school community means shaping a culture that reaches out and touches everyone: students, teachers, staff, administrators, parents, and community.

Symbolic bonds need to connect across the school's perimeter. They need to incorporate all constituents in a shared effort to both achieve results and to create an institution that produces widespread faith, hope, and confidence. Doing both requires the active involvement of everyone. The same sensitivity required for shaping culture internally must be applied to linking the school to parents and other members of the community.

The level of parent involvement depends on numerous factors. One of the more crucial factors is the extent to which the school's culture creates an inviting, open-door image and links to the values and sentiments of parents, community, and society. A school, by its essential nature, must be an open system with highly permeable boundaries.

Disconnections of the Past

Although most schools pay lip service to the importance of involving parents in the education of their offspring, the relationship between schools and parents has not always been robust. Smrekar's (1996) studies of three schools, for example, showed that parents are classified into one of three categories: committed partners, meddlesome intruders, or distracted absentees. The difference has more to do with the culture of a school than the attitude of parents.

In a perfect world, the communication channels between home and school would be buzzing with information, chatter, and news of the day. Unfortunately in many situations there is a shortage of connection. Part of the problem is that schools fail to fully grasp the realities of life on the home front, the day-to-day challenges with which parents wrestle. Or it may be that principals and teachers lack the sensitivity to appreciate cultural characteristics and differences among families in the community. Imagine how it feels for Hmong or Serbian, Korean, or Costa Rican parents to relate to teachers or principals. They may have difficulty with the language. Even more important, they may worry about the rituals and social norms that govern relationships between themselves and school authorities.

The culture of school needs to be deeply connected to the community through interactions, relationship, and activities. There must be time to talk, share, laugh, and tell stories about their children. There needs to be time to cry and worry, too. These connections build relationships that endure through hard times, as well as the good times. In many schools the principal has regular coffees or teas that bring in parents to chat about the school, share stories, and sharpen relationships. The openness and authenticity of dialogue creates connections and breaks down barriers.

Successful cultures try to find ways to increase

- *Convening*—bring parents and community members into the school to meet staff and students; proximity breeds understanding.

- *Conveying*—use multiple sources of communication with parents. Visit their homes, send e-mail, call, and send short positive notes; communication sends signals of engagement.

- *Collaborating*—include parents in planning, decision making, and implementing new ideas; empowerment fosters respect.

- *Conspiring*—work with parents to increase school funding, pass referenda, and gain resources from the district and local businesses; conspiring encourages dialogue.

- *Co-creating*—use the creative juices of parents and community organizations to produce television shows and podcasts, develop the arts, and add dazzle to the school's appearance; joint creating fosters close ties.

- *Celebrating*—recognize and commemorate parents, but also support the celebration of school staff by parent groups; mutual appreciation breeds trust and branding.

In all these ways, schools can connect with the community for mutual benefit and appreciation.

For example, in a New York City school, the demographics of a community had shifted almost overnight from a largely Hispanic to a predominately Korean population. School officials were initially perplexed and taken aback by the decreased parent contact with the school. Despite flyers, phone calls, and other inducements parents never showed up. During a faculty meeting a teacher suggested that they learn some Korean. The idea was met with overwhelming approval. The principal offered to call Berlitz the next day and arrange for lessons. Another teacher came up with a better proposal, "Let's have the students tutor us after school." A unanimous vote sealed the deal. Within two weeks, parents were flocking to the school to introduce themselves, inquire about their kids' progress, and offer assistance. Teachers were coached beforehand on the rituals of parent-teacher engagement and the role of teachers in Korean society. This awareness smoothed the process for both parties. These varied ways came together to build organic bonds with parents and community.

A Culture of Respect

A culture of respect is central to building ties with parents and community. Staff and administrators need to show this respect through their actions, words, and decisions. Respect is more than acceptance, rather, it requires a deeper sensitivity and appreciation of others—their core values and beliefs, situations, needs, ethnic folkways, and hopes for their children.

For example, in a southwestern elementary school, one principal built strong social ties by showing respect for the beliefs and values of the parents and community. At the Mexican Hat Elementary School in the Navajo lands, Principal Aaron Brewer knew that student success was tied to having positive relationships with parents. His respect for the traditions and beliefs of his parents was key to the way he operated. In one significant event, his symbolic leadership reinforced those ties.

One summer day, lightning struck a tree in the front of the school during a heavy storm. In some parts of the country this would only require the services of a local tree surgeon, but in Mexican Hat, the issue was more serious. In the Navajo nation, when lightning strikes a tree it imparts evil and negativity to the wood and the ground around it. Even being close may cause spiritual harm to children and elders. Students would not have returned to the school with the stricken tree nearby. Brewer knew this well and, in respect for the beliefs of the community, sought help from a local medicine man and tribal leaders.

It was clear that a medicine man was needed who had special knowledge and training in the healing ritual and song known as "The Lightning Way." This ritual needed to be completed appropriately for the place to be safe and to bring harmony back to the school.

Brewer spent several days looking for a medicine man who could enact the ritual. Covering hundreds of miles in his search, Brewer finally found a well-known healer who was willing to do the ceremony. The healer said that a ceremonial wedding basket was needed, specifically of willow, with the weaving pattern opening to the East, as well as sand from a cornfield. Also, to recognize its importance a small fee was required—of any amount. Traveling more miles in the beautiful country of the Four Corners, Brewer solicited contributions from fellow educators, and a local trading post contributed a lovely willow basket for the ceremony.

The medicine man arrived at the school and examined the tree. He conducted a complex and beautiful healing ceremony, placing the basket on a small mound of the sand and singing "The Lightning Way" song. Then part of the contaminated tree was placed in a special medicine pouch for transport many miles away to a tree hit by lightning in Monument Valley. There the spirits of the school tree were placed in the other lightning-struck tree. Upon returning to the school, the medicine man, the principal, staff, and others drank a ceremonial herbal tea poured carefully into the watertight willow basket. Water was sprinkled around the school, remaining trees, and vehicles to return positive spirits to the grounds. The ceremony, attended by parents, teachers, and others, was a powerful relationship-building event that respected the wishes and beliefs of the community.

This respectful, solemn, and cross-cultural happening was a powerful way for the school to alleviate the concerns about the damaged tree and to build respectful ties with the children, parents, and community. Students and parents returned happily to school as the year began (personal conversation with A. Brewer, 2008).

Respect must be constantly renewed and retained. Respect cements deep connections with parents and community.

A Climate of Trust

Every parent wants to trust the school and to be trusted. It is a two-way street. Parents want to trust that the school will do what is in the best interest of their child. Likewise, they want to feel they are trusted no matter what socioeconomic, racial, or ethnic place they come from. Trust is not bureaucratically determined—it is forged in the give-and-take of honest dialogue, open communication, and reliable positive interactions. In schools where there is a sense of trust, principals and teachers let others know them as people, ensure that there are times together around non-school issues (basketball games, picnics, cooking contests, reading groups), and show that they can always be counted on to be truthful—even when the message is painful. Trust is easy to damage, hard to establish, but remains one of the most important elements of parent and community ties (Tschannen-Moran, 2004). To build trust one must attend to

Time—trust requires time to get to know and accept others.

Tale-telling—trust needs stories, sagas, and legends to cement belief.

Traditions—trust grows with the knowledge that positive traditions will continue.

Ensuring Recognition

Neither an organization nor its clients will thrive unless there is celebration and recognition of successes, effort, and accomplishments. Just as in the business world Saturn invited car owners back to the factory to engage in a joint celebration of their automobiles (the drivers and the manufacturers), schools that bring parents into celebrations of their children's accomplishments—and perhaps even more important, recognizing and celebrating the role of parents themselves—similarly foster a culture of inclusion and connection. At Ganado Primary parents are celebrated for the ways they help their children learn to read. At Nativity parents are recognized for their engagement in the arts and global education arenas of the school. In one elementary school, parent volunteers are invited to a celebration lunch with long tables of food, a banner recognizing their assistance, and a huge thermometer noting the hundreds of hours of assistance they provided. A list of all the kinds of things they did (from copying to reading with students, from painting backdrops for the school play to editing the school-year DVD) run through a large-screen TV like credits in a movie. Throughout the recognition ceremony stories of caring and nurturing, supporting and helping are recounted by staff and administrators. Communal recognition glues the school and the community together in a celebration of commitment and caring.

In all these ways, the culture of the school builds bridges to parents and community, strengthens bonds, and reinforces their mutual commitment to every child.

Building a Brand

Parent and community relations are deeply sewn into the fabric of the school through connection, respect, trust, recognition, and valuing of the institution, thus creating a process known in the business world as *branding*. In business, *branding* means the development of an organization that not only does important work but also connects viscerally to clients and consumers.

Every school has a distinctive personality, its own character. It also has a reputation or image in the external world of parents and the public. The same is true of businesses. A company such as Saturn has a unique identity, which it conveys to customers who buy and drive the company's cars. It cultivates a close relationship with its suppliers because the material it receives affects the assembly process and, ultimately, the quality of the final product. Saturn goes to great lengths to build the reputation of its identity or brand, "A Different Kind of Company, A Different Kind of Car." Many of its commercials feature employees or customers. Many of the company's products rival the best that Japan produces. But much of its consumer appeal comes from its distinctive character. The company's external image is solidly rooted in its cultural uniqueness.

Schools need to establish a cultural uniqueness as well. They need to work with parents to show the quality of their "product"—student performances and achievements. Web sites, podcasts, newsletters, and ceremonies offer opportunities to show these accomplishments.

In schools the link between identity and image is complex. Unlike Saturn, a school's product is more ambiguous, hard to measure, and evanescent. Currently a school's quality is too often identified with scores on standardized tests. But most people would agree that there's more to it—a deeper set of accomplishments and goals. In most schools getting some agreement on these intangible outcomes of schools is difficult and even harder to measure.

Because of these things, every school needs to build and project a "brand" to build relationships, loyalty, and commitment among parents and in the community. As Fog et al. (2005) define it: "A brand is the perceived added value that a company or product represents, making us loyal in our preferences both to the company and its products. A strong brand is a combination of facts and emotions" (p. 20). A brand is based on values and clearly establishes how the enterprise makes a difference, how the school serves a deeper set of values in the community.

This deeper contribution is conveyed by portraying the core story, or culture, inside an organization—a school or a company—and outwardly to key stakeholders:

> A strong brand builds on clearly defined values, while a good story communicates those values in a language easily understood by all of us. A strong brand exists based on its emotional ties to the consumer or employee, while a good story speaks to our emotions and bonds people together. Ultimately, storytelling has the power to strengthen a brand both internally and externally. (Fog et al., 2005, p. 21)

Brands as Passions

Shaping a school or corporate culture requires building a brand that commands commitment and loyalty from employees and gains faith and support from customers and other external constituencies. A brand transforms an enterprise into a beloved institution and creates an emotional attachment. In the movie *Hoosiers*, the small town with a winning basketball team journeyed together hundreds of miles in school buses to see their boys play. Their passion passed viscerally to the team. When Coca-Cola changed its recipe in the 1980s the public was distraught to a degree unheard of for a product—the company soon changed back to the original secret recipe.

Whether it is a school, a university, or a consumer product such as Coke or L.L. Bean, Notre Dame or the Green Bay Packers, being a brand—an organization with a unique product demanding loyalty—creates strong ties and an allegiance that is unparalleled. In schools that are a brand this translates to commitment, involvement, trust, and achievement.

Branding in Schools

Private schools often have a brand—an identified sense of purpose, a core story, and a deep history. That is why parents pay tuition for their students to attend. The unique character of the school encourages believing that their child's education will be exemplary. Recent data show that private school teachers often have fewer degrees than their public school counterparts, but such facts are trumped by the faith and confidence parents have in the school they have chosen and are willing to pay for.

Charter and magnet schools, funded by public monies, must develop a brand in order to survive. A close synonym of the term *charter* is *character*, and each charter school strives to develop a unique culture or identity. This distinctive quality is displayed as way of attracting a compatible clientele. Thereafter stories of accomplishment and success, symbolic traditions, and meaningful symbols reinforce the brand. The schools must still achieve results on required tests, but parents already have an initial sense of connection and trust. Traditional schools often have similar brands—whether it is Stevenson High School or the Bronx High School for Visual Arts.

More public schools need to consider developing their own brand—their own unique, community-celebrating identity. It is more than just an aggressive job of marketing their character or simply broadcasting their test scores. It means building a sense of authentic understanding, appreciation, and commitment to the core symbols, traditions, and values of the school. It means transmitting the cultural core story across community boundaries.

It is not just creating a marketing department or launching an advertising campaign—that's not the point. There are more than enough channels to build community commitment. A principal recently bemoaned the lack of a public relations staff. But everyone in the school is a marketing agent, a cheerleader, and dream sender. All these informal public relations staff must be committed to the bedrock purpose and culture of the school to be able to communicate its significance to parents and the community.

East Bay Community Corps Charter School

East Bay Community Corps Charter School serves students in the inner city of Oakland, California. The school's mission is to prepare students to assume productive future roles in the workplace and their community:

> The EBCC Charter School was created out of the belief that public schools must prepare students for the challenges, opportunities, and responsibilities of life in a democratic, pluralistic society. Through service learning, the curriculum and culture of the school integrates service, spiritual development, and creative expression across a full range of academic subjects. (Deal & Hentschke, 2004, p. 185)

Located in a tough neighborhood, dealing with many students with previous behavioral problems, and pursuing long-term goals difficult to measure, the first challenge was creating some glue that would hold the school in concert: "Our task during the first month was to develop a school culture . . . routines and rituals that have brought our school together" (p. 190).

For example, every Monday morning staff and students assemble for a schoolwide gathering. Initially, they sit in silence on the floor of a large music room. Then adults and children are invited to share their thoughts and reflections with group. On Friday an end-of-the-week celebration gives people a chance to honor and praise one another. The event ends with the school song and a sense of community.

Since the school's beginning, parents have been actively involved. The school assumes from the beginning that parents love their kids and want to help out, even though poverty presents some vexing exigencies. Their assumption has paid dividends through volunteering, support, caring, and trust. The school is on the way to becoming a brand.

Ties to Parents and Community

There is no question that the school culture must develop deep and enduring ties to parents and community. By building connections, respect, trust, recognition, and branding, schools and community can become a powerful force for the good of all children. But getting there will require leaders who are able to assume multiple symbolic roles.

12

Strengthening Culture
Eight Essential Roles

Culture crops up in response to persisting conditions, novel changes, challenging losses, and enduring ambiguous or para-doxical puzzles. People create culture; thereafter it shapes them. But we have also shown that school leaders can nudge the process along through their conversations, decisions, public pronouncements, and actions.

Effective school leaders are alert to the opaque issues agitating beneath a seemingly rational veneer of activity. They read between the lines to decipher complex cultural codes and struggle to figure out what's really going on. Once they get a bead on a situation, they ponder with staff about whether and how to shape or reshape existing realities. In effect, they are asking three basic questions:

1. What is the culture of the school now—its history, values, traditions, assumptions, and ways?
2. What can we do to strengthen aspects of the culture that already fit people's images of an ideal school?
3. What can be done to change or reshape the culture when we see a need for a new direction?

As they labor to meld past, present, and future into a coherent cultural tapestry, school leaders assume several important symbolic roles.

Reading the Current School Culture

How do school leaders read and shape the cultures of their respective schools? To find out, we borrow from anthropology, history, and sociology for metaphors for school leaders' roles: those of historian, anthropological sleuth, visionary, icon, potter, poet, actor, and healer.

It is important to remember the wide-ranging nature of school leaders' unofficial power to reshape school culture toward an "ethos of excellence" and to make quality an authentic part of the daily routine of schools. As discussed earlier, school leaders must understand their school—its patterns, purposes served, and origins. Trying to change a culture without understanding it is a sure-fire recipe for stress and ultimate failure. Leaders must look below the surface to formulate an accurate explanation of what is really going on. To be effective, school leaders must read and understand their school and community culture: its past, its present, and its beliefs about the future.

Reading a culture takes several forms: watching, sensing, listening, interpreting—using all of one's senses and even employing intuition when necessary. These analytic processes are key to successful leadership.

First, leaders must listen to the echoes of school history, as we noted in Chapter Three. The past exists in the cultural present. For instance, remember the large, diverse middle school whose culture devoted to family and caring stems from a tradition developed decades before when a teacher developed cancer and everyone pitched in to help her out. Or the suburban school outside a large city that was burdened with a checkered history of perceived failures and disappointments—leading to a jaded and skewed sense of hopelessness on the part of students, teachers, administrators, parents, and the community. Knowing the past and how it still affects the hearts and minds of staff and community is a key to understanding the present.

Second, leaders should take stock of the current circumstances. The existing mores, values, rituals, and ceremonies are immediate determinants of actions, thoughts, and moods. Although these influences may be hard to pinpoint, they are never invisible to the heart or soul. The at-hand ways of doing things will persist unless reshaped or "recultured" (Fullan, 2001a). The leader needs to unpack and understand the culture, how it came to be, the strength and modes of its influence, and who its prime beneficiaries and most formidable guardians are.

Third, leaders must listen for the deeper dreams and hopes the school community holds for the future. Every school is a repository of unconscious sentiments and expectations that carry the code of the collective dream—the high ground to which they aspire. This represents emerging energy that leaders can tap and a deep belief system to which they can appeal when articulating what the school might become. In a middle school with a strong culture, the future is envisioned and discussed throughout the spring during meetings, informal coffees, and after school. New ideas and programs add hope and energy to the present. But in some schools there are no hopes or dreams for the future; the next year is seen as an empty and frightening slate, or, alternately, a drudgery to be faced.

School leaders can size up the current culture by posing several key questions about the current realities and future dreams of the school (Deal & Peterson, 1990):

What are the social rituals of interaction and support?

How and when (if at all) are classroom successes shared and recognized?

What subcultures exist inside and outside the school? What are their values?

Who are the recognized (and unrecognized) heroes and villains of the school?

How is the work of teaching defined—as job or calling?

What do people say (and think) when asked what the school stands for? How is conflict typically defined? How is it handled?

What events are assigned special importance?

How are newcomers welcomed?

What do people wish for? Are there patterns to their individual dreams? What does the school's architecture convey?

How is space arranged and used?

Are student work and accomplishments displayed?

What are the key ceremonies and stories of the school?

Shaping a School Culture: The Roles of School Leaders

When school leaders feel they understand a school's current way of life, they can evaluate the need to reshape or reinforce it. Valuable aspects of the school's existing culture can be reinforced, problematic ones revitalized, and toxic ones given strong antidotes.

Ideally, everyone in a school should share leadership. Leadership in successful schools is parceled out generously to staff and community (Spillane, Halverson, & Diamond, 2003). The idea of a single omniscient leader who does it all is misleading, except when staff are unwilling or unable to pick up the slack.

Consequently, the eight symbolic leadership roles discussed in this chapter can be assumed by principals, teachers, staff members, custodians, parents, community members, and others. Cultural leaders reinforce the underlying mores, values, and beliefs in subtle and often important ways. They shore up the central mission and purpose of the school. They create and sustain motivation and commitment through rites and rituals. Leadership at its best is shared, with everyone pulling together in a common direction.

Now let's look more closely at the eight essential leadership roles:

Historian: seeks to understand the social and normative past of the school

Anthropological sleuth: analyzes and probes for the current array of cultural traditions, values, and beliefs

Visionary: works with others, including leaders in the neighboring community, to characterize a portrait of the ideal school

Icon: affirms values through dress, behavior, attention, actions, and routines

Potter: shapes and is shaped by the school's symbolic webbing of heroes, rituals, traditions, ceremonies, symbols; brings in staff who share core values and helps them find the right seat "on the bus" (Collins, 2001)

Poet: uses expressive language to reinforce values and sustains the school's best image of itself

Actor: improvises in the school's predictable dramas, comedies, and tragedies

Healer: oversees transitions and changes; heals the wounds of conflict and loss

School Leaders as Historians

As effective school leaders probe deeply into defining events that have given rise to the symbolic texture of a school, they realize that echoes of past crises, challenges, and successes reverberate in the here and now. Leaders perpetuate a pageant that demonstrates where the school has been as a key factor in interpreting present practices and ways. Staff and parents take on this role, for example, whenever new staff arrive or new parents join the community.

One of the best ways of tracking the past is to construct an organizational time line depicting the flow of events, ideas, and key characters over several decades. This time line provides a chronological portrait of the events, circumstances, and key leaders who shaped the personality of the school.

At Monona Grove High School in Wisconsin the construction of a new building and the passage into a new millennium prompted a look back. Developing an in-depth historical time line of the prior three decades showed the flow of events, the influences of people, and the challenges and successes that helped foster the school's evolution. In the rearview mirror, things are closer and clearer than they first appear.

School Leaders as Anthropological Sleuths

Anthropological sleuths are a cross between Margaret Mead and Columbo, CSI and Law and Order. As dogged cultural detectives, school leaders listen and look for clues and signs in the school's present behavioral rituals and in the physical displays of symbols and artifacts. They unearth mores and values in the daily doings. School leaders must decode the pottery shards and secret ceremonies of daily activity in teachers' lounges, staff workrooms, and hallway greetings to access veiled features of the culture. Nothing is ever as it seems, and these sleuths find unexpected interpretations of common human activity.

For example, in one innovative school, teachers started wearing the DARE drug program badge that states, "Just Say No." They did it not to reinforce drug awareness week but to uphold their desire to slow the pace of curricular change. They all knew they had taken on too much. Knowing the significance of the badge was important to understanding what was really going on. And in Ganado Primary the displays of superb local weavers along with the student newspaper and school awards highlight not just local crafts but also the importance of celebrating accomplishments and reaffirming the school's dedication to creativity and artistry.

School Leaders as Visionaries

In addition to their roles as historian and anthropologist, school leaders can't escape their duties as visionaries. Through a careful probe of past and present, they need to ferret out an understandable sense of what the school can become, a shared dream of an upbeat future. Visionary leaders continually find ways to communicate communal hopes and wishes, capturing the essence of the school's purpose and mission. To arrive at a shared vision, teacher-leaders and administrators listen closely for the cherished dreams that bubble up from people's heads and hearts. Sometimes these dreams become mission statements, but other times they take on the form of stories, commentaries, or emblems. The vision may not be shared in exactly the same way by everyone, but overall there is a sense that this is what we can become, this is where we are headed.

Visionaries exist anywhere in a school's pecking order. For example, in Chicago's Piccolo Elementary School the president of the local school council, a parent and community leader, joined with the principal to identify and communicate communal hopes and dreams. Together, with others, they worked to develop a caring, safe, and academically focused learning environment. Another example: at Hollibrook Elementary, the principal and the teachers jointly shared and protected the school's dream as staff and administration changed. When Suzanne Still, the principal, and some teachers left for other positions, those remaining indoctrinated the new principal and staff into the existing path the school was taking. Even then, a vision is never static. It must be reinforced, renewed, and celebrated.

School Leaders as Icons

Everyone pays attention to what leaders do even more closely than they listen to what they say. Both deeds and words get people's attention, whether it is the principal's efforts to foster more collaboration or encouraging creative use of the Internet. Who school leaders are—what they do, attend to, get excited about, or seem to appreciate—is constantly scrutinized and interpreted by students, teachers, parents, and members of the community. Leaders' interests and actions send powerful messages. They signal their values and beliefs. Above all else, leaders are cultural "teachers" in the best sense of the word.

We rarely realize an action's symbolic value when it occurs; more often its significance seeps in later. For example, the principal's morning "building tour" may be, on one level, a functional walk to look into potential trouble areas or to spot building maintenance problems. But teachers and students may see the same stroll as a symbolic event, a ritual demonstrating that the principal cares about classrooms, teaching, students, and learning. Similarly, the visit of a teacher-leader to another's class to observe a unique lesson can send the message that good instruction is valued and respected.

Schools are filled with many routine tasks that often take on added significance. A classroom visit, building tour, or faculty meeting may be nothing more than routine—or it can become a symbolic expression of shared values and beliefs. Routines become significant when imbued with pomp and pageantry.

Almost all actions of school leaders can have symbolic content when a school community grasps the actions' relevance to cultural ideals. The arrangement of space sends cultural signals. For example, the location, accessibility, decoration, and arrangement of a principal's office are significant. One principal works from her couch in an office near the school's entrance; another is hidden in a corner suite behind a watchful, stern, and protective secretary. One principal decorates her office walls with students' work; another displays athletic trophies, public service awards, posters of favorite works of art, and photographs of his family. These cultural artifacts are indicators of what a principal sees as important.

The arrangement of classrooms also sends a powerful message. Is student work displayed? Is it current? In one school visited in April there were extensive displays of student work—none

more recent than November. The students and community pay
heed to such minute details. Is there a wide variety of learning
activities, materials, and books readily available? Do teachers
have a professional library, awards, or certificates for professional
institutes attended? How are the desks arranged? Rows? Circles?
Physical arrangements reverberate with important clues about the
culture.

A principal is always on duty, and little things mean a lot
twenty-four hours a day. What car a leader drives, his or her
clothes, posture, gestures, facial expression, sense of humor, and
personal idiosyncrasies send signals of formality or informality,
approachability or distance, concern or lack of concern for people.
A wink following a reprimand can have as much effect on a child
as the verbal reprimand itself. A frown, a smile, a grimace, or a
blank stare—each may send a potent message. Do staff interact
with students and parents when they cross into school territory?
Are energy and joy apparent in the faces of teachers? Is laughter
and humor evident?

One principal told us that he assesses his emotional state each
day before going into the school as a way of shaping and preparing
for his interactions with people. This is an important reflection of
emotional intelligence and will help him monitor the emotional
content of messages he will send that day.

Time is also crucial. How leaders spend their time and where
they focus attention sends strong signals about what they value.
A community quickly discerns discrepancies between espoused
values and true values by what issues receive a leader's time and
attention. The appointment book and daily schedule show what a
principal cares about. Whether staff take time to attend and engage
in discussions with parents during Parent Association Meetings
or site council gatherings demonstrates their commitment to the
community. In one large high school, the principal does an informal
tally every Wednesday to estimate how she has spent her time in
various areas so she can adjust and send the right messages for the
rest of the week, if needed.

School leaders signal appreciation officially through celebrations and public recognition and rewards. Informally, their daily behavior, demeanor, and emotional energy communicate their preferences about quality teaching, acceptable behavior, and desired cultural traditions.

Staff and students are particularly attentive to the values displayed and rewarded by various school leaders in moments of social or organizational crisis. But a quick "thanks, great job," a hand-written "I appreciate what you are doing," or dropping by class to thank someone can be equally significant. An e-mail, recognition on the school Web site, or inclusion in the principal's column in the newsletter can also recognize and show appreciation for innovation, the caring support of a student, or a successful display of good teaching techniques. Whatever the medium, the message should be clear, authentic, and tied to the deeper mission of the school.

The form, emphasis, and volume of memos, e-mails, podcasts, blogs, and newsletters communicate as strongly as what is written. E-mails may be a source of inspiration, a celebration of success, or a collection of bureaucratic jargon, rules, and regulations. Class or departmental newsletters or e-mails can send a message to parents that communication and connection are important. Even the appearance of written material or the organization of a Web site will be noticed, from the informality of the penciled note to the care evidenced by the way the Web site responds to what a parent needs.

The Internet has transformed how leaders communicate their principles. The school's Web site now sends powerful messages to the community about the school. One must ask: Is the Web site easy to navigate, attractive, and filled with clear and useful information? Does the look and feel of the Web site suggest the caring, nurturing, productive values of the school? Pride, humor, affection, and even fatigue displayed in words and Web sites communicate what a school stands for. The Web site for the Nativity School, for example, includes core values, programs, and messages about what is happening. It is clear and well organized and very popular with parents.

Taken together, all aspects of a leader's behavior form a public persona that carries symbolic import. It comes with the territory of being a school leader and plays a powerful role in shaping the culture.

School Leaders as Potters

School leaders contour the elements of school culture (its values, ceremonies, and symbols), much the way a potter shapes clay—patiently, with skill, occasionally creating a new form by accident and sometimes with a clear idea of what the pot will eventually look like. Most often, however, the destiny of a particular art form is a subtle interplay between the artist and the material. As potters, school leaders shape the culture in a variety of ways.

Leaders Infuse Shared Values and Beliefs into Every Aspect of the School Day and Beyond

Although the principal often, formally and informally, articulates the philosophical principles that embody what the school stands for, successful schools distribute this responsibility throughout the staff. Staff increasingly communicate the core values, model what is important, and tell the core story of the school to new staff, recently added students, and new parents.

An invaluable service is rendered as the principal and other leaders express a school's values and beliefs in a form that makes them memorable, easily grasped, and engaging. Teachers are powerful communicators and should be offered the opportunity at ceremonies, celebrations, meetings, and gatherings to share their views of what the school stands for. Whenever they meet parents in the hallway, run into a school board member in the grocery store, or jog with a local businesswoman, what they say and do creates an image of the school as compellingly as if they were giving a speech or writing a mission statement.

In a western school the principal and staff gather each year to discuss the meaning of the school's mission and ways to share that undertaking with others through anecdotes from classrooms, stories of connection and learning, recounting of the history and founding of the school, and analogy and metaphor. These sessions enrich the ways staff, who deeply believe in the school, can convey to others what they feel about the institution.

Values and beliefs are often condensed into slogans or mottos that help communicate the character of a school. Of course, to ring true they must authentically reflect the school's practices and promises. These shorthand descriptors must be credible, honest, and trustworthy. For instance, (1) "Every child a promise"; (2) "A commitment to People. We care. A commitment to Excellence. We dare. A commitment to Partnership. We share"; and (3) "A Community of Learners" (Deal & Peterson, 1990).

In some schools, symbols take the place of slogans but play a similarly expressive role. One middle school's values are embodied in the symbol of a frog. The frog reflects the school's commitment to caring and affection that eventually can turn all children into "princes and princesses." We see symbols in many schools. For example:

- At Ganado Primary the detailed, locally woven Navajo rugs on the walls shout quality and reinforce a tribal belief that the knowledge of weaving is part of a longer tradition of learning and expertise.

- At a high school in the Salt Lake City area, an impressive collection of student artwork communicates the dedication to creativity and the importance of art (the art is purchased with an endowment given to commemorate the untimely death of a student).

- In a northern Wisconsin school, the display of Hmong hand-stitched wall hangings tell detailed stories of

Hmong parents' journey from war-torn Cambodia and celebrate the importance of knowing one's history.

- In suburban Chicago, a school displays the growth of student performance on a massive chart visible as one enters the lobby. The message supports the planning and achieving of learning.

Leaders Celebrate Heroes and Heroines, Anointing and Recognizing People Who Make a Difference

Key individuals in most schools, past and present, exemplify shared virtues, model dedicated service and caring connections, and radiate commitment. Heroes and heroines, living and dead, personify values and serve as role models for others. They push us all to be better than we might think we can be.

Anyone may qualify for special status and recognition through words or deeds that reflect what a school holds most dear. Like vivid stories of Amelia Earhart or Charles Lindbergh, Mother Teresa or Martin Luther King, Jr., stories of local heroes and heroines help motivate people and bond them to the virtues of the school. When heroes exemplify qualities a school wants to reinforce, leaders can recognize these individuals publicly. When challenges seem to drain energy, the stories of a school heroine can buoy morale. Schools can commemorate teachers or administrators who have put in the extra effort that embody what is best about educators. Just as businesses, hospitals, or military units recognize their finest role models, schools do this with words, pictures, plaques, or special ceremonies:

- In an outlying school a retired teacher, renowned for her ability to help struggling students learn to read, returned every week to work with the most challenged and challenging students. Over time she saved dozens of students from the jaws of illiteracy.

- In a southern middle school, everyone knew "Martha," the experienced English teacher who, with family gone years before, always stayed after school to help students who struggled with writing. She always seemed able to identify those needing assistance and knew how to motivate them to spend extra time to master the work.

True heroes and heroines don't have super powers; they are regular people who, through caring and dedication, go beyond what is expected. For the school they become important symbols and exemplars.

Leaders Observe Rituals as a Means of Building and Maintaining Esprit de Corps

School leaders contour cultures by encouraging rituals that celebrate and reinforce important ideals. As noted previously, everyday tasks take on added significance when they symbolize something special and when they buttress a sense of purpose and bond people in a common quest.

For example, a new superintendent of schools opened his first districtwide convocation by lighting a small lamp, which he labeled the "lamp of learning." After the event, no one mentioned the lamp. But the next year, prior to the convocation, several people inquired: "You are going to light the lamp of learning, aren't you?"

Rituals take various forms (Deal & Peterson, 1990). Some are social and others center on work. Surgical teams scrub for seven minutes, although bacteria are destroyed by modern germicides in thirty seconds. Members of the British artillery, when firing a cannon, still feature an individual who holds his hand in a position that once kept the horse from bolting because "that's the way it has always been done." Other rituals revolve around greetings and relationships. Americans shake hands, Italians hug, and the French kiss both cheeks when greeting or parting. In the 2008 election, controversy swirled around presidential candidate Barack Obama's congratulatory "fist punch" with his wife. In a Florida school, the staff meeting begins with a ritual storytelling—stories of the past month's accomplishments, funny situations, and significant challenges overcome. This ritual sharing is glue for the social bonds of the staff.

Meetings, parties, informal lunches, and school openings or closings provide opportunity for rituals. As we saw in Chapter Seven, Bob Herring, principal at Nativity School, closed meetings by offering an opportunity for anyone to share stories of positive events. In this setting, issues can be aired, accomplishments recognized, disagreements expressed, or exploits retold. These rituals connect people to each other and tie them with deeper values that are otherwise difficult to express.

Leaders Perpetuate Meaningful, Value-Laden Traditions and Ceremonies

Schoolwide ceremonies allow us to put cultural values on display, retell important stories, and recognize the exploits and accomplishments of important individuals. These special events tie past, present, and future together. They intensify everyone's commitment to the organization and revitalize educators for challenges that lie ahead.

When an authentic ceremony is convened in a hallowed place, given a special touch, and accorded a special rhythm and flow, it builds momentum and expresses sincere emotions. Planning and staging these events is often done with extreme care. Encouraging and orchestrating such special ceremonies provide still another opportunity for leaders to shape—and to be shaped by—the culture of the school. Here is an example:

One group of parents—with input from the high school leadership—planned a joyous celebration for the school's teachers. They decorated the cafeteria with white tablecloths and silver candleholders. They went to the superintendent and asked permission to serve wine and cheese and arranged for a piano bar where teachers and parents could sing together. Each teacher was given a corsage or a ribbon. The supper was potluck, supplied by the parents. After dinner the school choir sang. Several speakers called attention to the significance of the event. The finale came as the principal recognized the parents and asked everyone to join her in a standing ovation for the teachers. The event was moving for both the teachers and the parents, and has become a part of the school's tradition.

School Leaders as Poets

We should not forget the ways, both straightforward and subtle, that leaders communicate with expressive language in media ranging from memos to mottoes to sagas and stories, as well as in informal conversation. Words and images invoked from the heart and soul convey powerful sentiments. "The achievement scores of my school are above the norm" conveys a very different image from "Our school is a special temple of learning."

Acronyms can separate insiders from outsiders to the school community and tighten camaraderie. (They can also exclude people.) PSAT, CTBS, NCLB, PLC, AYP, or SAT may carry different meanings to educators than to the public. Idioms and slogans ("Every child a promise" or "Onward to excellence") may condense shared understandings of a school's values. However, hypocrisy in such slogans can alienate those who hear them. Consider the principal in the satirical book *Up the Down Staircase* (Kaufman, 1965), who would say, "Let it be a challenge to you" in the face of problems that were obviously impossible to solve.

Metaphors provide "picture words" that consolidate complex ideas into a single, understandable whole. Whether students and teachers think of a school as a factory or a family will have powerful implications for day-to-day behavior. One school's description of itself was, "If our school were an animal it would be a chameleon because it changes color every time a new fad comes along," whereas another school stated, "Our school is like an Octopus, reaching out in all directions for new ideas and connected in the center by our shared values."

As we have seen, one of the highest forms of evocative communication is the story. A well-chosen story provides a powerful image that addresses a question without compromising its complexity. Stories position complicated ideas in concrete terms, personifying them in flesh and blood. Stories carry values and connect abstract ideas with sentiment, emotions, and events.

Stories told by or about leaders help followers know what is expected of them. Stories accentuate what is valued, looked after, and rewarded for old-timers and greenhorns alike. For example, the parents of a third-grade student informed the principal that they were planning to move into a new house at Christmas and would therefore be changing schools. He suggested they tell the teacher themselves, since she took a strong personal interest in each of her students. They returned later with the surprising announcement that they were postponing their move. The principal asked why. The mother replied, "When we told Mrs. Onfrey about our decision she told us we couldn't transfer our child from her class. She told us that she wasn't finished with him yet."

By repeating such stories, leaders reinforce the magical values and beliefs of teaching and learning. Sagas—stories of unique accomplishment, rooted in history and held in sentiment—can convey core values to all of a school's constituents. They can define for the outside world an "intense sense of the unique" that captures imagination, engenders loyalty, and secures external resources and support.

School Leaders as Actors

Cultures are often characterized as theater, that is, the stage on which important events are dramatized. If "all the world's a stage," then aspects of the life of a school are fascinating whether they are comedy, tragedy, or some unique mixture. Technically, these have been called "social dramas," various stages of goings-on in a school that blend all forms of theater into a delightful human pageant.

Much of this drama bubbles up during routine activities. Periodic ceremonies, staged and carefully orchestrated, provide intensified yet predictable excitement in any organization. In crises or in critical incidents (like the murder of a student in the school yard, or the untimely passing of a beloved teacher) a culture opens itself to unforgettable moments and defining events.

A critical incident like a school closing offers leaders a significant opportunity to sponsor a social drama that can reaffirm or redirect cultural values and beliefs. For example, a principal was concerned about the effect of a school merger on the students and the community. He convened a transition committee made up of teachers and community members to plan, among other things, a ceremony for the last day of school. On that day, the closing school was wrapped in a large red ribbon and filmed from a helicopter. When wreckers had demolished the building, each student, teacher, parent, and observer was given one of the bricks tied with a red ribbon and an aerial photograph of the school tied with a red bow (Deal & Peterson, 1990).

Such drama provides a heightened opportunity and an energized sensibility among staff and community to make a historical transition and reaffirm cultural ties within the school community. Rather than inhibiting or stifling such dramas, school leaders may seize them as an opportunity to resolve differences and redirect the school.

Principals and teacher-leaders can be actors in a comedy, too. At Jefferson Middle School in Madison, Wisconsin, an early principal who was a serious instructional leader took on a different persona during the yearly "Follies." This talent show featured dozens of acts by students, but the principal always came out and provided a humorous skit dressed as Elvis, Superman, or a magician. He was able to demonstrate his creativity, humanity, and silly side at the Follies—and reinforce the culture of inventiveness and individuality as well.

Social dramas and conflicts can be improvisational theater with powerful possibilities to reaffirm or alter values. In a political sense, events such as faculty or student conflicts are arenas with referees, rounds, rules, spectators, fighters, and seconds. In the arena, conflicts are surfaced and decided rather than left lingering and seething because they have been avoided or ignored. Such avoidance often leads to the development of toxic cultures or nasty subcultures. Arenas provide school leaders significant opportunity to wrestle things out in a controlled public forum instead of slugging things out behind the scenes in unregulated combat. Social drama enacted as contained "sporting events" can hash out festering grudges and lance old wounds while often reaffirming or redirecting the values and beliefs of the school.

Improvisational theater offers a chance to peek behind the veneer of everyday transactions and behind the masks we wear. Seeing ourselves as we really are often opens possibilities to change the script. A district team at a cultural workshop was experiencing great difficulty with an assignment. Other teams had gone back to their districts to retrieve artifacts to present their district's cultural profile following lunch. This group was arguing, and some of the exchanges were becoming heated shouting matches. Several people walked away. Others sat silently, refusing to participate. Things were going downhill fast. Then the superintendent said, "Wait a minute, this is us! This is our culture! Bring the others back." For an hour, the team reconstructed a meeting that had resulted in a disastrous event marking the district's twenty-fifth anniversary. When the teams returned, this group reenacted the meeting, a presentation so funny that people were laughing with tears rolling down their cheeks. Weeks afterward, the superintendent reported that the session triggered some profound changes in how things were done, both in the district and in individual schools.

Symbolic leaders know their roles in the multitude of social dramas that make up a school's expressive life. They engage in authentic, meaningful theater every day, encouraging other members of the cast to play their parts as well.

School Leaders as Healers

School cultures are stable but not static, and changes do occur. Especially when changes cause the existing cultural fabric to fray or unravel, symbolic wounds cause distress and pain. School leaders can play key roles in acknowledging these transitions—whether school consolidations or closings, new instructional practices, or staff turnover—healing whatever injuries they create and helping the school adapt to the loss of its traditions and ways. Leaders serve as healers in many ways.

Leaders Mark Beginnings and Endings

Schools celebrate the natural transitions of the year. Every school year has a beginning and an end. Beginnings are marked by convocations to end the summer and outline the vision and hopes for the coming year. Endings are marked by graduations, bittersweet events that unite members in a common celebration of their accomplishments but mark the end of a page in their lives.

Leaders Remember and Recognize Key Transitions in the Occupational Lives of Staff

Changes of employment are episodic transitions that a principal may use to reaffirm the school's culture and the continuity of its core values. Newcomers need rites of initiation. Even transfers, reductions in force, terminations, and firings-for-cause are ruptures that require symbolic recognition.

In a Massachusetts elementary school, primary students named hallways after teachers who had been let go in the wake of a taxpayer rebellion that required tremendous cost reductions in nearly every school in the state (Deal & Peterson, 1990). In another school the transition to tenured status is not simply a "whew," but rather a time of joy and formal entry into the traditional fraternity of teachers. Staff and administrators come together to welcome the newly tenured teacher with stories of past heroines, sagas of teaching savvy, and a ceremonial presentation of the school logo embedded in a paperweight symbolizing that the anointed teacher is a member-in-full-standing.

Leaders deal directly and openly with critical, difficult, and challenging events in the lives of staff and students, always aware of the message they are sending. Unpredictable, calamitous events in the life of the school, such as a death or a school closing, are upsetting to all members of a school community. These transitions require recognition of pain, emotional comfort, and hope. Unless transitions are acknowledged in public cultural events, loss and grief will accumulate. For example, following the death of several classmates in a car accident, a school and its community gathered at funerals, memorial services, and informal get-togethers to remember and eulogize the students. These events helped the community cope with its hurt and sadness and over time replaced sharp pain with warm memories.

Too often, the technical side of leadership—planning, supervision, evaluation, discipline, decisions, and deadlines—eclipses the available time and willingness of principals and other leaders to assume much-needed symbolic roles. When that happens, schools become sterile, incapable of reaching the hearts and souls of students and teachers or earning the faith and confidence of parents and local residents. By expanding their repertoire of symbolic responsibilities, school leaders can make a real difference. Their artistry can help galvanize a diverse group of people into a cohesive community whose members are wholly committed to a beloved institution.

We explore the unique ways that school leaders can mold culture over time through blending technical and symbolic actions—becoming bifocal leaders—in the next chapter.

13

Living with Paradox
The Bifocal Principal

We believe America's schools are currently awry. Decades of reform have attempted to make them more rational, efficient, and technically sophisticated. We believe schools need a fresh dose of symbolism to revive their cultural roots. To achieve this objective requires a profound shift in how school administrators think about schools and their roles. Fundamentally, they need to become cultural stewards as well as structural wardens. But there is a danger lurking in this argument. In our efforts to make schools more spiritual, it is all too easy to overlook the importance of structural clarity and technical competence. The goal should be striking a balance or symmetry between rationality and spirituality.

There is the rub. Most Americans are prone to dualistic thinking, to seeing the opposing parts as competing segments rather than unifying essence:

> Although at first view nature's poles present themselves as opposite and mutually antagonistic, on closer inspection we realize that they are complementary; one cannot exist without the other. Without the female, there could be no male, and without the male there could be no female. The lungs both expand and contract continuously. If movement in either direction were to stop, life would cease. Were man to know no sadness, he would never know joy; without the experience of

failure, he would know no success; without a knowledge of sickness, he would know no health. The universe and our knowledge of it are therefore constituted of the endless to and fro movement of life from any pole to its complementary opposite. (Foy, 1980, p. 32)

This either-or mindset dominates our approach to educational improvement. We tend to see solutions to problems in schools as choices between extreme alternatives: structural or cultural, rational or spiritual. Polarities are seldom perceived as the warp and woof of the same fabric or integral parts of a balanced composition. In much Western thought, puzzling situations are considered simplistic problems to be solved with predetermined answers rather than puzzling dilemmas begging a balanced judgment. Those who pass reform legislation or work in schools sometimes apply this antagonistic view of opposites in thinking about what should be done to improve schools. Typically, both legislators and school administrators seek structural answers to education's persistent spiritual challenges. In 1994 we identified this issue in *The Leadership Paradox* and see this challenge continuing unabated (Deal & Peterson, 1994).

Dualistic thinking leads people to view managing and leading as different, inherently conflicting, approaches. Many administrators thus think they need to pick one orientation over another, to focus mainly on either technical *or* symbolic aspects of their work—but not both at the same time. Principals often find themselves in a predicament of trying to figure out who they want to be, which way to behave, what to emphasize. Should they emulate the rational management model exemplified by Robert McNamara or pattern themselves after the artistic symbolic orientation of Martin Luther King, Jr.? Either choice creates its own dilemmas. As Pirsig states:

Because we're accustomed to it, we don't usually see that there is a third possible logical term equal to yes or no which is capable of expanding our understanding in an unrecognized direction. We don't even have a term for

it, so I'll have to use the Japanese Mu . . . . Mu means "no
thing" . . . . It states the context of the question in such
a way that a yes or no answer is in error and should not
be given. Unmask the question is what it says. (1984,
p. 288)

Unmasking the question means confronting the possibility that
principals can create both meaning and order. They can be both
supporters of change and defenders of the status quo. Principals can
find a balance point between being traditional or innovative, tight
or loose, inflexible or creative. They can embrace paradoxes and
puzzles of their work as the fulcrum for creating new approaches to
leadership.

The idea of Mu, of finding a "nonanswer" to perplexing questions, seems strange. It introduces the notion of paradox, a seemingly
contradictory situation or statement that runs counter to common
sense and yet appears to be true. How can a pointillist painter like
Seurat produce masterpieces of merged colors and complex form
with a multitude of closely spaced dots? How does the Möbius
strip seem to have three dimensions, yet one is able to draw a
continuous line around it, moving onto both sides, and never pick
up the pencil or cross an edge as though on a flat surface (personal
conversation with Norman Webb, 1993)? How can one see both
near and far? How can architecture be both functional and artistic?
In schools, complicated puzzles may only be addressed successfully
through balanced, bifocal actions: those that are both technical and
spiritual. Such even-handed actions provide simultaneous opportunities for both management and leadership, for movement and
stability.

Paradoxes of the Principalship

Dilemmas that arise in schools each day require new ways of
combining leading and managing. We need to think of leadership as intertwined with management in an intricate knot. This

tie is interwoven with strands of managing people, time, and instruction in unison with infusing a school with passion, purpose, and meaning.

Paul Houston, executive director of the Association of School Administrators (AASA), for example, developed his "ten teachings for leading by ambiguity" around the philosophy of contradiction and paradox. He suggests that leadership should exhibit (Houston, 1990, p. 22)

- Interdependent autonomy

- Flexible integrity

- Confident humility

- Cautioned risk-taking

- Bifocal vision

- Wobbly steadiness

- Skeptical belief

- Thin-skinned empathy

- Lowly aloofness

- Childlike maturity

Although these ten teachings may appear as mixed messages to dyed-in-the-wool dualistic thinkers, they open new possibilities for receptive school principals. They lead to the Taoist concept of *wu-wei*, the place between doing nothing at all and forcing actions no matter what. As Watts writes, "Wu-wei ... is what we mean by going with the grain, rolling with the punch, swimming with the current, trimming sails to the wind, taking the tide at its flood, and stooping to conquer" (Watts, 1975, p. 76). Centering on the balance point allows principals to maintain a middle position between the extremes of overly tight managerial control and overzealous symbolic commitment.

In Taoist traditions, philosophers use the concepts of Yin and Yang to depict opposites that when combined make a unified whole. One thinks of man and woman, love and hate, war and peace, status quo and innovation—each making the other possible. The Yin-Yang concept represents a seeming duality that in fact expresses an implicit unity. In baseball, without the offensive batter there can be no defensive play. In nature, without the death of the caterpillar there is no butterfly. In schools, there can be no new hiring without retirement or transfer; often new programs cannot be instituted without the discontinuation of old ones; and new forms of staff collaboration cannot take place without the end of isolation. Watts notes, "The art of life is not seen as holding to Yang and banishing Yin, but as keeping the two in balance, because there can't be one without the other" (Watts, 1975, p. 21).

The same need for balance is true of the oft-cited management-leadership polarity. The concept of paradox in a principal's work stresses the ability to embrace supposedly opposing poles to become a technical artist or an artistic technician, an organizer and an inspirer. By merging different, seemingly conflicting roles, school leaders can bring harmony and balance to the situation and deal with complex puzzles at the same time.

Principals address polarities simultaneously as a way of accomplishing at least two things with a single action—shaping culture while developing a plan, promulgating policy through poetry and stories, using traditions and ceremonies to inform and restructure. Every event or situation presents opportunities for leading while managing, managing while leading. For busy principals, this approach creates a new cache of available time. For schools, this helps address the challenge of getting results while maintaining confidence and faith, building esprit de corps while managing day-to-day minutiae. Ambiguities can be dealt with in a new way, through embracing paradox and seeking harmony among competing values, ideas, and actions. A study of three leaders demonstrates how this idea can work.

Good Leaders Give Mixed Signals

Several years ago, Bower studied three highly effective leaders to uncover the reasons for their success (Bower, 1989). Over a three-year period, she observed and interviewed a hospital administrator, a grocery-store manager, and a high school principal. She also interviewed their subordinates. She was particularly concerned with how these leaders send and receive signals from subordinates. She found some interesting patterns that illustrated paradoxes in their work and demonstrated how they balanced leading and managing. The three leaders communicated in a variety or ways. They sent signals

- Of what is expected, appreciated, and preferred by "being with" rather than "being around" people

- Through questioning that promotes the belief that subordinates are the experts

- Through the selection and installation of new members

- By nurturing a defined cultural core causing members to remain faithful

- Informally through the network of cultural carriers

- Through open, inclusive, and high-variety communication

- Through a common vocabulary keyed to an ethic of service and a spirit of collaboration

- Through the content and manner of staff development

- By maintaining the facility to highlight values of pride, care, and commitment to quality

- By serving themselves as signals of what is important

These patterns are consistent with those found in the contemporary literature about leadership and management. They are also supportive of many of the ideas already presented about the various ways principals deal with their schools.

But as Bower burrowed more deeply into the behavior of these three leaders, she stumbled onto some unanticipated and perplexing patterns. Given prevailing assumptions about effective leadership, she had expected that the leaders would give clear, consistent signals. Instead, she found their signals were seemingly mixed and contradictory yet effective and harmonizing in many ways. Within the context of each organization, these apparently conflicting signals were not seen as confusing but were well understood and widely accepted. Staff members interpreted them as different positions that taken as a whole were not in opposition. Instead, the differences provided balance and unity. Rather than canceling out or undermining each other, contradictions supported, sustained, and complemented one another; they took the form of paradox. By embracing the paradoxical nature of their work and by blending multiple messages and roles, a leader addresses contradictions as a way to achieve balance, unity, and harmony that distinguish a robust culture.

Bower's work suggests that leaders help people think, seek their own answers, and make decisions within the boundaries of a dynamic continuum. Leaders encourage followers to be spontaneous and orderly, creative and precise, imaginative and factual.

They find their own equilibrium to keep themselves on center. Leaders are like benevolent Zen masters, renowned for that impatience with novices who try to become too logical:

> A monk asked the master Ts'wu-wei for what reason the Bodhidharma had come from India. The master answered: "Pass me the chin-rest." As soon as the monk had passed the chin-rest, the master whacked him over the head with it. That is all there is to the story. A chin-rest is a board to support the head during long meditation; and the moral of the story is evidently: don't try to reason—meditate. Through meditation and an occasional whack on the head monks arrive at the meaning of the statement "One in all and all in one." (Koestler, 1961, p. 235)

Most principals have little time for meditation. Yet they get whacked on the head all the time by problems and crises. More time to reflect and create new modes of reflection may provide a pathway through the puzzles and inconsistencies of the school day. In the words of Joseph Campbell, "By putting oneself in accord with [the way]—one's time, one's world view, oneself—one accomplishes the ends of life and is at peace in the sense of being in harmony with all things" (Campbell, 1991). Furthermore, facing the unavoidable paradoxes of work through new approaches to school leadership may help principals deal more effectively as the demands of the position increase, complications multiply, and ambiguities of purpose become more opaque. This harmony between rationality and spirituality creates a dynamic equilibrium, a foundation for strong cultures (Bower, 1989).

Embracing paradox is a way to work toward balance and harmony. To clarify the idea of paradox and the blending and balancing of work's opposites, we present in some detail a portrait of one of Bower's subjects, Paul Morris, principal of Oakwood Middle School.

His creative responses to six paradoxes of leadership and the commingling of multiple roles demonstrate how complexity may encourage leaders to reflect and create harmony in difficult situations.

The paradox of role expectations: meeting role expectations requires creating your own. Do what you are told; do what you are not told.

Work in schools often demands accommodating new expectations. Teachers spoke of feeling in charge of their work and being able to shape their own roles. The school's media specialist remarked, "Mr. Morris lets me do mostly what I want." Morris himself observed, "I look for teachers who see their role as much broader than I can describe." Teachers purchase their own supplies and do not submit lesson plans: "Some principals require teachers to turn in lesson plans every Friday. They never look at them, and if they do, don't really know what they are looking for. I look at lesson plans when I visit classrooms. I just can't imagine going through them in stacks every week."

By contrast, teachers noted that they felt their responsibilities were clear-cut. They were held accountable for assigned tasks and asked to follow specific rules and procedures. Department heads had monthly meetings with the principal, followed by team meetings with their departments. Morris expected them to carry out assigned tasks while constantly searching for new ways of doing what they were assigned.

The paradox of performance: it is right to be wrong in order to be right. Mistakes are expected; do it right.

At Oakwood School, mistakes are readily admitted. A teacher related a story about an after-school program that failed:

> It was a special program designed to work with eighth graders who are at risk. This means they will probably drop out before they graduate.... There were nine students in the program when it began. After two weeks

one student was left.... I was embarrassed. Mr. Morris called me in and said, "Mildred, do you know how many programs similar to this haven't made it? We'll think of something else." We had a long talk and I left his office. I felt as if I hadn't really been a failure.

On another occasion, a physical education teacher was summoned to the principal's office for not teaching an area assigned to him: "I didn't like to teach health; so I just didn't do it. Well, Mr. Morris called me in one time and said, 'Dave, you're not teaching health. Why?' After some discussion I left, and now I am teaching health."

Mr. Morris expects people to do things right, while simultaneously tolerating mistakes. He resolves the apparent contradiction that it is right to be wrong in order to be right.

The paradox of problem perception: problems are best solved by allowing them to be problems. Problems are unavoidable; avoid problems.

On the one hand, Morris communicates that problems are normal occurrences to be accepted: "Just don't make a big deal out of problems." On the other hand, he prides himself on avoiding problems related to mandated reforms: "I read all the stuff from central staff and the state, gobs of stuff, and then I decide what I will give to the teachers and what I won't. Some of these guys [references to other principals] get into a lot of trouble—they create their own problems—because they pass things on down rather than deciding what is important and what can be dismissed."

The contradiction between accepting and avoiding problems is a normal part of life at Oakwood. Working to avoid problems is balanced with knowing problems occur.

The paradox of pride: pride in being the best comes from knowing that we are not good enough. Be proud to be the best. We *aren't* good enough.

At Oakwood, the teachers and staff speak with a sense of reverence about their high standards and performance. They believe their school to be one of the best in the state. Frequent award ceremonies, plaques, and letters of recommendation reinforce their pride. Each fall a dramatic production celebrates the previous year's accomplishment.

At the same time, the people at Oakwood are constantly looking for new ways to become better. Morris makes this search for improvement very clear: "We couldn't be in the business of education and not want to learn and improve." Feeling pride and, at the same time, the deep need to improve helps drive change.

The paradox of control: by letting go of control, control remains. The leader is in control. The leader does not control.

"Mr. Morris has control of things; he knows his business" is a common perception at Oakwood. In other words, he knows what is going on inside the school and buffers it against external influence. As he puts it, "If I followed every rule that comes across my desk, I would not be here talking to you today."

But in same breath, Morris recognizes that he cannot control most outside influences and relinquishes control inside: "I hire good teachers and then I support them as they work with the children." Control at Oakwood School is in balance; keeping control and letting loose occur simultaneously. Control is distributed and enhances collaboration, exchange of ideas, and a sense of shared commitment to the school.

The paradox of concern: acting in a caring way may not mean that the leader is always caring. The leader is tender and cares for individuals. The leader is tough and cares about the organization.

Paul Morris exudes a caring, sensitive attitude, but it is supported by clear standards. He obviously cares about teachers, staff members, and students and treats them lovingly and tenderly. At the same time, he is tough. He dismissed a teacher who could not manage a class. He expelled students, one of whom later got in trouble outside. He rearranged schedules that require teachers to change in mid-year routines they had enjoyed and found comfortable for a long time. Everyone knows that they are valued as human beings but are all responsible for serving the school's charges.

Instead of giving simplistic straightforward signals, Paul Morris sent complex mixed ones. For every statement or action, there was its opposite: "work together—be autonomous"; "think things through—act"; "be cautious—take risks." Bower argues that apparent contradictions brought unity and balance to his organization, as well as to those of the other two leaders. Unraveling the puzzles or balancing opposites helped subordinates maintain a healthy tension between alternatives. These leaders not only saw the possibilities of both yes and no but they acted within their environments in ways that promoted the balance. The pivotal points for these leaders centered on role expectations, performance, problem perception, pride, control, and concern. As they steered their organizations and were themselves steered, they balanced the Yin and Yang of the pivot points.

Although none of the three leaders was conscious of it, all three were intuitively in tune with paradoxical thinking: the principle of polarity is not to be confused with ideas of opposition or conflict. Leadership is lived in the dialectic or tension. As Watts writes, "Our overspecialization in conscious attention and linear thinking has led to the neglect, or ignorance of the basic principles and rhythms of the process [of living], of which the foremost is polarity" (1975, p. 21).

It is clear that school and other leaders face many paradoxes. Principals and teacher-leaders need much work to balance and blend leadership and management through paradox.

Unearthing Paradoxes of School Leaders' Work

As noted earlier, schools are challenging, ambiguous, and demanding organizations. The vast array of complex tasks, conflicting pressures, and thorny dilemmas creates a constant state of activity and challenges. Paradox confronts all leaders in the school from principals to teachers, from parents to students.

In addition to those identified by Bower, school leaders often deal with many other paradoxes of work.

People don't work for rewards. Reward people. Teachers and staff find their greatest meaning and reward by having students learn and grow (Lortie, 1975). Yet they also respond to formal recognition, informal rewards, and professional support for their hard work and success. In positive cultures the deeper connection to educational values drives work, but people should be recognized for their accomplishments and service.

Plans always must be revised. Plan carefully. Planning is important to building motivation and coordination for a new program or curriculum. But as action is taken, unpredictable surprises and changing situations make evolutionary planning necessary (Louis & Miles, 1990). Developing flexibility can bring stability and ultimately produce a more challenging work environment.

If you keep changing, you will never get it right. Keep changing. Studies of school improvement point out that schools will be most successful when they are continuously improving— when change occurs within a community of learners (Fullan, 2001b). But without stability, it is hard to perfect promising practices. Finding the balance point between stability and constant change keeps a school on its toes while remaining grounded.

Education is serious work and should be approached seriously. Lighten up and have fun. Schooling remains one of the most important and serious endeavors of any society. But seriousness must be counterbalanced with humor, fun, light-heartedness, and joy. Hard work and dedication can and should be combined with whimsical stories, comical memories, and enjoyment.

Coordination is unfeasible. Tighten up. Schools have become so complex, with so many specializations and subspecializations, programs, and activities that synchronization among groups, units, classrooms, and programs is beyond grasp. But without enough bringing together of diverse labors, schools can disintegrate into a chaos of disjointed and conflicting efforts.

Follow central office directives. Be creatively insubordinate. School principals cannot afford to become such mavericks that they end up transferred, fired, or demoted. Nor can they be so passive that they do not discover ways to bend rules so that the learning needs of children are served. Finding the right mixture of the "independent subordinate" and "loyal deviant" is a requisite of the job (see Morris et al., 1984).

Test scores are the only true measure of educational outcome. Use test scores as one among other valued measures. Many of the important outcomes of education remain ignored by current laws. It is critical to show how well a school is performing on routine indicators of learning. Schools should be constantly searching for and developing ways to appraise other enduring (if intangible) aspects of a school's sacred mission. Don't ignore test scores, but don't be consumed by them.

Allocate resources equally. Distribute resources where needed most. School leaders constantly deal with trade-offs between equity (allocating resources universally) and the demand for quality (investing resources where they will do the most good). The goal is to find a shared sense of quality-directed equity.

Don't change things too fast. Change quickly to make a difference. School improvement invariably creates alterations in educational patterns and practices. Principals regularly seek to walk a tightrope between speed and caution in introducing new programs and approaches. Going too fast derails change; going too slowly decreases success.

Don't make snap decisions. Act before you are sure. Merging leadership and management requires balance between action and reflection, risk-taking and caution. Leaping before you look causes plans to go awry; too much looking prior to leaping creates paralysis that prevents actions from ever being taken. Harmony occurs through reflective action and active reflection.

Delegate to others. Do it all yourself. The issue of sharing and distributing leadership remains one of the core dilemmas of schools. The principal must be willing to be out in front to get things done right, but he or she must have faith in the lead of others. Without tension between leading and following, leaders either become overwhelmed or take the rap of others' mistakes.

Each of these paradoxes haunts school leaders every minute of every day. It is not easy to strike a workable midpoint between the technical and symbolic dualities of school leaders' work. The Yin and Yang, symbolic and structural, are part of a larger unified whole. One supposedly taps the left part of our brain, the other the right hemisphere. A bifocal leader is able to interweave these roles. One set of issues is usually in the foreground; the other provides a backdrop; just as quickly as the ground becomes the figure or the figure becomes the ground. The balanced interplay of seeming opposites helps capture both present and future, technical and symbolic simultaneously.

This is how technical and symbolic issues play out in schools—harmony and balance, blending and balancing. When a principal is dealing with goals, it is against a backdrop of cultural values. When a principal is telling a story, it is done in a context of rational activity. A formal e-mail may also have a second life as a symbol. A ceremony may make a recent new program understandable or heal the wounds of past skirmishes. In sum, bifocal leaders are able to view every part of each day through two lenses and use whichever one the occasion requires. In their heads and through their actions, they are able to balance and blend logic and artistry, dancing on the juncture of the two. In doing so, they help create schools that are technically sound as well as symbolically attuned. The next chapter illustrates how the balance can be achieved by accomplishing two ends with one action.

14

Achieving Balance
Meeting Cultural and Structural Demands

As already noted, over the years of top-down reform, schools have struggled to become more rational by concentrating on developing standards and measuring outcomes. Accountability pressures have centered attention on standardized achievement tests as the sole indicator of a school's effectiveness. The federal No Child Left Behind Act (NCLB) has taken reform a step further by putting teeth in the legislation. Schools that fail to meet an Average Yearly Progress (AYP) target are placed on probation. If they continue to fail to measure up, they are penalized and risk being shut down. In tightening structurally, the culture of most schools has been compromised or severely maimed. Teaching to the tests has become the norm; professional pride and morale has reached low ebb. This seems ironic, since most evidence points to cultural cohesion and buoyancy as the primary predictors of school effectiveness.

The main task ahead is to restore the balance between rigor and vigor that keeps a school structurally well ordered and symbolically well knit. Since the demands on time and attention are so overwhelming, how can a principal blend cultural sensitivity with technical efficiency? How can rational acts serve cultural needs and vice-versa?

Symbolic Functions of Structure

There can be an enormous overlap and blending of technical and symbolic issues in key actions. In this chapter we describe some central ways that principals use significant technical activities to shape the culture and vice-versa.

Retirement as Anointing

Retirement has its technical aspects: completing contractual arrangements, replacing personnel, and making sure that the appropriate benefits flow to the retiree. But it also provides an opportunity for showcasing important values. Retirement under any circumstances is an uneasy and painful process, both for those who leave and for those who remain. It involves reliving past experiences, accepting the transience of life, and ending professional relationships and a lifelong career. Retirement is an important time for healing the hurt and loss of a valued member of the community. It is also a moment for communicating shared values of loyalty, commitment, and caring. Retirements are as important to those who continue on as they are to those who are leaving. The design of a retirement event requires careful, sensitive symbolic attention. It is another solid benchmark in the emerging history of a school.

In an Iowa elementary school, the principal planned a joint retirement for two teachers who had each served the school over thirty-five years. Graduates from decades past told stories about the retirees. The staff celebrated their dedication and loyalty. As a final gesture, the principal presented to the teachers the doorknobs from the classrooms in which they had taught—mounted on walnut plaques.

Coordination to Build Cultural Networks

Coordination ensures that events and activities are sequenced properly and efficiently. It minimizes problems of mutual interdependence in the complex mix of individuals, class schedules, and materials. The type of coordination chosen reflects what a school values. Vertical coordination, through either command or rules, emphasizes the value of authority and a belief that people in top positions have a better idea than those further down about getting things to work effectively. Lateral coordination supports the value of collegiality and the idea that integration happens best when people synchronize activities through face-to-face dialogue.

Schools with site-based management have extra planning periods for teachers to work on governance issues, thus communicating the importance of collaboration. Other schools involve staff members in deciding teacher schedules and sports events. Collaborative coordination increases the ties between teachers and builds informal cultural networks.

Communication as Cultural Signals

Communication is one of the most important aspects of life in human organizations. Technically, communication involves distributing information so that everyone knows what is happening and how their work affects others. Like coordination, communication can take many different forms. Choices about how best to convey information are based as much on values and beliefs about interchanges as on technical criteria of what is most efficient. Signals help shape the school culture.

Memos are commonplace items in schools. Memoranda and written documentation provide durable information, promote high degrees of accuracy, and offer a formal audit trail that can sometimes pinpoint where communication breaks down. Memoranda can also signal a sense of professional collegiality or one of impersonality and the sense that communication is a one-way street. Symbolically words and format of memoranda connect to larger purposes and values. For example, memos in one school feature its mission and motto, as well as children's drawings on each page.

In an Alabama school, meetings begin with another form of communication: stories of success shared by faculty or staff. These stories keep people up-to-date on what is happening and furnish an arena to celebrate small successes.

Communication can take place in formal meetings or face to face. Meetings are a technically efficient way of passing along information. But without openness and trust, these time-intensive encounters are no better than a public reading of verbal memos. Good conversation involves a mutual process of advocacy and inquiry in which people listen as well as they speak. Open meetings are a sign of cohesive cultures in which signals are collectively sent and interpreted. Face-to-face exchanges, properly constructed, offer crucibles in which shared values are forged and concentrated. To be effective, authentic dialogue between principal and staff requires a value of openness and a belief in the process.

Professional dialogue can be one of the most powerful anchors of a cohesive culture. It indicates that the principal and staff are colleagues. It conveys a strong belief in face-to-face discourse as a quick and direct way of gathering information and communicating with others.

Teacher Promotion as Cultural Celebration

The promotion of teachers to tenured status satisfies contractual and statutory requirements. In a technical sense, tenured teachers operate under a different set of legal conditions. Unlike probationary teachers, they are subject to dismissal only through due process and for unique problems. But the granting of tenure has an expressive, symbolic side as well. It marks the transition from novice to expert, a symbolic journey into the sacred profession of teaching and into full membership in the school community.

In a northwestern district, teachers go through a legislated tenure process similar to that of other districts. What is different is the way the district treats the process. In a ceremonial ritual, newly tenured teachers are accepted into the profession of teaching. It is a festive occasion complete with academic robes, speeches about the values of teaching, and other accoutrements of a major and meaningful event. Teacher promotion is a way of publicly communicating and reinforcing the important values and beliefs of both the profession and the school district.

School Closing as Function and Ritual

Schools are usually closed because of safety problems, space needs, or demographic changes. A school closing creates enormous technical challenges. Specific criteria guide decisions about which schools to close. Moving from an existing school to a new site requires planning and coordination. Equipment and people must be moved as efficiently and effectively as possible.

But the closing of a school is also a wrenching cultural calamity. Staff members need to deal with the grief and loss of the old school. Even in a new setting, memories, old stories, and nostalgia still abound. A physical move does not break existential attachments and emotional ties. Finding a way to make the technical logistics of boxing up and moving on a healing transition ritual is a challenge. Properly orchestrated, wakes, funerals, mourning periods, and memorials help people let go and move on emotionally and spiritually, as well as physically. In one Milwaukee high school, a DVD of pictures, music, and performances from prior years eased the transition—the building was closed, but the history was saved.

Even young children seem to realize the importance of marking transitions with ritual. Following a taxpayers' rebellion in Massachusetts, schools were forced to terminate personnel as a way to keep budgets in balance. In one elementary school, five teaching positions were eliminated. The school lost five of its best-liked teachers. One day, the students on their own organized an event to commemorate the departed teachers. They named a different hallway after each of the teachers by posting their names on the hallway walls. Physically the teachers were gone, but the ritual ensured their memory would remain with the school.

Seasonal Actions as Symbols

Dramatic opportunities arise around all routine annual events or cycles. Symbolic passages in the academic calendar join people to each other and to their visions and traditions. The opening of school, for example, is an important event. From a technical standpoint, summer plans are put into action, students are assigned to classrooms, and teachers receive the resources and materials they will need to achieve important instructional objectives. But the beginning of school is also an annual transition ritual that sets the tone for the year. It is a time to acculturate new members and show them the ropes. Time is provided for teachers to disconnect themselves from summer vacation and reconnect with each other and with shared professional values that will guide the year's instruction. For example, a West Virginia district hosted a massive celebration of school opening with a focus on deeper values. Speeches, bands, and hot-air balloons marked the festive transition and conveyed the importance of everyone's contribution to learning (personal communication with L. McCue, 1989).

Getting started after vacation or holidays requires special attention; routines and rules must be reestablished and functional roles, relationships, and authority patterns must be reaffirmed. Moreover, reentry offers an opportunity to reinforce schoolwide values and to remind teachers of their sacred trust.

Vacations also need to be appropriately launched. The school year's end is a particularly powerful cultural event. Healing the loss felt by teachers whose classes were a joy, celebrating goals accomplished, and reflecting on the joys and travails of a year left behind offer a chance to bury the old year but also to celebrate hopes for the future. To mark this event, one school meets after all the administrative details have been completed. People are expected to tell one story of the year that touched them, cheered them, or made them proud. Awards for challenges met (sometimes a decorated helmet) are presented, and hopes and plans for the coming year are shared.

When activities marking transitions are carried out with their dual (symbolic as well as technical) purpose in mind, an added benefit is achieved with little extra effort. But it does not stop there. In its play, the porpoise prepares for defending itself and getting food. The same is true in all organizations. Expressive, symbolic activity also has functional value. In this section, we have focused on "porpoiseful" purpose. In the next, we look at the other side of the coin: purposeful play.

Purposeful Play

More often than we realize, our modern way of thinking causes us to view the symbolic side of organizations as fun and fluff. But just as routine can become ritual, ritual can serve functional purposes. Symbolic activity often produces tangible results, better coordination, and well-functioning schools. Symbols and expressive activity serve as implicit sources of direction, communication, and coordination.

History as Policy

Policy is usually intended to establish a specific course of action or a uniform code of behavior. Even so, most people recognize the gap between the intentions of a policy and its actual consequences. One reason is that historical precedent is at work, dictating what people actually do. Echoes of the past sculpture actions of the present more powerfully than we realize. We typically do not do things because policies say so. We do them because we have always done them that way, because they are part of the unwritten cultural rules. Knowing how things got where they are (the school's past) is a crucial first step in trying to change behavior. Recreating or reinterpreting cultural history can have more influence than establishing a formal policy. Times gone by establish informal precedent through tradition and serve as a vital source of unwritten policy.

For example, a principal of a large high school called on older teachers to recreate the three-decade history of the institution for the entire faculty. As the pageant unfolded, members of the group saw how they had drifted far from their original roots and forgotten what they stood for. Actions had become devoid of meaning. Rather than trying to reform the school, the principal was asking them to revive a glorious past.

A middle school that had formerly been a junior high gathered all the trophies, academic awards, old basketballs, and other memorabilia of past successes in a glass display when the school reopened. While emphasizing continuity with what went before, this event also helped put the old times in perspective. The school entryway is now ablaze with student work and its new statement of values—thus signaling a symbolic statement of what is important now.

Reliving past successes and challenges can communicate norms of behavior, values, and goals as effectively as any job description or plan. Yet stories from times past can also connect to deeper wells of purpose and help move the culture forward.

Values as Goals

Goals, tangible ends to strive for, are often defined carefully and measured systematically. Values, by contrast, are the intrinsic qualities an organization stands for, what it considers good and virtuous. Values are frequently expressed in abstract symbols or metaphorical stories. They can be interpreted in a variety of ways, thus giving them more elasticity and flexibility than concrete goals. Determining how well an organization is living up to its values is more a subjective than an objective exercise. Despite this fact, values often serve as goals to be achieved, ends to be attained.

A middle school's core value, "reaching for excellence," encourages students to excel at whatever they do. School achievement scores have improved significantly since the value was articulated. The principal attributes the rise in scores to a symbolic commitment: "The test scores by themselves were never goals that motivated students to achieve. But our shared commitment to striving for the best performance possible, while not tangible or specific, has made a big difference in what we can accomplish."

Values are communicated in everything a school leader does, writes, or speaks. Consistency in behavior and connection to convictions about student learning and growth serve to mold core values as well as to encourage progress.

Heroes as Supervisors

Supervision is typically a first-hand, on-the-spot, face-to-face activity. Supervisors observe subordinates and either provide compliments for a job well done or make suggestions for improvement. Effective supervision requires both direct observation and concrete feedback. Though these are important, there are less tangible forms of supervision that have an implicit, indirect effect on how people do their jobs.

All people have heroes or heroines whom they try to emulate. People carry images and stories of human exemplars and often, consciously or otherwise, look to them for direction and guidance. Heroes and heroines exert considerable influence on how principals or teachers go about their daily duties. They function as supervisory ghosts looking over the shoulder to offer advice and suggestion. As one teacher put it, "Even though she'll never know it, Ms. Jones is with me every day I teach. She was the best teacher I ever had. In my head, I have conversations with her about how to handle situations. She is a great source of guidance and support even though she's been dead for years." Identifying and recognizing educational heroes and heroines is an effective alternative source of supervision.

Stories as Coordination

Synchronizing diverse efforts is generally accomplished through planning, formal meetings, or hierarchical control. Stories have a similar impact in less formal ways. Stories carry values and archetypes that let everyone know what is valued and expected.

One school's story of how everyone pitched in during a snowstorm is told over and over. Normally each person did his or her own thing in isolation. But in order to survive, it was necessary for people to work closely together; there was no time for planning or conflict. People found that they could work together informally in a way heretofore impossible—even with all their meetings and planning. The story perpetuates the tradition of their cooperation and success.

At another institution, Frank Boyden, the original headmaster of Deerfield Academy, told the story of the superb teacher who chose to stay on staff and thus forgo an offer with a large salary increase from another school because he believed in the values of Deerfield (McPhee, 1966).

Stories tie staff members to the shared successes of the school and delineate the valued roles they can play. They can also illuminate the puzzles and paradoxes of work.

Rituals as Rules

Rules regulate behavior in an authoritative way. Rituals do the same thing through implicit understandings of underlying norms and values. Violating a stated rule will result in answering to someone in authority. Failing to follow the correct protocol of an unstated ritual invites social sanctions from everyone.

In Dayton's Allen Elementary School, values (such as fairness and industriousness) are identified in a word of the week. The word is posted on bulletin boards, appears on cafeteria placemats, and is discussed each day in every classroom. Every Friday, the entire student body and faculty gather around the flagpole to watch a skit put on by students to dramatize what the word means. The principal notes the impact of the ritual on behavior: "The whole school revolves around teaching the values represented in the word of the week."

The problem with rules is that they are "made to be broken" because they are usually enforced by authority figures. Rituals dictate behavior in less visible and obtrusive ways. Conformity to professional values is an individual's moral obligation, carefully monitored by the entire group. For example, at Audubon Elementary School in Baton Rouge, Louisiana, a ritual exchange of information on upcoming workshops or seminars works better than rules requiring that the information be posted.

Rituals are routines that have deeper norms and values embedded in them. Rituals that support collaboration, collegiality, and renewal powerfully promote school improvement.

Ceremonies as Communication Media

As previously stated, the beginning and end of a fiscal or school year and special events should be marked by celebration. Ceremonies provide a cultural space in which stories are told, rituals are enacted, and heroes and heroines are anointed or remembered. During these special events, there is a deeper form of communication that takes place below the surface. Celebrations join past, present, and future. While bonding people to one another and to the important values they share, celebrations provide a functional means for communication. They link myth and structure so that with tangible form myth becomes animate.

Jo Ann Harrison, principal of a new school in Broward County, Florida, launched the year with an announcement: the school had been adopted by the city baseball team. In an opening session, each teacher was presented with a baseball, autographed by all the team players. As each teacher was presented the gift, the principal commented on why he or she had been selected as part of the new instructional "team."

The ending of an urban junior high school's year offers another example. During the year, an informal faculty group compiled examples of errors or failures on the part of teachers, administrators, and staff members. A closing ceremony featured these goofs in Academy Awards style. Nominations were made for the FOOGIES award (Fremont Order of Goofs in Educational Settings). The recipient received a statue of a horse's rear end. The school recognized the importance of taking risks and making mistakes on behalf of educational improvement in a humorous but ceremonial way.

Ceremonies are powerful community events that can build a shared identity, spirit, and commitment. They also communicate goals and role expectations and reinforce formal relationships and authority.

Informal Players as Functional Roles

As noted earlier, every school creates a network of informal cultural players. These people also occupy formal roles, such as teacher, secretary, or custodian, but their unofficial duties put them in charge of traditions and symbols. Their cultural responsibilities also have functional consequences.

In a California junior high, the custodian was the school's informal priest. His intimate knowledge of the history of the school was shared with all new teachers. He was their main source of "the way we do things around here." Although all new teachers receive a faculty handbook outlining formal policies, their behavior is shaped more powerfully by the informal rules passed on by the custodian. Storytellers, in spreading the lore, serve as informal coordinators. As we have already seen, stories have synchronization value—if widely shared. For instance, a school that has been implementing a number of new instructional and assessment approaches, seeking grants regularly, and using site-based decision making has a staff member who knows all the stories of the school. She is available whenever visitors arrive.

Few groups really have communication problems. Although the formal system may be inadequate at times, the "grapevine" usually keeps everyone up-to-date. In a southern high school, a math teacher who served as the chief gossip went so far as to have a business card made listing his title as "rumor control." As the school's eyes, ears, and voice, he ensures that everyone, including the principal, knows what everyone else is doing. Neither official e-mails nor formal announcements over the school's public address system are as effective as this informal network.

Memoranda as Poetry

Memoranda are often mundane and downright boring. As a result, they are disposed of before being read or scanned with little joy or attention. Really vivid memos, however, can be more functional in communicating important issues to different groups. The "Fat Lady Sings" memo from a middle school provides an excellent example of how memoranda can become more functional when they have pizzazz. Such announcements serve their intended purpose of circulating information but do so in an interesting way.

———

The Fat Lady Sings

"Success is a journey, not a destination."

February 12, 1985

I ONLY HAVE A PEN   Please bring a #2 pencil in today's faculty meeting to fill out a SACS questionnaire.

LOCKED OUT   Is there any reason for the lounge to be locked in the morning? Some of us come early, and we are unable to sign in.

BLACKOUT   Why are there no lights in the front hall on the third floor? Are we on an austerity campaign? Someone falling, tripping, or hiding will ultimately cost more than light bulbs.

CHANGES ON THE WAY   At the volunteer faculty meeting yesterday afternoon, the following concerns were discussed:

1. Too many interruptions over the PA system: The PA system will normally be used only during homeroom and the LAST FIVE MINUTES of the school day. At any other time, it will be used only in cases of emergency.

2. Conflicting information and directions given by the office: Any information/directions printed in the Fat Lady should be considered accurate and final. If the information or directions are later changed, the "buzz words" will be "Contrary to what has been said in the Fat Lady."

3. New procedures that change the schedule of the school day: Change will always cause some frustration. Although the office will attempt to inform teachers beforehand, teachers are also responsible for suggesting ideas/opinions/concerns to the office. Teachers must trouble-shoot—just as administrators do. All of us are responsible for the policies of the school.

I'LL BELIEVE IT WHEN I SEE IT   David Jackson from computer service called and said our report cards should be ready by Wednesday. Keep your fingers crossed.

TO THE OFFICE   Thank you from Susan, Patti, Wallace, Colette, Janet, and Nancy for not interrupting the last ten minutes of our seventh-period classes yesterday with announcements.

Play as Work

During the past two or three decades, schools have been under pressure to clarify goals, set measurable objectives, evaluate teachers and programs more systematically, and rationalize procedures. Teaching has become hard work, and time spent "on-task" has become a measure of successful instruction. Play has become a marginal activity, but it is crucial to the development of young people.

Decreasing play in schools is counterproductive because play has important functional outcomes. It relieves tension, keeps people from getting so tight that they cannot work well, and brings them together. More important, play is a primary source of creativity and invention. Albert Einstein once commented that the gift of fantasy was more meaningful to him than his talent for absorbing knowledge. In order to work better, schools may have to encourage people to play more. One principal, for example, promised to eat fried worms if all the students in school read six books each over vacation (they did, and he kept his promise—although their task was certainly more pleasant than his). After successful test scores were made public, another principal spent the day on the roof accompanied by his desk, chair, and telephone.

Playfulness communicates the human acceptance of mistakes, the pleasure of success, and the importance of humor. The seriousness of schooling is actually enhanced by the use of play.

Final Thoughts

Effective schools are those that balance structure and culture in a dynamic tension that keeps the fulcrum point on center. In blended schools, principals need to encourage dramatic routine and functional drama, "porpoiseful" policy and purposeful play.

Bifocal principals understand the importance of viewing schools as productive factories and as value-shaping temples. But more important, they understand how routine activities must reflect the culture and how rituals can also serve formal purposes. By simultaneously making routines dramatic and rituals functional, principals and other school leaders work to develop meaningful, productive schools for themselves, their staffs, and their students. Meaning and production come together in a balanced school that is existentially buoyant and instructionally efficient, precious and proficient, beloved and focused. Symbolic and technical perspectives, rather than remaining separate and antagonistic, combine to create a high-quality school with deep values and efficient roles. What does the future hold for America's schools? Can a better balance between metrics and meaning be achieved?

15

Conclusion
Opportunities for the Future

There is nothing like a young life with great potential. And a quality education is one of the best ways to ensure that every promising young person comes to fruition as a well-adjusted, fully skilled adult. It is the way a nation offers hope and opportunity, a sense of self, and the skills to succeed.

Students deserve the best schools we can give them—schools full of heart, soul, and ample opportunities to learn and grow, a place of hope and a chance to shine. Too often, students are being shortchanged. They are stifled by sterile, toxic places that turn them against learning rather than turn them on to it. Many tune out; others drop out.

Our efforts at educational improvement often do not work to guarantee good schools for everyone. Reforms that focus only on changing structures or increasing school accountability will never succeed in building positive organic forms that will serve all our students. Reforms that bring new technologies or higher standards won't succeed without being embedded in supportive, spirit-filled cultures. Schools won't become what students deserve until cultural patterns and ways are shaped to support learning. Leadership from throughout the school will be needed to build and maintain such positive, purposeful places to learn and grow.

As we traverse the new millennium, school leaders will grapple with both paradox and opportunity. How well they balance opposing forces and find promising pathways will have a tremendous impact on America's future.

Paradox, Culture, and Leadership

In the future, school leaders will face five central paradoxes in their work. As leaders, they cannot solve a paradox the way a problem is solved. A leader must discover ways to harmonize and find the right balance among conflicting values. The five paradoxes are as follows:

Paradox of purpose. Leaders need to build and maintain a shared purpose while encouraging enough creative diversity to ensure continued growth for students and staff. Shared purpose is key to quality schools, but it is equally important to nurture diverse views, be open to innovation, and encourage flexibility for the sake of progress. *Shared* means everyone both inside and outside the school.

Paradox of people. Leaders must be caring and supportive of people who work in schools but also must champion and protect the integrity and common good of the institution. This is one of leadership's deepest and most challenging paradoxes. As schools empower, motivate, and nurture staff and parents, they must do so for the common good of students, the school, and society at large.

Paradox of change. Leaders must perpetuate what is thriving in the present while reaching for what may be even better in the future. They must both embrace change and remain the same. They must balance the status quo with future improvements. They must balance the development of core skills with the development of the child.

Paradox of action. Leaders must take time to reflect on purpose and potential but must also make decisions and take action. It is always a balancing act: reflecting on ideas about what to do and implementing what appears to be a satisfactory decision (Palmer, 1990). Leaders must do both well. They must visualize new purposes and better directions while bringing new possibilities to reality.

Paradox of leading. Leadership must come from the principal, but he or she cannot be the only source of leadership. To sustain strong, positive cultures, leadership must come from everyone. It must be distributed, shared, and truly democratic, based on trust, authenticity, and core values.

New Opportunities, New Challenges

In this new millennium, school leaders will encounter a number of critical opportunities to lead their schools. If not addressed, these opportunities will be lost:

Opportunity of purpose. Central to successful schools is a powerful sense of purpose that is focused on students and learning. Developing and articulating a higher calling is the foundation of a strong culture.

Opportunity of place. Schools are complex, demanding institutions. School leaders must make these special places where students, staff, parents, and community members feel welcome, safe, and appreciated. A positive "ethos of place" should permeate everything that goes on. Messages of principle should be everywhere.

Opportunity of people. People are the central resources in any organization. When leaders invest in a culture that nurtures and challenges staff, students, and community, it pays off in learning outcomes. Putting time into shaping a culture that motivates and inspires people is the venture capital of schools.

Opportunity of competence. Human beings crave competence. Everyone wants to do well. The challenge and opportunity for school leaders is to nourish the know-how of staff and students in their work, their thinking, and their daily actions. Through competence, expertise, and knowledge comes achievement.

Opportunity of commitment. School leaders will need to build or, in some cases, resurrect commitment to schools and education. The past decade has disheartened many about the possibilities of education and the potential of schools. School leaders from every corner of the school need to relentlessly build commitment, a sense of brand, and a deep feeling of connection to this place called school.

Opportunity of celebration. School leaders need to find exciting ways to celebrate accomplishments of the culture—both large and small. Schools are living, breathing organisms that need nourishment. In order to thrive, people need to come together in community to celebrate accomplishment, hard work, and dedication. By celebrating the best of what the school has done in ceremony, song, or words, everyone exalts in the accomplishments of compatriots.

Opportunity of caring. Finally, school leaders face the need to bring caring back to schools (Noddings, 1992; Beck, 1994). Schools and classrooms demand much from their inhabitants. Teaching and learning, while rewarding, is hard work. By establishing schools as caring places, the culture becomes more humane and kind.

Paradox versus opportunity, standards versus spirit, test scores versus stories—the list of dilemmas school leaders will face in this new century goes on and on. But in our view, unless we can restore the sacred stature of education, very little will help us achieve our hopes and dreams. Teachers need once again to believe in themselves and relish the opportunities they have to make a real difference. Communities need to reexamine the role schools play in society; that is, the role of balancing cognitive achievement with character development.

We began this book by taking another look at what really makes businesses succeed. Too often, schools are asked to master the wrong lessons about what makes a successful organization tick. Clear goals, rational structures, high standards, and accountability are only part of why a business succeeds. The real lesson is how business leaders are able to infuse passion and purpose into an enterprise and build a common spirit and cohesive culture.

Herb Kelleher, former CEO of Southwest Airlines, gave a speech to employees on the occasion of the launch of Southwest's "Symbol of Freedom" campaign. He reminded people of Southwest's central mission: making it possible for anyone to visit a relative, attend a wedding, be at a friend's funeral, or go somewhere just for the fun of it. "Giving people the freedom to fly is," he said, "Southwest's higher calling and ennobling purpose" (Kelleher, 1997). As Southwest employees come to work each day, they are not just answering phones, taking tickets, loading bags, or fueling aircraft. Their collective efforts are making it possible for others to enjoy the fruits of life.

In education, our higher calling or ennobling purpose is even more majestic. We are giving young people a chance to thrive and succeed in the world. Previously we quoted part of a larger statement by Tracy Kidder. The larger statement offers a luminous conclusion. In his book *Among Schoolchildren* (1989), Kidder paints education's sacred mission in lyric prose:

> Teachers [and other school leaders] usually have no way of knowing that they have made a difference in a child's life, even when they have made a dramatic one. But for children who are used to thinking of themselves as stupid or not worth talking to or deserving rape and beatings, a good teacher can provide an astonishing revelation. A good teacher can give a child at least a chance to feel "*She* thinks I'm worth something, maybe I am." Good teachers [and good school leaders] put snags in the river of children passing by, and over the years, they redirect hundreds of lives. Many people find it easy to imagine unseen webs of malevolent conspiracy in the world, and they are not always wrong. But there is also an innocence that conspires to hold humanity together, and it is made up of people who can never fully know the good they have done. (pp. 312–313)

The core leadership challenge of the coming decades is to build schools in which every child can grow and every teacher can make a difference. Such sentiments flourish in a culture where learning and caring are valued and where stories, rituals, and ceremonies provide zest and buoyancy to the world's most sacred profession. School leaders can make a difference by restoring hope, faith, and a shared spirit to the place called school.

Strong cultures produce dense leadership—every member becomes champion, visionary, and poet. As teachers and parents become leaders—cultural icons for the deeper values of the school—the school becomes more than a building with instructional materials. It becomes an institution with history, values, purpose and pride, stories and beliefs.

Conclusion

As we have seen in the preceding chapters, school cultures are complex systems. Leaders need the skills and knowledge to uncover a culture's deeper history; the techniques to assess current conditions and values, and, most important, the ability to be symbolic leaders, reinforcing cultural values and ways in their daily work. For some leaders, these skills can be developed on the job; others will develop them through preparation programs. But many leaders will need in-depth professional development opportunities with adequate time to reflect, analyze, and interpret their culture.

If a company can motivate employees to pour their hearts into selling coffee (or motorcycles or cars), then schools should be able to motivate staff to pour themselves into teaching. Schools that are toxic should be provided the support, leadership, and charge to renew themselves. Schools that are dangerous to the health and learning of students and staff alike need to be transformed or reformed into positive, meaningful institutions. And, finally, schools that have a rich and robust culture need the strength and resources to nurture and sustain their valued institutions.

References

Abplanalp, S. (2008). *Breaking the low-achieving mindset: A S.M.A.R.T. journey of purposeful change*. Madison, WI: QLD Learning (Quality Leadership by Design).

Baldridge, J. V., & Deal, T. E. (1975). *Managing chance in educational organizations: Sociological perspectives, strategies, and case studies*. Berkeley, CA: McCutchan.

Barth, R. S. (1991). *Improving schools from within: Teachers, parents, and principals can make the difference*. San Francisco: Jossey-Bass.

Beck, L. G. (1994). *Reclaiming educational administration as a caring profession*. New York: Teachers College Press.

Big quiz 2007: The year in business. (2007, Dec. 30). *Seattle Times*. Retrieved February 24, 2008, from Seattle Times database.

Bissinger, H. G. (1991). *Friday night lights: A town, a team, and a dream*. New York: HarperPerennial.

Bolman, L. G., & Deal, T. E. (2001). *Leading with soul: An uncommon journey of spirit*. San Francisco: Jossey-Bass.

Bolman, L. G., & Deal, T. E. (2003). *Reframing organizations: Artistry, choice, and leadership* (3rd ed.). San Francisco: Jossey-Bass.

Boloz, S. (1997). *The C diet.* Unpublished manuscript.

Boyd-Dimock, V., & Hord, S. M. (1994–1995). Schools as learning communities: Issues about change. *SEDL, 4*(1). Retrieved Aug. 5, 2008 from http://www.sedl.org/pubs/catalog/items/sch11.html

Bower, M. (1966). *Will to manage.* New York: McGraw-Hill.

Bower, P. B. (1989). *Living the leadership paradox: The pivotal points of leaders' signals and signaling.* Unpublished doctoral dissertation, George Peabody College.

Bowerman, W. J. (1991). *High-performance training for track and field.* Champaign, IL: Leisure Press.

Bruce, K. M., & Newmann, F. M. (2004). Key link. Successful professional development must consider school capacity. *Journal of Staff Development, 25*(1), 26–30.

Bryk, A., Lee, V. E., & Holland, P. B. (1993). *Catholic schools and the common good.* Cambridge, MA: Harvard University Press.

Campbell, J. G. (1991). *The power of myth.* New York: Anchor.

Carter-Scott, C. (1991). *The corporate negaholic.* New York: Villard.

Clark, B. (1972). The organizational saga in higher education. *Administrative Science Quarterly, 17,* 178–184.

Clark, E. (2004). *Around the corporate campfire: How great leaders use stories to inspire success.* Sevierville, TN: Insight.

Collins, J. C. (2001). *Good to great: Why some companies make the leap—and others don't.* New York: HarperBusiness.

Collins, J. C., & Porras, J. I. (1997). *Built to last: Successful habits of visionary companies.* New York: Harper Business.

Cutler, W. W. (1989). Cathedral of culture: The schoolhouse in American educational thought and practice since 1820. *History of Education Quarterly, 29,* 1–40.

Deal, T. E., & Hentschke, G. C. (2004). *Adventures of charter school creators: Leading from the ground up.* Lanham, MD: Scarecrow Education.

Deal, T. E., & Kennedy, A. A. (1982). *Corporate cultures: The rites and rituals of corporate life.* Reading, MA: Addison-Wesley.

Deal, T. E., & Key, M. K. (1998). *Corporate celebration: Play, purpose, and profit at work.* San Francisco: Berrett-Koehler.

Deal, T. E., & Peterson, K. D. (1990). *The principal's role in shaping school culture.* Washington, D.C.: U.S. Department of Education.

Deal, T. E., & Peterson, K. D. (1994). *The leadership paradox: Balancing logic and artistry in schools.* San Francisco: Jossey-Bass.

Denning, S. (2005). *Leaders' guide to storytelling.* San Francisco: Jossey-Bass.

Driver, C. E., & Levin, H. M. (1997). *The dilemma of principal succession in restructuring schools.* Unpublished manuscript, Accelerated Schools Project, Stanford University.

DuFour, R. (1998). Why celebrate. *Journal of Staff Development, 19*(4), 58–59.

DuFour, R. (2007). Professional learning communities: A bandwagon, an idea worth considering, or our best hope for high levels of learning? *Middle School Journal, 39*(1), 4–8.

Eder, D. J. (2007). Bringing Navajo storytelling practices into schools: The importance of maintaining cultural integrity. *Anthropology and Educational Quarterly*, 38(3), 278–96.

Fog, K., Butz, C., & Yakaboylu, B. (2005). *Storytelling: Branding in practice*. Berlin: Springer.

Foy, N. (1980). *The yin and yang of organization*. New York: Morrow.

Fullan, M. (1998). Leadership for the 21st century: Breaking the bonds of dependency. *Educational Leadership*, 55(7), 6–10.

Fullan, M. (2001a). *Leading in a culture of change*. San Francisco: Jossey-Bass.

Fullan, M. (2001b). *The new meaning of educational change* (3rd ed.). New York: Teachers College Press.

Geertz, C. M. (1973). *The interpretation of cultures*. New York: Basic Books.

Gerstner, L. V. (2002). *Who says elephants can't dance? Leading a great enterprise through dramatic change*. New York: HarperCollins.

Goddard, R. D., Hoy, W. K., & Hoy, A. W. (2004). Collective efficacy beliefs: Theoretical developments, empirical evidence, and future directions. *Educational Researcher*, 33(3), 3–13.

Goldberg, M. S., & Feldman, S. (2003). *Teachers with class . . . True stories of great teachers*. Kansas City, MO: Andrews McMeel Publishing.

Heath, C., & Heath, D. (2007). *Made to stick: Why some ideas survive and others die*. New York: Random House.

Hindo, B. (2007, June 11). At 3M, a struggle between efficiency and creativity. *Business Week*, 8–12.

Hopfenberg, W. S., Levin, H. M., & Associates. (1993). *The accelerated schools resource guide*. San Francisco: Jossey-Bass.

Houston, P. D. (1990). Zen and the art of school management. *Executive Educator*, 12(10).

Houston, P. D., & Sokolow, S. L. (2006). *The spiritual dimension of leadership: 8 key principles to leading more effectively*. Thousand Oaks, CA: Corwin Press.

Hoy, W. K., & Woolfolk, A. E. (1993). Teachers' sense of efficacy and organizational health of schools. *The Elementary School Journal*, 93(4), 355–372.

Johnson, M. (1995). Hollibrook elementary school: A case study. In R. T. Clift & P. W. Thurston (eds.), *Distributed leadership: School improvement through collaboration*. Greenwich, CT: JAI Press.

Johnson, S. M. (1990). *Teachers at work: Achieving success in our schools*. New York: Basic Books.

Kaufman, B. (1965). *Up the down staircase*. Englewood Cliffs, NJ: Prentice-Hall.

Kelleher, H. (1997). *Southwest: A symbol of freedom*. Internal publication of Southwest Airlines, video.

Kidder, T. (1989). *Among schoolchildren*. Boston: Houghton Mifflin.

Kilmann, R. H. (1985). *Five steps for closing culture-gaps*. In R. H. Kilmann, M. J. Saxton, & R. Serpa and Associates

(Eds.), *Gaining control of the corporate culture*. San Francisco: Jossey-Bass.

Kilmann, R. H., Saxton, M. J., & Serpa, R. (1985). *Gaining control of the corporate culture*. San Francisco: Jossey-Bass.

Koestler, A. (1961). *The lotus and the robot*. New York: Macmillan.

Kotter, J. P., & Heskett, J. L. (1992). *Corporate culture and performance*. New York: Free Press.

Kruse, S. D. (1996). *Collaboration efforts among teachers: Implications for school administrators*. Paper presented at the Annual Meeting of the University Council for Educational Administration (10th, Louisville, KY, October 25–27, 1996).

Kruse, S. D. (1999). Collaborate. *Journal of Staff Development*, 20(3), 14–16.

Kruse, S. D., & Louis, K. S. (1997). Teacher teaming in middle schools: Dilemmas for a schoolwide community. *Educational Administration Quarterly*, 33(3), 261–289.

Kübler-Ross, E. (1970). *On death and dying*. New York: Macmillan.

Kubler-Ross, E. (2000). *Life lessons: Two experts on death and dying teach us about the mysteries of life and living*. New York: Scribner.

Ladson-Billings, G. (1994). *The dreamkeepers: Successful teachers of African American children*. San Francisco: Jossey-Bass.

Lambert, L. (2002). A framework for shared leadership. *Educational Leadership*, 59(8), 37–40.

Leithwood, K., & Louis, K. S. (Eds.). (1998). *Organizational learning in schools.* Lisse, the Netherlands: Swets and Zeitlinger.

Levine, D. U., & Lezotte, L. W. (1990). *Unusually effective schools: A review and analysis of research and practice.* Madison, WI: National Center for Effective Schools Research and Development.

Little, J. W. (1982). Norms of collegiality and experimentation: Workplace conditions of school success. *American Educational Research Journal,* 19(3), 325–340.

Lopez, B. (1998). *Crow and weasel.* San Francisco: North Point Press.

Lortie, D. C. (1975). *Schoolteacher.* Chicago: University of Chicago Press.

Louis, K. S. (1994). Beyond "managed change": Rethinking how schools improve. *School Effectiveness and School Improvement,* 5(1), 2–24.

Louis, K. S. (2006). Change over time? An introduction? A reflection? *Educational Administration Quarterly,* 42(1), 165–173.

Louis, K. S., & Miles, M. B. (1990). *Improving the urban high school: What works and why.* New York: Teachers College Press.

Love, L. (2008). *The story of the custodian.* Unpublished manuscript.

Martinez, L. (1989). Unpublished doctoral dissertation, Peabody College, Vanderbilt University, Nashville, TN.

McCain, J., & Salter, M. (2008). *Hard call: Great decisions and the extraordinary people who made them.* New York: Twelve.

McPhee, J. (1966). *The headmaster: Frank L. Boyden, of Deerfield.* New York: Farrar, Straus and Giroux.

McLaughlin, M. (1995). Keynote address at the annual conference of the National Staff Development Council, Chicago, December.

Meier, D. (1995). *The power of their ideas: Lessons for America from a small school in Harlem.* Boston: Beacon Press.

Meier, D., & Schwartz, P. (1995). Central park east secondary school: The hard part is making it happen in democratic schools. In M. W. Apple & J. A. Beane (Eds.), *Democratic Schools.* Alexandria, VA: Association for Supervision and Curriculum Development.

Moore, S. F., & Meyerhoff, B. G. (1977). *Secular ritual.* Assen: Van Gorcum.

Morris, V. C., Crowson, R., Porter-Gehrie, C., & Hurwitz, E. (1984). *Principals in action: The reality of managing schools.* Columbus: Merrill.

Neibuhr, R. (1984). *The irony of American history.* New York: Scribner.

Neil, D. (2007, April 1). Starbucks nation. *Los Angeles Times West Magazine,* I–46.

Newmann, F. M., & Associates (1996). *Authentic instruction: Restructuring schools for intellectual quality.* San Francisco: Jossey-Bass.

Newmann, F. M., Bruce, K. M., & Youngs, P. (2000). Professional development that addresses school capacity: Lessons from urban elementary schools. *American Journal of Education,* 108(4), 259–299.

Noddings, N. (1992). *The challenge to care in schools: An alternative approach to education.* New York: Teachers College Press.

O'Brien, T. (1998). *The things they carried: A work of fiction.* New York: Broadway Books.

Ott, J. S. (1989). *The organizational perspective*. Pacific Grove, CA: Brooks/Cole.

Owen, H. (1987). *Spirit: Transformation and development in organizations*. Potomac, MD: Abbott.

Palmer, P. J. (1990). *Leading from within: Reflections on spirituality and leadership*. Washington, DC: The Servant Leadership School.

Peterson, K. D., & Bamburg, J. (1993). *Case studies in successful urban school leadership*. Unpublished manuscript, North Central Regional Educational Laboratory, Oak Brook, Ill.

Peterson, K. D., & Brietzke, R. (1994). *Building collaborative cultures: Seeking ways to reshape urban schools*. Urban Monograph Series. Oak Brook, Ill.: North Central Regional Educational Laboratory.

Pinkerton, E. (2007). Unpublished manuscript.

Pirsig, R. M. (1984). *Zen and the art of motorcycle maintenance: An inquiry into values*. New York: Morrow.

Pondy, L. R. (1976). Leadership as a language game. In M. McCall and M. Lambert (Eds.), *Leadership: Where else can we go?* Durham, NC: Duke University Press.

Purkey, S. C., & Smith, M. S. (1983). Effective schools: A review. *Elementary School Journal*, 83(4), 427–452.

Raffaele, P. (2007, December). Keepers of the lost ark? *Smithsonian Magazine*, 40–41.

Reed, K. (2001). *The rituals of air warfare*. Unpublished manuscript.

Reitzug, U. C., & Reeves, J. E. (1992). "Miss Lincoln doesn't teach here": A descriptive narrative and conceptual analysis of a principal's symbolic leadership behavior. *Educational Administration Quarterly, 28*(2), 185–219.

Ricks, T. E. (1997). *Making the corps.* New York: Scribner.

Rodriguez, R. (1982). *Hunger of memory: The education of Richard Rodriguez.* Boston: Godine.

Rossman, G. B., Corbett, H. D., & Firestone, W. A. (1998). *Change and effectiveness in schools.* Albany: State University of New York Press.

Rutter, M., Maughan, B., Morrtimore, P., Ouston, J., & Smith, A. (1979). *Fifteen thousand hours.* Cambridge, MA: Harvard University Press.

Saphier, J., & King, M. (1985). Good seeds grow in strong cultures. *Educational Leadership, 42*(6), 67–74.

Schultz, H., & Yang, D. J. (1997). *Pour your heart into it: How Starbucks built a company one cup at a time.* New York: Hyperion.

Schein, E. H. (1985). *Organizational culture and leadership* (1st ed.). San Francisco: Jossey-Bass.

Schein, E. H. (2004). *Organizational culture and leadership* (3rd ed.). San Francisco: Jossey-Bass.

Show tracker: "Battlestar" kills Starbuck, but how dead is she? (2007, March 5). *Los Angeles Times.* Retrieved April 1, 2007, from Los Angeles Times database.

Smrekar, C. (1991). *The voice of parents: Rethinking the intersection of family and school.* Unpublished manuscript.

Smrekar, C. (1996). *The impact of school choice and community: In the interest of families and schools.* Albany: State University of New York Press.

Spillane, J., Halverson, R., & Diamond, J. (2003). Towards a theory of leadership practice: A distributed perspective. *Journal of Curriculum Studies*, 36(1), 3–34.

Starbucks must find lost "soul," Schultz says. (2007, February 24). *Seattle Times*. Retrieved October 18, 2007, from http://SeattleTimes.nwsouce.com/html/businesstechnology/2003586922starbucks24.html

Talbert, J. E., & McLaughlin, M. W. (1994). Teacher professionalism in local school contexts. *American Journal of Education*, 102(2), 123–153.

Trice, J. M., & Beyer, J. M. (1985). Using six organizational rites to change culture. In R. J. Kilmann, M. J. Saxton, & R. Serpa (Eds.), *Gaining Control of the Corporate Culture*. San Francisco: Jossey-Bass.

Tschannen-Moran, M. (2004). *Trust matters: Leadership for successful schools*. San Francisco: Jossey-Bass.

Tyack, D., & Cuban, L. (1995). *Tinkering toward utopia: A century of public school reform*. Cambridge, MA: Harvard University Press.

Tyack, D., & Hansot, E. (1982). *Managers of virtue: Public school leadership in America, 1820–1980*. New York: Basic Books.

Vydra, J. (1998). *Three cases of culture building*. Unpublished manuscript.

Waller, W. (1932). *The sociology of teaching*. New York: Wiley.

Waters, J. T., Marzano, R. J., & McNulty, B. (2004). Leadership that sparks learning. *Educational Leadership*, 61(7), 48–51.

Watts, A. (1975). *Tao: The watercourse way*. New York: Pantheon.

Witherspoon, G. (1995). *Dynamic symmetry and holistic asymmetry in Navajo and Western art and cosmology.* New York: P. Lang.

Wolff, K. H., & Moore, B. (1967). *The critical spirit; essays in honor of Herbert Marcuse.* Boston: Beacon Press.

Wright, E. (1999). *Why I teach: Inspirational true stories from teachers who make a difference.* Rocklin, CA: Prima.

Index

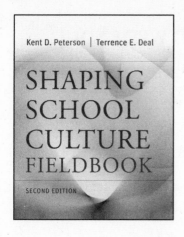

SHAPING SCHOOL CULTURE FIELDBOOK

2nd Edition

Terrence E. Deal | Kent D. Peterson

ISBN: 978-0-7879-9680-2
Paperback

An essential complement to
Shaping School Culture: Pitfalls, Paradoxes, and Promises, 2nd Edition

In *Shaping School Culture Fieldbook, 2nd Edition*, the authors apply their expanded model for use in group planning and training sessions involving the whole school. Drawing on the authors' extensive research and school contacts across the country, the *Fieldbook* includes hands-on strategies and exercises for helping school leaders to:

- Uncover a school's hidden values, beliefs, and assumptions

- Think through and implement a "culture building" process

- Work out appropriate stories, metaphors and symbols to represent a school

- Devise rituals and ceremonies for enriching the school experience

- Build understanding through 50 field-tested exercises and activities

- Rethink leadership practices in light of educational and cultural needs

- Take specific action steps to identify, transform, and heal a 'toxic' or dysfunctional school culture.

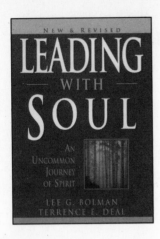

LEADING WITH SOUL
An Uncommon Journey of Spirit

New & Revised

Lee G. Bolman | Terrence E. Deal

ISBN: 978-0-7879-5547-2
Hardcover

"Bolman and Deal understand that organizations are filled with living, breathing, feeling human beings, people who need more than a paycheck, more than a performance review, more than a promotion. This is a deceptively powerful realization for any leader." —Patrick Lencioni, author, *The Five Temptations of a CEO: Obsessions of an Extraordinary Executive*

"No two authors are better equipped than Bolman and Deal to address and answer the seminal dilemma of our time—the difference between making a living and making a life. They lead the way to discover how to lead a spirited life." —Warren Bennis, distinguished professor of business administration, University of Southern California; author, *Managing the Dream*

Since its original publication in 1995, *Leading with Soul* has inspired thousands of readers. Far ahead of its time, the book bravely revealed the path to leadership to be a very personal journey requiring knowledge of the self and a servant-leader mentality.

Now, in this revised edition, authors Bolman and Deal address such issues as the changing nature of work, the new face of today's workforce, and the greater need for an infusion of soul in the workplace. They also include real-life stories from readers of the first edition, and answer key questions that those readers raise. As vital as ever, this revisited narrative of an executive and his quest for deeper meaning continues to point the way to a more fulfilling work experience.

More Resources From the Authors

Reframing Organizations
Artistry, Choice, and Leadership

4th Edition

Lee G. Bolman | Terrence E. Deal

ISBN: 978-0-7879-8798-5 Hardcover
ISBN: 978-0-7879-8799-2 Paperback

The Classic Leadership Resource Now In Its 4th Edition!

First published in 1984, Lee Bolman and Terrence Deal's best-selling book has become a classic in the field. Its four-frame model examines organizations in terms of factories, families, jungles, and theaters or temples:

- The Structural Frame: how to organize and structure groups and teams to get results

- The Human Resource Frame: how to tailor organizations to satisfy human needs, improve human resource management, and build positive interpersonal and group dynamics

- The Political Frame: how to cope with power and conflict, build coalitions, hone political skills, and deal with internal and external politics

- The Symbolic Frame: how to shape a culture that gives purpose and meaning to work, stage organizational drama for internal and external audiences, and build team spirit through ritual, ceremony, and story

This new edition contains a wealth of new examples from both the private and the nonprofit sectors. In addition, the book offers updated content and expanded discussions of self-managing teams, dramaturgical and institutional theory, change theory, the "blink" process, "black swans," and gay rights. An Instructor's Guide is available online.

MORE RESOURCES FROM THE AUTHORS

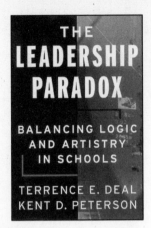

THE LEADERSHIP PARADOX
Balancing Logic and Artistry in Schools

Terrence E. Deal | Kent D. Peterson

ISBN: 978-0-7879-5541-0
Paperback

"School leaders, as well as aspiring principals and observers of the principalship, will delight in this distinctive, playful, and insightful look at the art and craft of leading a modern-day school."—Roland S. Barth, educator and author of *Improving Schools from Within*

"The Leadership Paradox *pushes our understanding of the complexity of the principal's work to new levels. It should be required reading for those who are or aspire to be principals and for those who prepare, train, or supervise them."*—Laraine Roberts, director of research and development, California School Leadership Academy

As leaders and managers, principals must continually blend the symbolic and technical aspects of their role, embracing each complexity with confidence, enthusiasm, and skill. *The Leadership Paradox* draws from organizational and management theory to reveal the art and logic of school leadership.

Instead of viewing leadership and management as opposing factions, the authors show how these two ideals can serve as complements in building powerful school culture. They also share real-life stories and examples of school leaders who have learned to adopt a bifocal approach and integrate the contradictions of their work.

Practical yet inspiring, this volume presents a wealth of insights for principals, superintendents, school board members, and other educational leaders.

MORE RESOURCES FROM THE AUTHORS

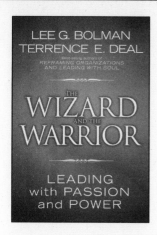

THE WIZARD AND THE WARRIOR
Leading with Passion and Power

Lee G. Bolman | Terrence E. Deal

ISBN: 978-0-7879-7413-8
Hardcover

"The 'gold standard' for looking at leadership. The Wizard and the Warrior is about fighting the good fight, but not losing sight of the magic—it is about making the word flesh. This is a must-read for anyone who cares about becoming a better leader." —Paul D. Houston, executive director, American Association of School Administrators

The Wizard and the Warrior gives leaders the insight and courage they need to take risks on behalf of values they cherish and the people they guide. Great leaders must act both as wizard, calling on imagination, creativity, meaning, and magic, and as warrior, mobilizing strength, courage, and willingness to fight as necessary to fulfill their mission.

Best-selling authors Lee Bolman and Terrence Deal present the defining moments and experiences of exemplary leaders such as David Neeleman (CEO of Jet Blue), Mary Kay Ash, Warren Buffet, Anne Mulcahy, Thomas Keller (head chef of French Laundry), and Abraham Lincoln—all of whom have wrested with their own inner warrior and wizard.

These engaging, realistic case studies are followed by commentaries that will raise questions and suggest possibilities without rushing to resolution or simple answers.

Armed with this book's expanded repertoire of possibilities, the reader can become more versatile and imbue work and life with power and passion.